CLONE

™

CREATED BY DAVID SCHULNER

DAVID SCHULNER
AARON GINSBURG
WADE MCINTYRE
WRITERS

JUAN JOSE RYP
ARTIST

ANDY TROY
COLORIST

RUS WOOTON
LETTERER

SEAN MACKIEWICZ
EDITOR

JUAN JOSE RYP
AND ANDY TROY
COVER

CREATED BY DAVID SCHULNER

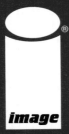

IMAGE COMICS, INC.
Robert Kirkman – Chief Operating Officer
Erik Larsen – Chief Financial Officer
Todd McFarlane – President
Marc Silvestri – Chief Executive Officer
Jim Valentino – Vice-President

Eric Stephenson – Publisher
Ron Richards – Director of Business Development
Jennifer de Guzman – Director of Trade Book Sales
Kat Salazar – Director of PR & Marketing
Jeremy Sullivan – Director of Digital Sales
Emilio Bautista – Sales Assistant
Branwyn Bigglestone – Senior Accounts Manager
Emily Miller – Accounts Manager
Jessica Ambriz – Administrative Assistant
Tyler Shainline – Events Coordinator
David Brothers – Content Manager
Jonathan Chan – Production Manager
Drew Gill – Art Director
Meredith Wallace – Print Manager
Monica Garcia – Senior Production Artist
Jenna Savage – Production Artist
Addison Duke – Production Artist
Tricia Ramos – Production Assistant
IMAGECOMICS.COM

For SKYBOUND ENTERTAINMENT

Robert Kirkman - CEO
J.J. Didde - President
Sean Mackiewicz - Editorial Director
Shawn Kirkham - Director of Business Development
Helen Leigh - Office Manager
Brian Huntington - Online Editorial Director
Lizzy Iverson - Administrative Assistant

For international rights inquiries,
please contact: foreign@skybound.com

WWW.SKYBOUND.COM

CLONE VOL. 3 TP. ISBN: 978-1-60706-939-3. First Printing. Published by Image Comics, Inc. Office of publication: 2001 Center Street, 6th Floor, Berkeley, CA 94704.

CHAPTER 11

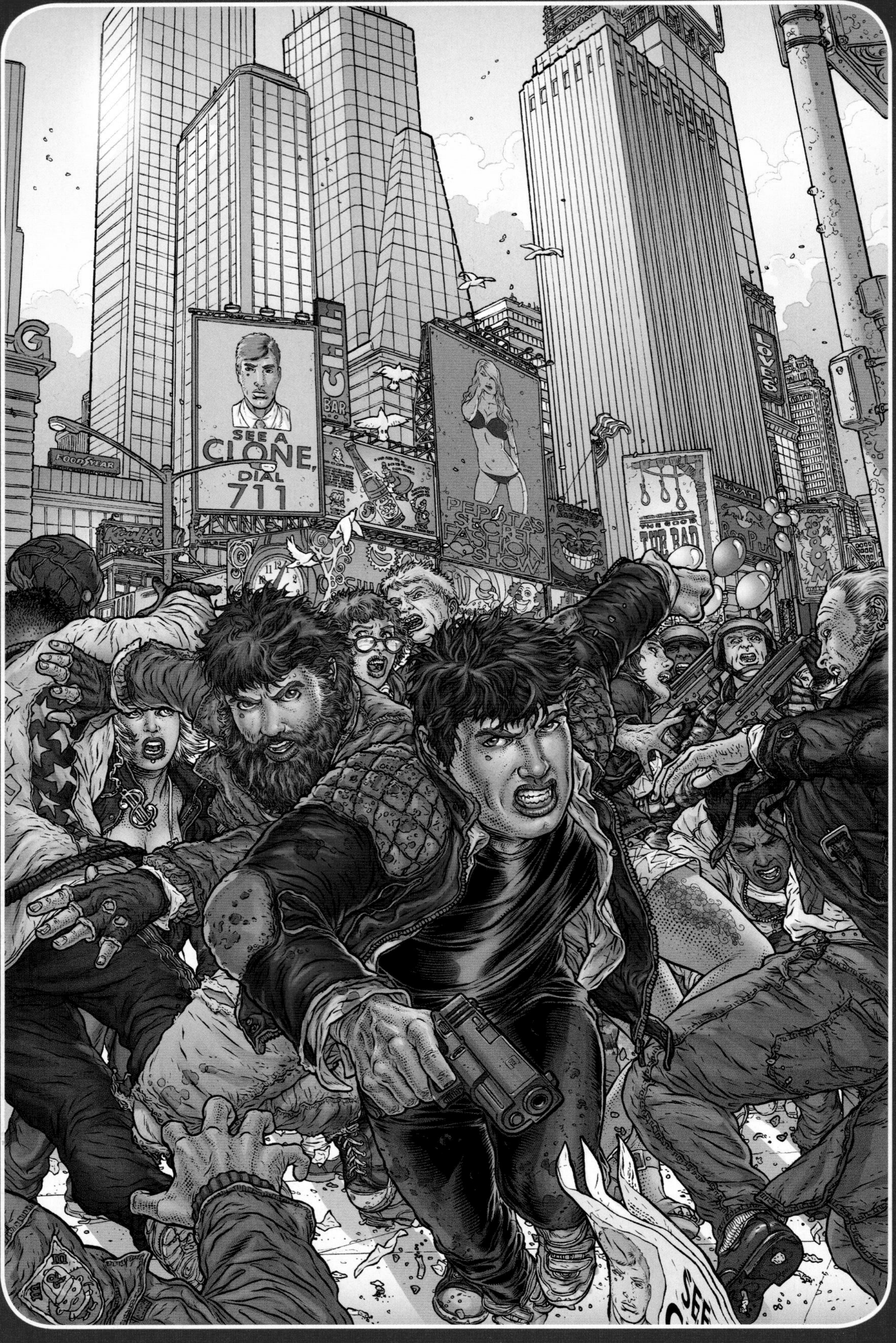
SEE A CLONE, DIAL 711
BAR
GOODYEAR
PEPOTA'S SECRET FASHION SHOW

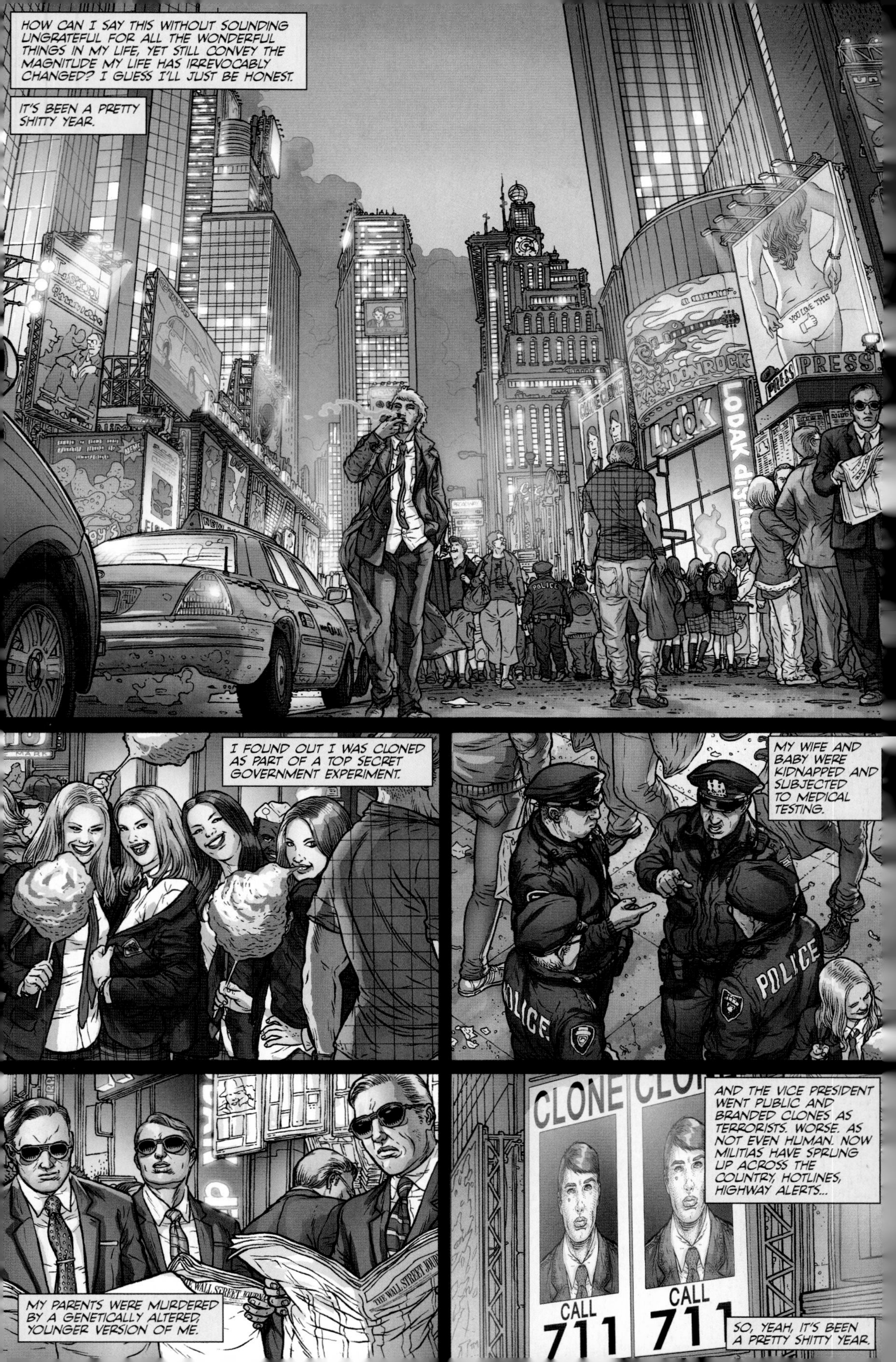
HOW CAN I SAY THIS WITHOUT SOUNDING UNGRATEFUL FOR ALL THE WONDERFUL THINGS IN MY LIFE, YET STILL CONVEY THE MAGNITUDE MY LIFE HAS IRREVOCABLY CHANGED? I GUESS I'LL JUST BE HONEST.
IT'S BEEN A PRETTY SHITTY YEAR.
KARTOONROCK
LODAK
LODAK digital
CLONE CLONE
PRESS
POLICE
YOU LOVE THIS
I FOUND OUT I WAS CLONED AS PART OF A TOP SECRET GOVERNMENT EXPERIMENT.
MY WIFE AND BABY WERE KIDNAPPED AND SUBJECTED TO MEDICAL TESTING.
POLICE
POLICE
THE WALL STREET JOURNAL
MY PARENTS WERE MURDERED BY A GENETICALLY ALTERED, YOUNGER VERSION OF ME.
CLONE
CALL 711
CALL 711
AND THE VICE PRESIDENT WENT PUBLIC AND BRANDED CLONES AS TERRORISTS. WORSE. AS NOT EVEN HUMAN. NOW MILITIAS HAVE SPRUNG UP ACROSS THE COUNTRY, HOTLINES, HIGHWAY ALERTS...
SO, YEAH, IT'S BEEN A PRETTY SHITTY YEAR.

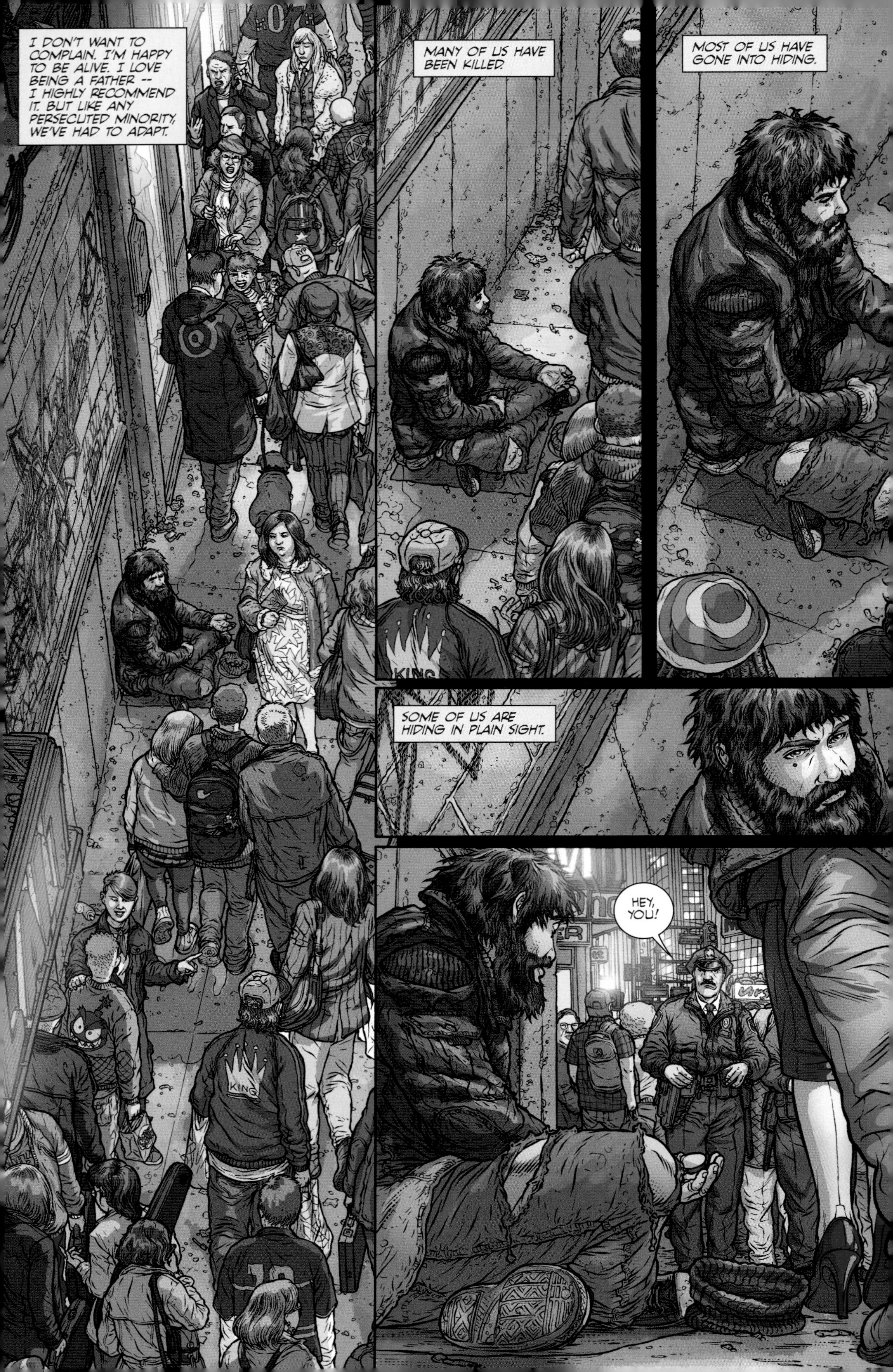
I DON'T WANT TO COMPLAIN. I'M HAPPY TO BE ALIVE. I LOVE BEING A FATHER -- I HIGHLY RECOMMEND IT. BUT LIKE ANY PERSECUTED MINORITY, WE'VE HAD TO ADAPT.
MANY OF US HAVE BEEN KILLED.
MOST OF US HAVE GONE INTO HIDING.
KING
SOME OF US ARE HIDING IN PLAIN SIGHT.
HEY, YOU!
KING

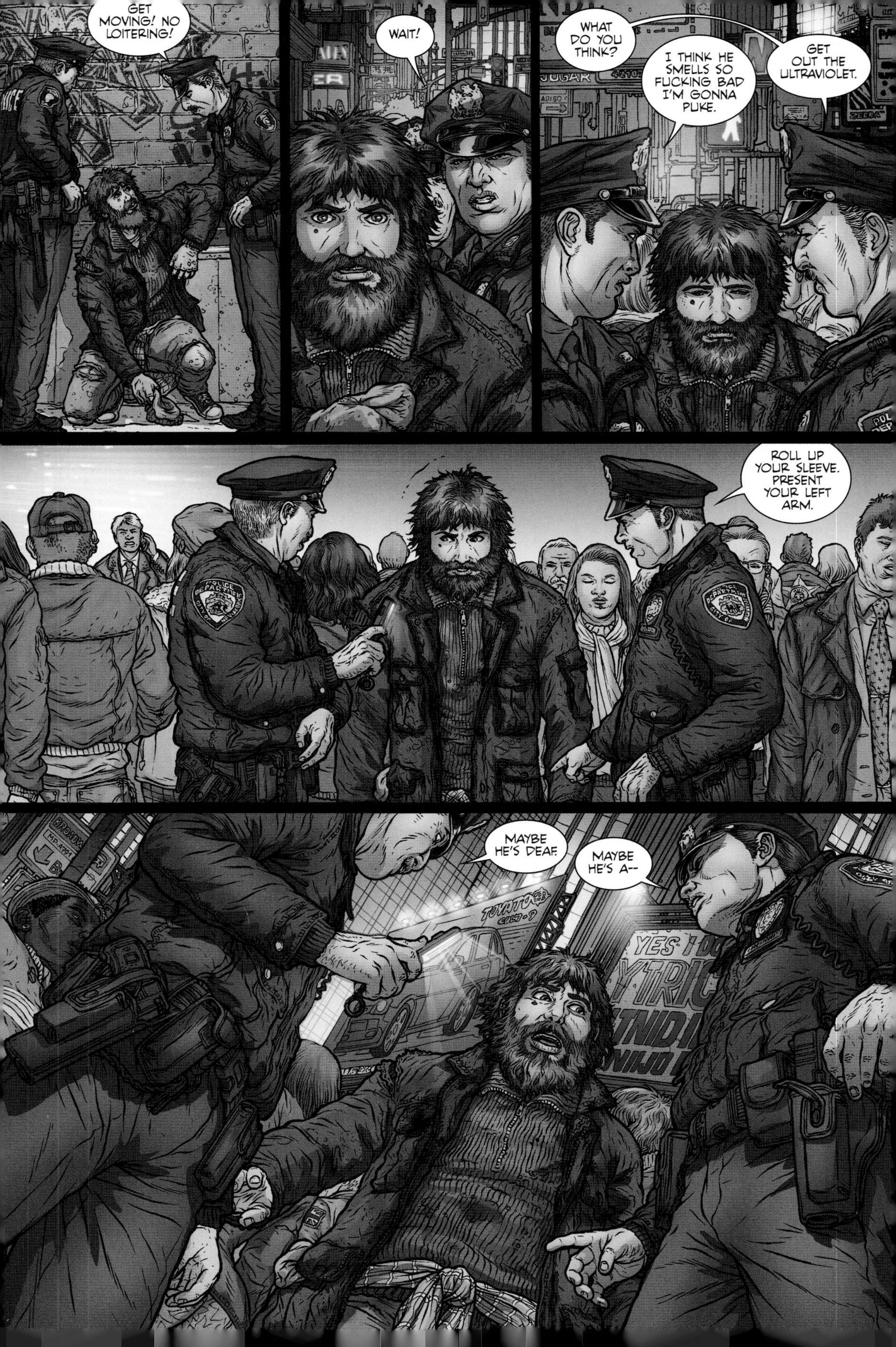
GET MOVING! NO LOITERING!
WAIT!
WHAT DO YOU THINK?
I THINK HE SMELLS SO FUCKING BAD I'M GONNA PUKE.
GET OUT THE ULTRAVIOLET.
ROLL UP YOUR SLEEVE. PRESENT YOUR LEFT ARM.
MAYBE HE'S DEAF.
MAYBE HE'S A--

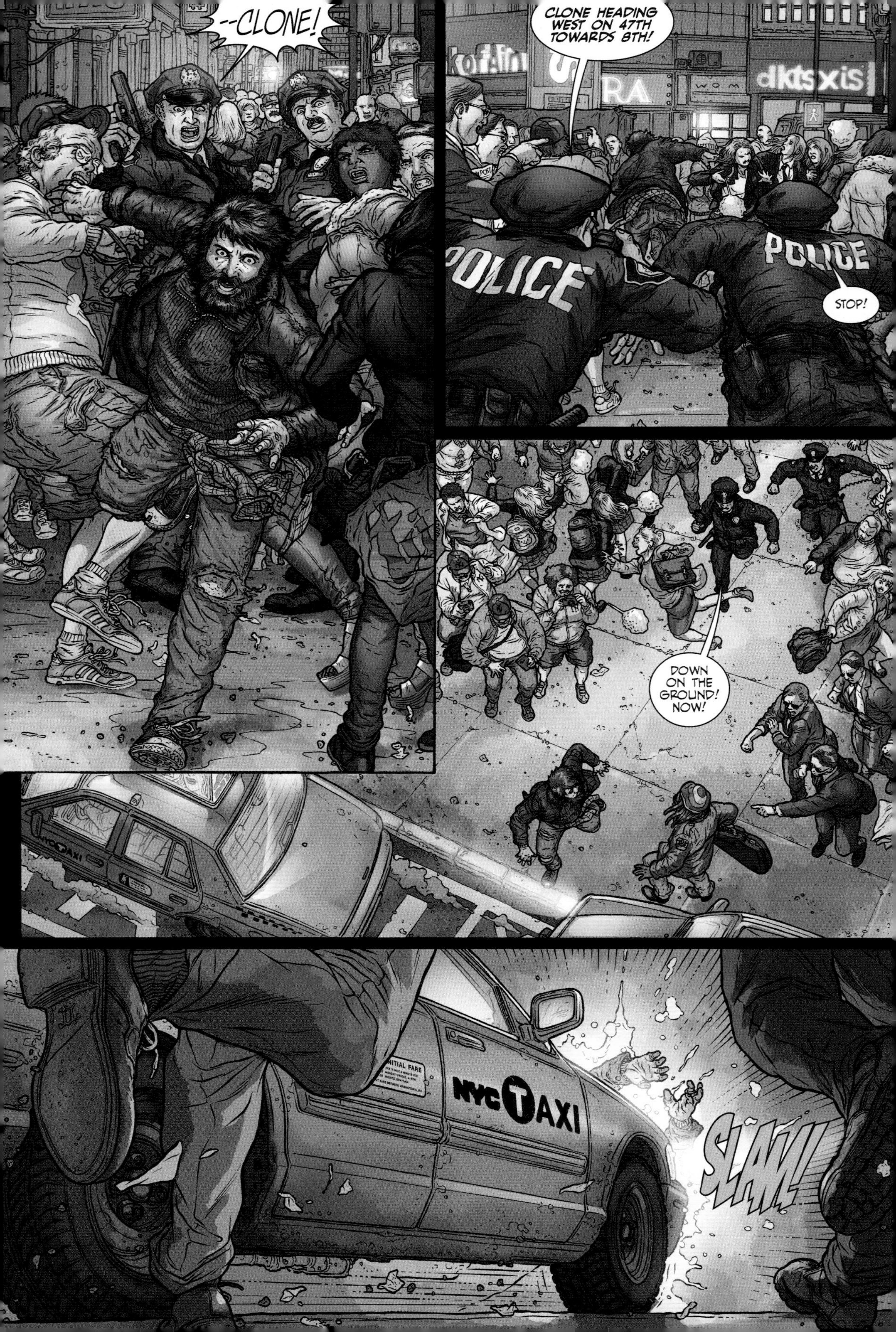
--CLONE!
CLONE HEADING WEST ON 47TH TOWARDS 8TH!
POLICE
POLICE
STOP!
DOWN ON THE GROUND! NOW!
NYC TAXI
SLAM!!

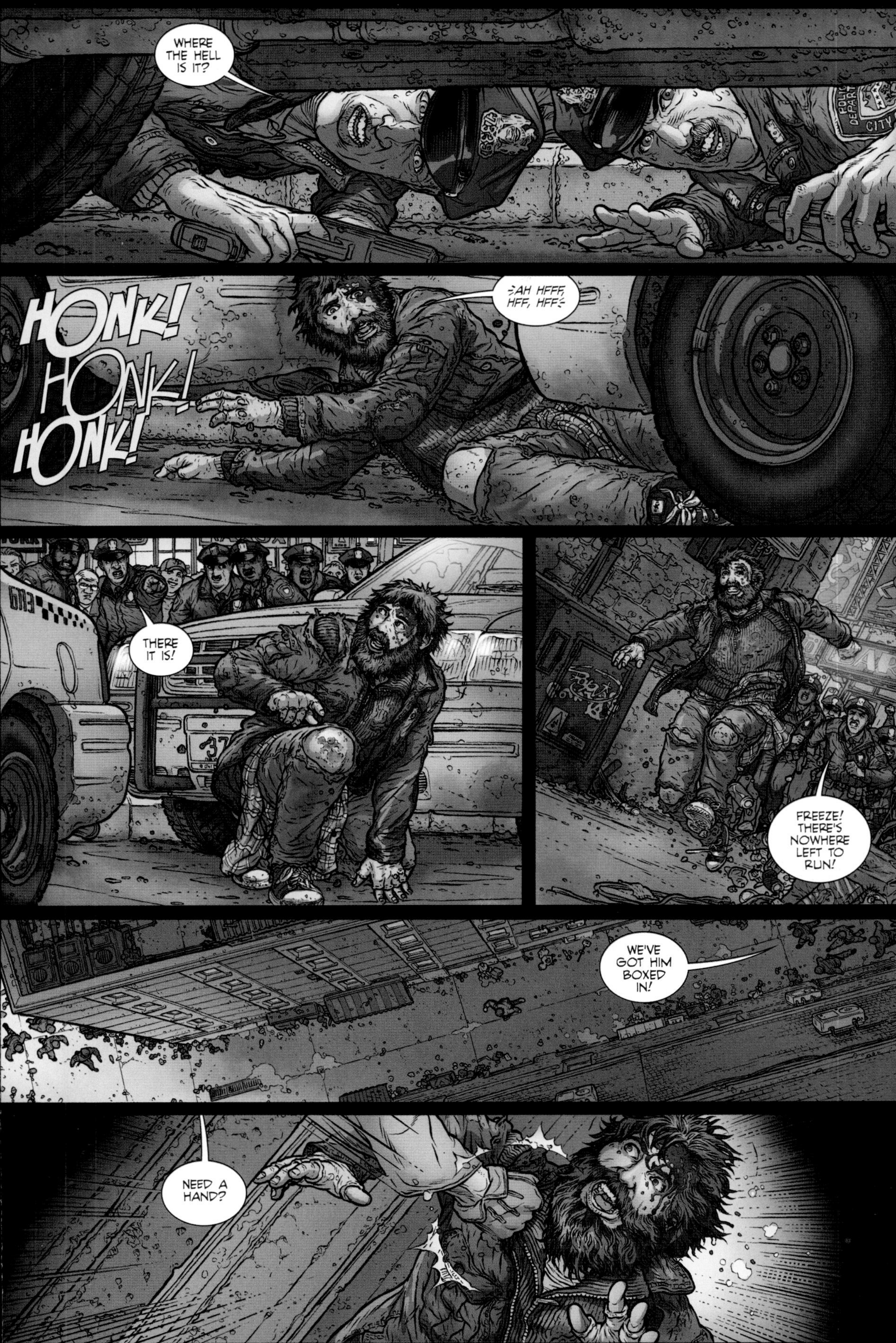
WHERE THE HELL IS IT?
HONK! HONK! HONK!
=AH HFFF, HFF, HFF=
THERE IT IS!
FREEZE! THERE'S NOWHERE LEFT TO RUN!
WE'VE GOT HIM BOXED IN!
NEED A HAND?

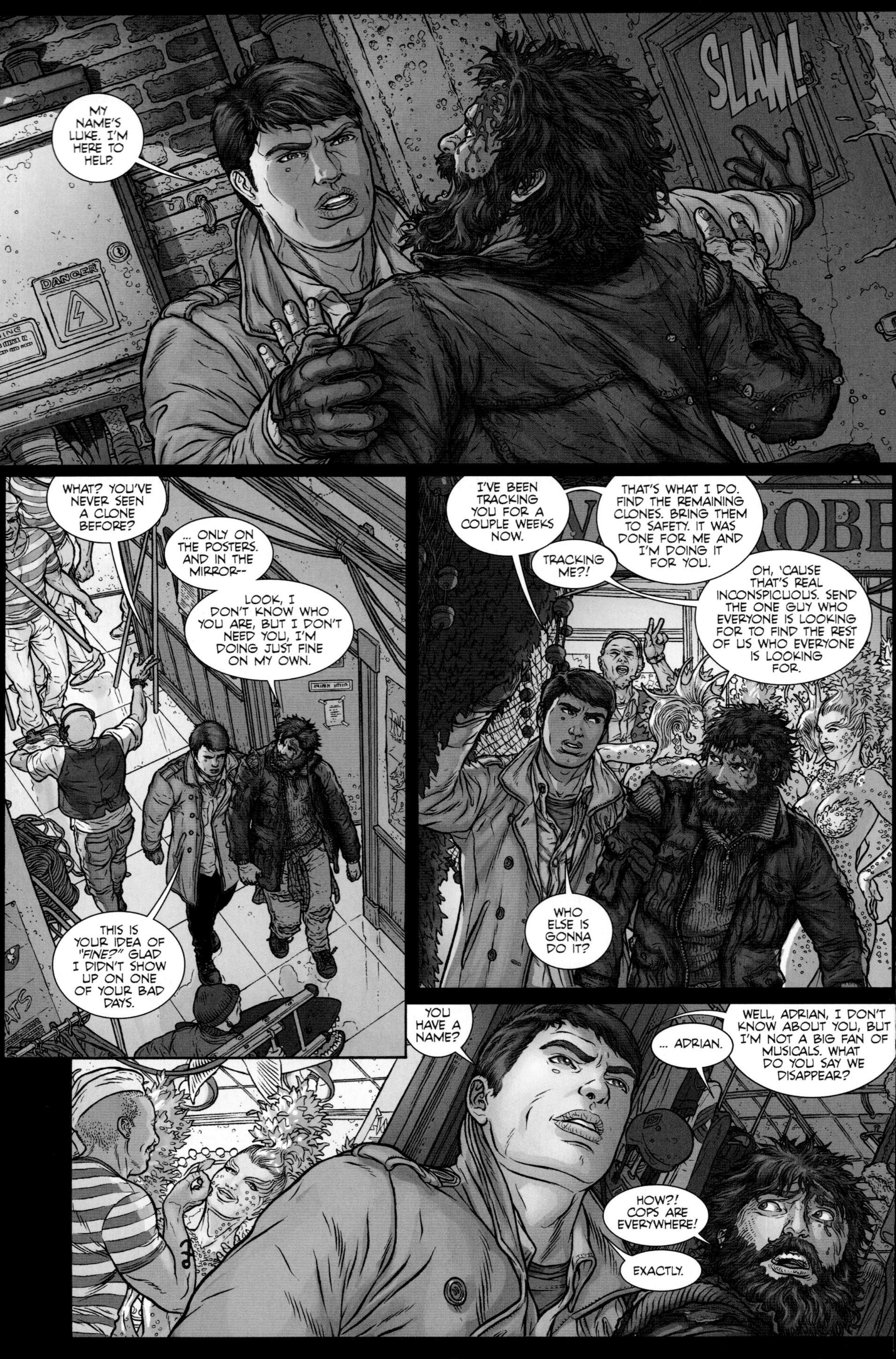
SLAM!
MY NAME'S LUKE. I'M HERE TO HELP.
DANGER
WHAT? YOU'VE NEVER SEEN A CLONE BEFORE?
... ONLY ON THE POSTERS. AND IN THE MIRROR--
LOOK, I DON'T KNOW WHO YOU ARE, BUT I DON'T NEED YOU, I'M DOING JUST FINE ON MY OWN.
THIS IS YOUR IDEA OF "FINE?" GLAD I DIDN'T SHOW UP ON ONE OF YOUR BAD DAYS.
I'VE BEEN TRACKING YOU FOR A COUPLE WEEKS NOW.
TRACKING ME?!
THAT'S WHAT I DO. FIND THE REMAINING CLONES. BRING THEM TO SAFETY. IT WAS DONE FOR ME AND I'M DOING IT FOR YOU.
OH, 'CAUSE THAT'S REAL INCONSPICUOUS. SEND THE ONE GUY WHO EVERYONE IS LOOKING FOR TO FIND THE REST OF US WHO EVERYONE IS LOOKING FOR.
WHO ELSE IS GONNA DO IT?
YOU HAVE A NAME?
... ADRIAN.
WELL, ADRIAN, I DON'T KNOW ABOUT YOU, BUT I'M NOT A BIG FAN OF MUSICALS. WHAT DO YOU SAY WE DISAPPEAR?
HOW?! COPS ARE EVERYWHERE!
EXACTLY.

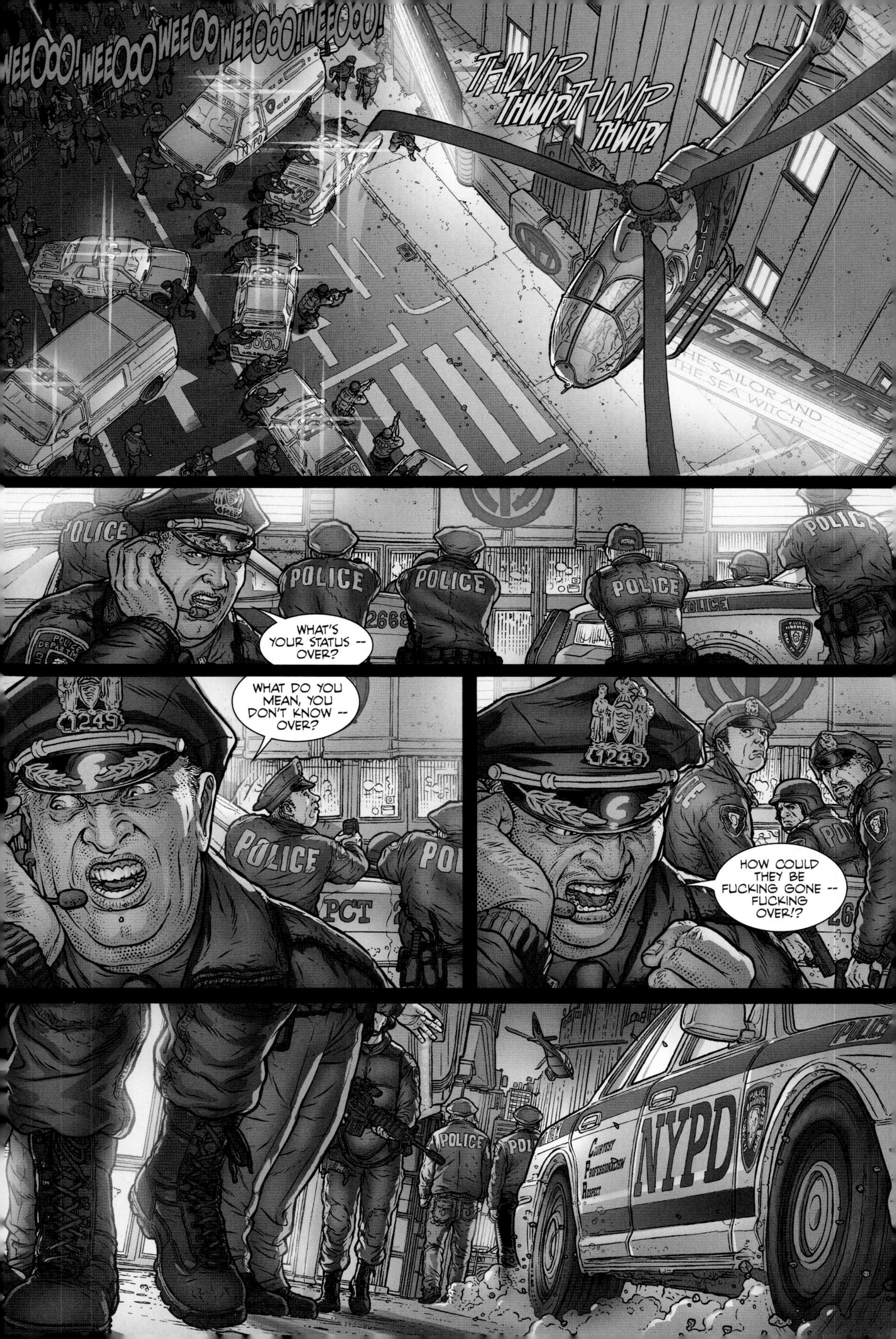
WEEOOO! WEEOOO WEEOO WEEOOO! WEEOOO!
THWIP THWIP! THWIP THWIP!
THE SAILOR AND THE SEA WITCH
WHAT'S YOUR STATUS -- OVER?
WHAT DO YOU MEAN, YOU DON'T KNOW -- OVER?
HOW COULD THEY BE FUCKING GONE -- FUCKING OVER!?
NYPD
COURTESY PROFESSIONALISM RESPECT

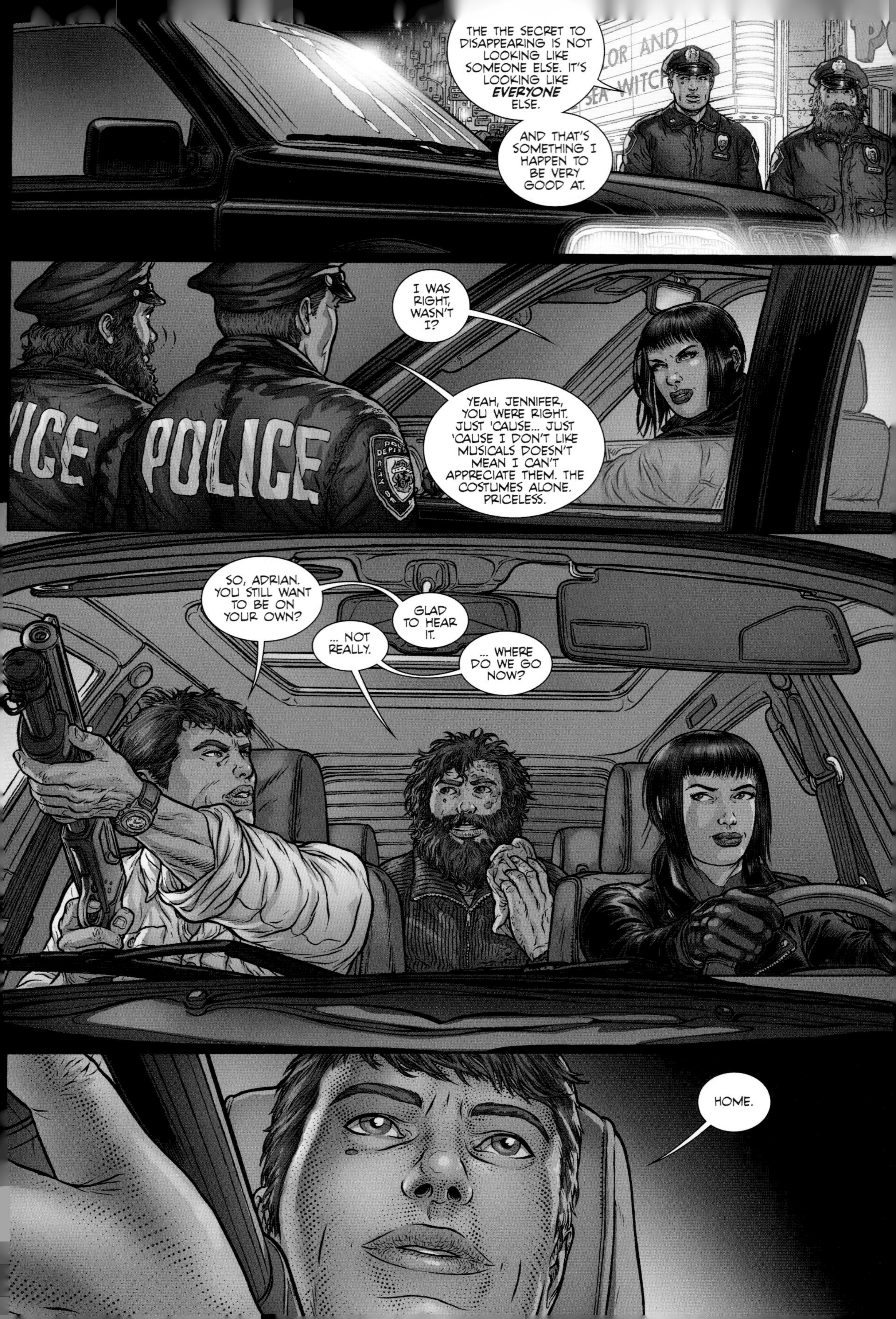
THE THE SECRET TO DISAPPEARING IS NOT LOOKING LIKE SOMEONE ELSE. IT'S LOOKING LIKE **EVERYONE** ELSE.
AND THAT'S SOMETHING I HAPPEN TO BE VERY GOOD AT.
I WAS RIGHT, WASN'T I?
YEAH, JENNIFER, YOU WERE RIGHT. JUST 'CAUSE... JUST 'CAUSE I DON'T LIKE MUSICALS DOESN'T MEAN I CAN'T APPRECIATE THEM. THE COSTUMES ALONE. PRICELESS.
POLICE
SO, ADRIAN. YOU STILL WANT TO BE ON YOUR OWN?
... NOT REALLY.
GLAD TO HEAR IT.
... WHERE DO WE GO NOW?
HOME.

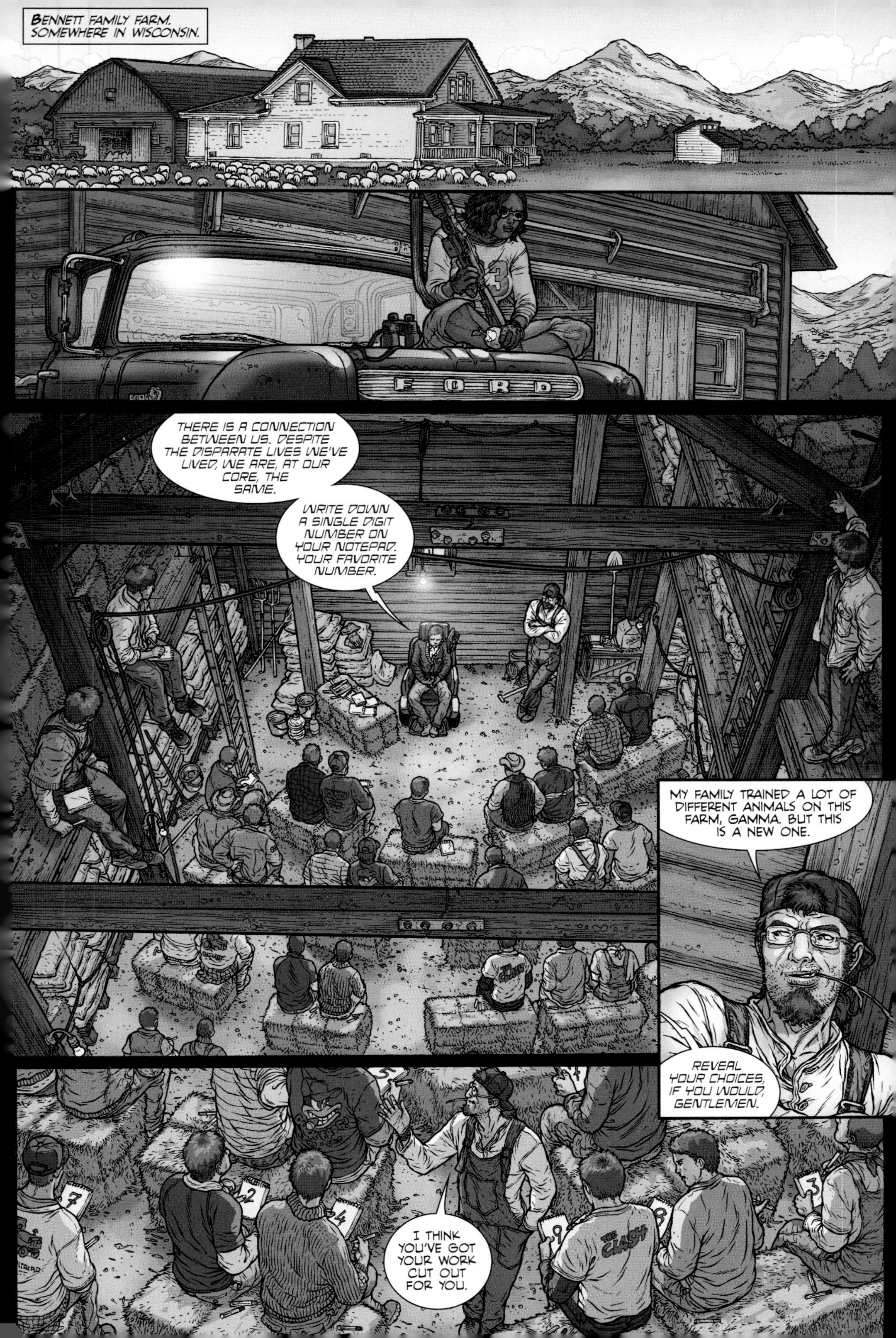

BENNETT FAMILY FARM. SOMEWHERE IN WISCONSIN.
FORD
THERE IS A CONNECTION BETWEEN US. DESPITE THE DISPARATE LIVES WE'VE LIVED, WE ARE, AT OUR CORE, THE SAME.
WRITE DOWN A SINGLE DIGIT NUMBER ON YOUR NOTEPAD. YOUR FAVORITE NUMBER.
MY FAMILY TRAINED A LOT OF DIFFERENT ANIMALS ON THIS FARM, GAMMA. BUT THIS IS A NEW ONE.
REVEAL YOUR CHOICES, IF YOU WOULD, GENTLEMEN.
I THINK YOU'VE GOT YOUR WORK CUT OUT FOR YOU.

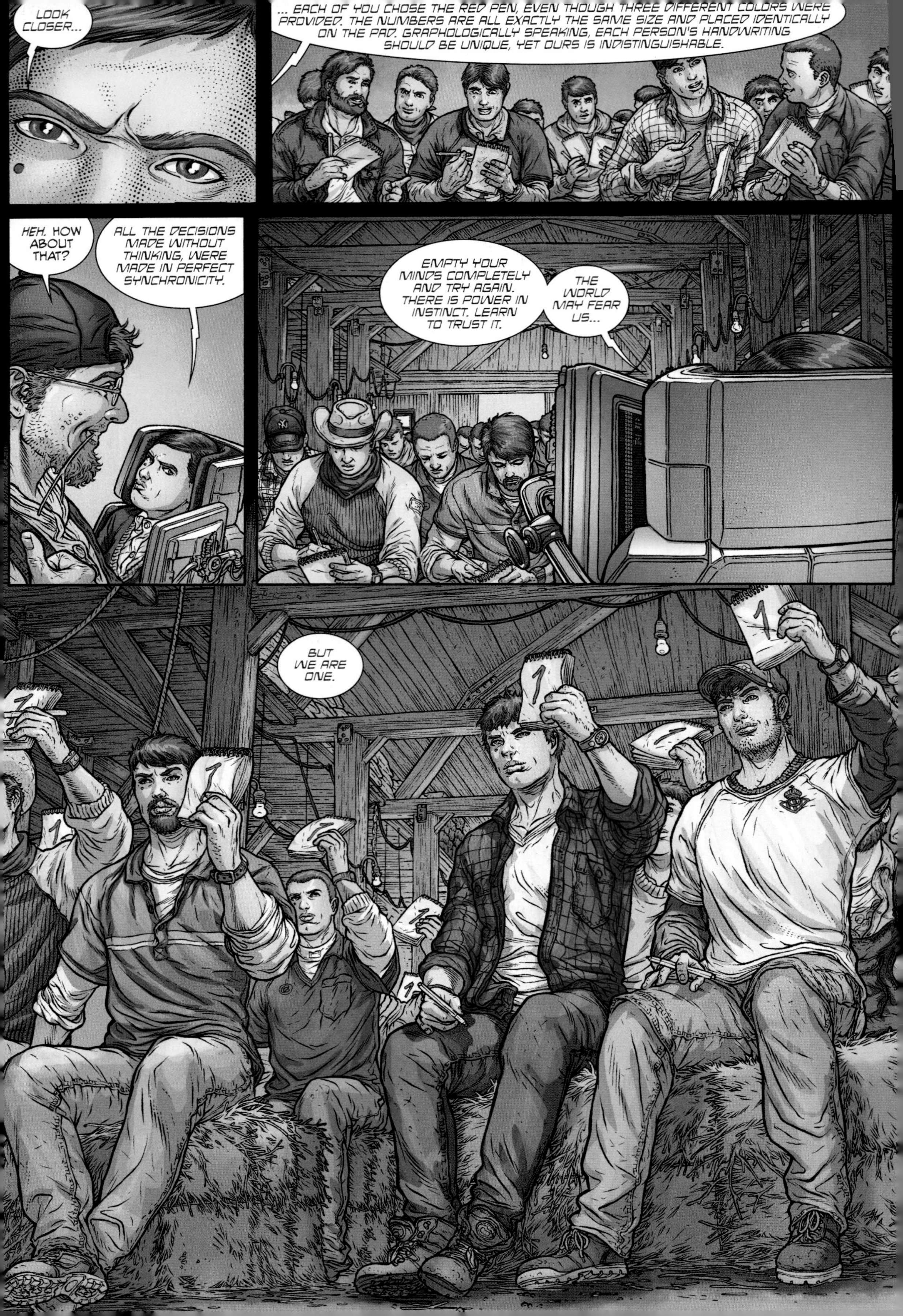
LOOK CLOSER...
... EACH OF YOU CHOSE THE RED PEN, EVEN THOUGH THREE DIFFERENT COLORS WERE PROVIDED. THE NUMBERS ARE ALL EXACTLY THE SAME SIZE AND PLACED IDENTICALLY ON THE PAD. GRAPHOLOGICALLY SPEAKING, EACH PERSON'S HANDWRITING SHOULD BE UNIQUE, YET OURS IS INDISTINGUISHABLE.
HEH. HOW ABOUT THAT?
ALL THE DECISIONS MADE WITHOUT THINKING, WERE MADE IN PERFECT SYNCHRONICITY.
EMPTY YOUR MINDS COMPLETELY AND TRY AGAIN. THERE IS POWER IN INSTINCT. LEARN TO TRUST IT.
THE WORLD MAY FEAR US...
BUT WE ARE ONE.

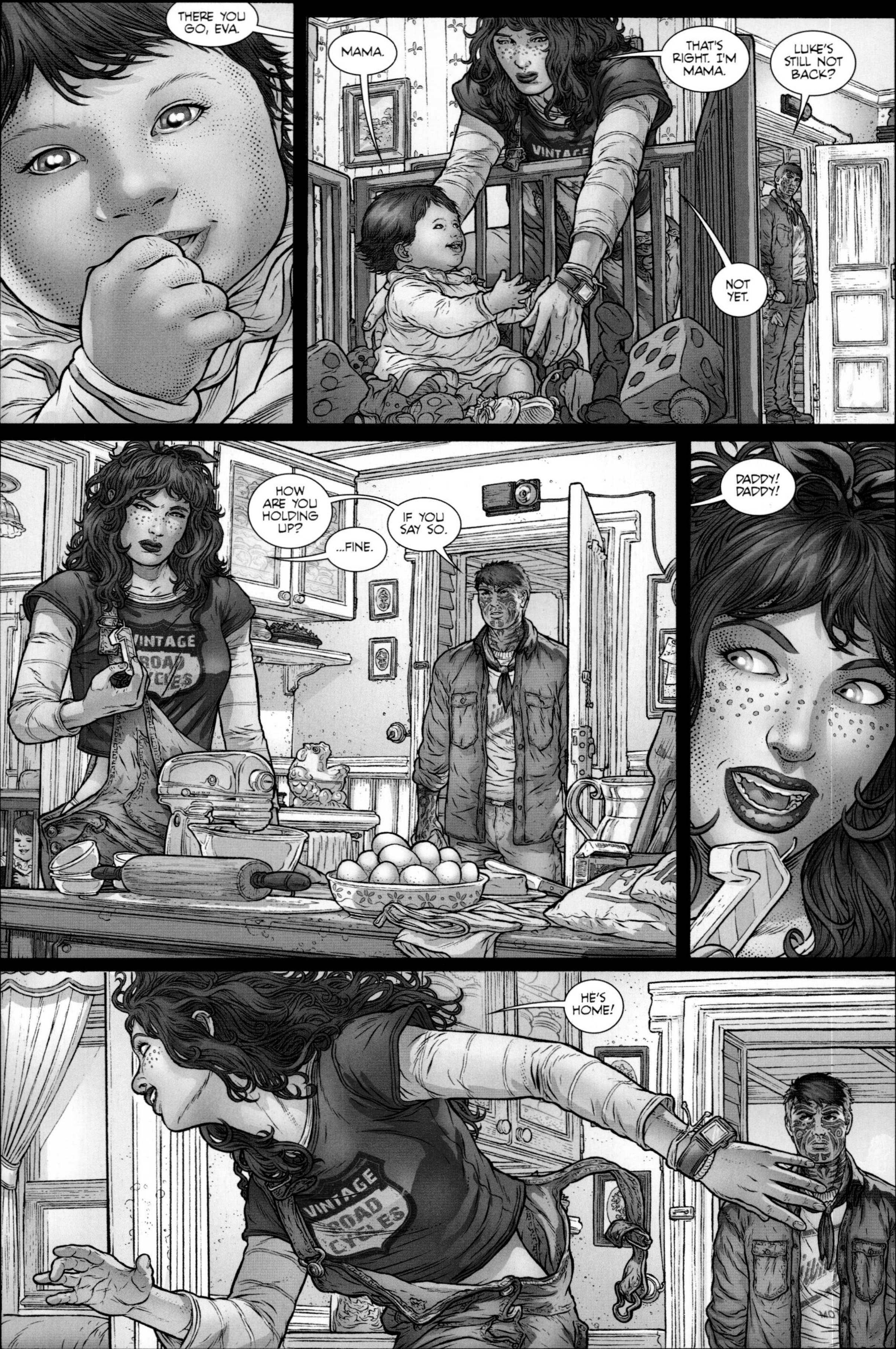
THERE YOU GO, EVA.
MAMA.
THAT'S RIGHT. I'M MAMA.
LUKE'S STILL NOT BACK?
NOT YET.
VINTAGE
HOW ARE YOU HOLDING UP?
...FINE.
IF YOU SAY SO.
VINTAGE ROAD CYCLES
DADDY! DADDY!
HE'S HOME!
VINTAGE ROAD CYCLES

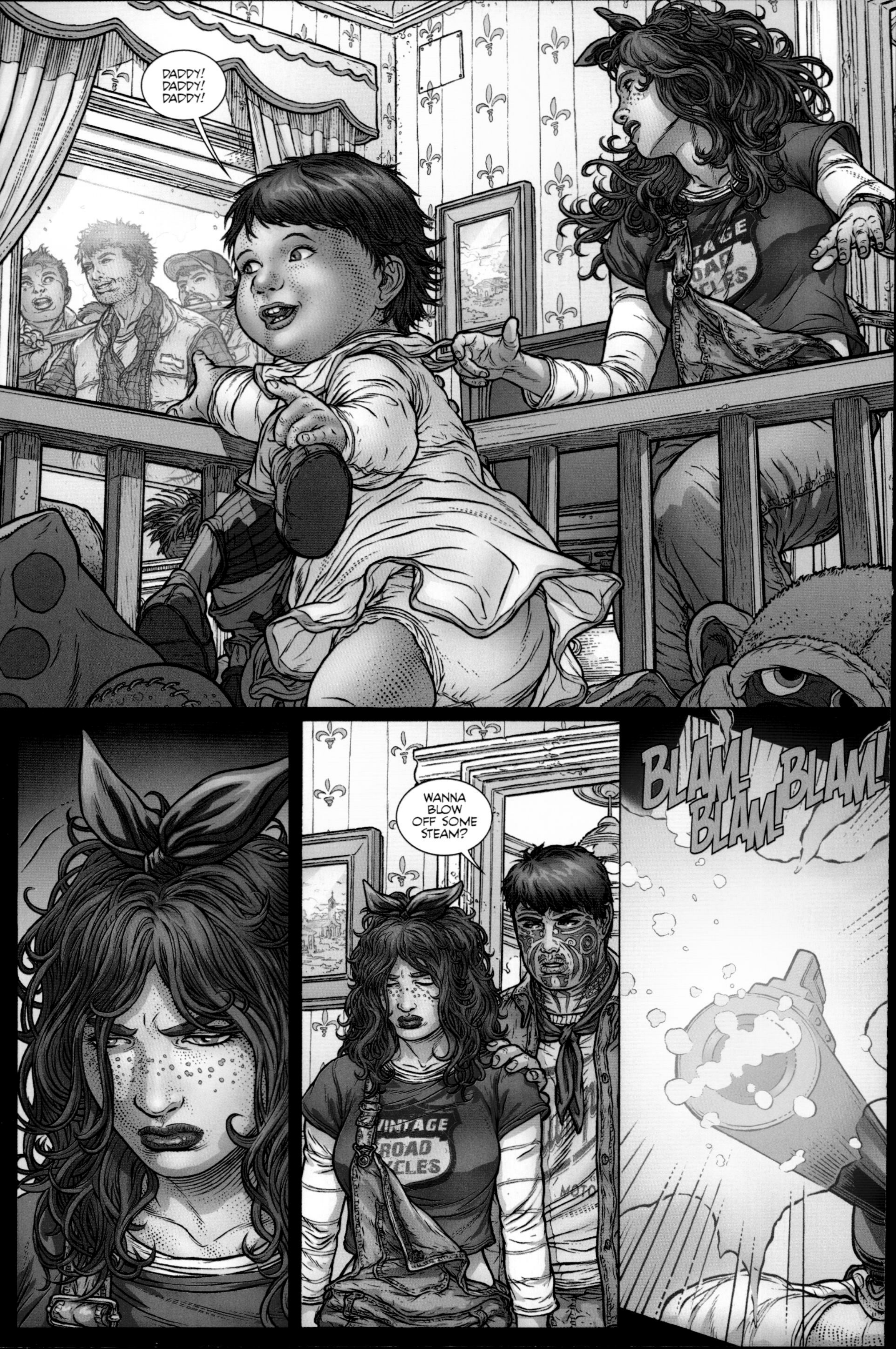
DADDY! DADDY! DADDY!
WANNA BLOW OFF SOME STEAM?
BLAM! BLAM! BLAM!

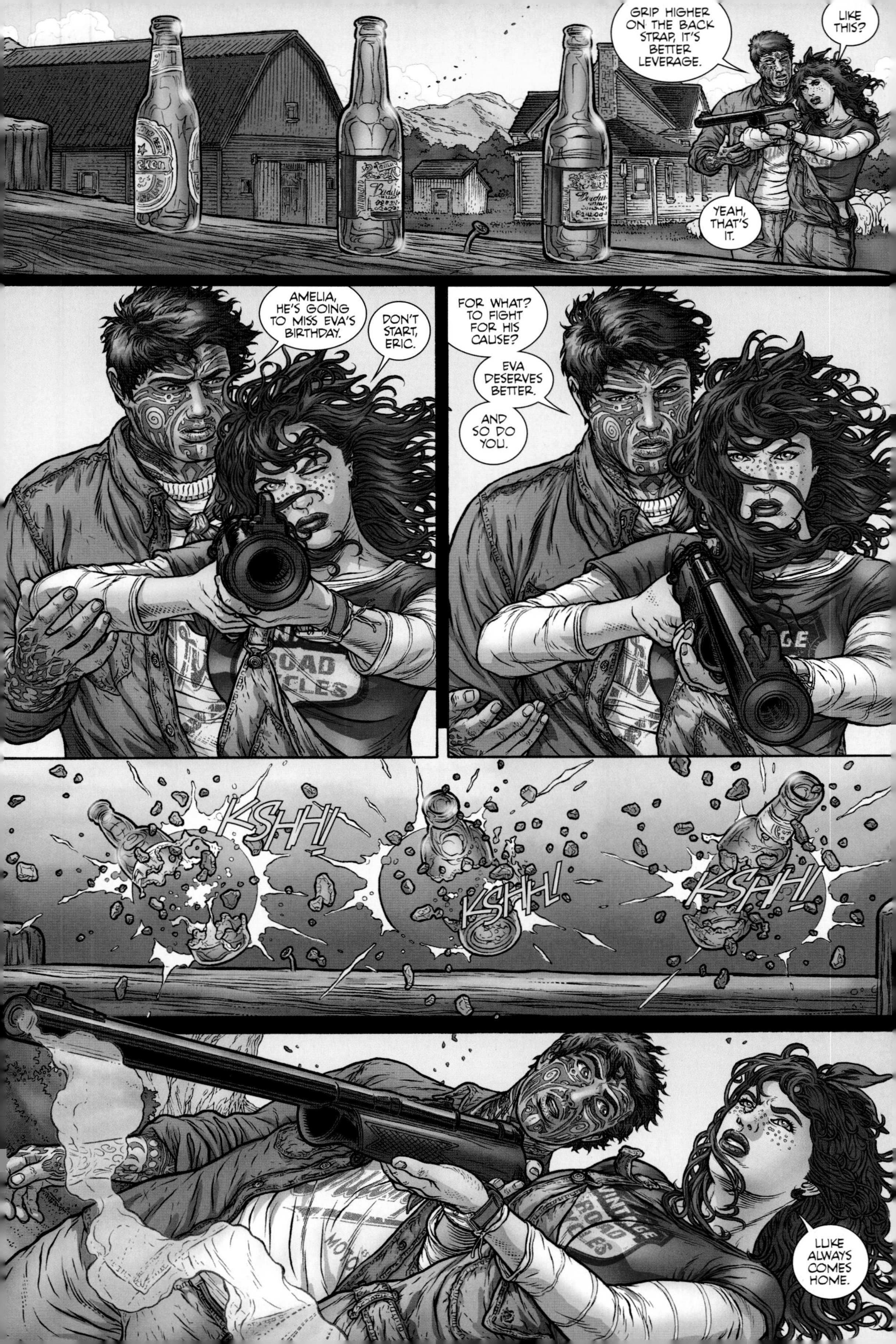

GRIP HIGHER ON THE BACK STRAP, IT'S BETTER LEVERAGE.
LIKE THIS?
YEAH, THAT'S IT.
AMELIA, HE'S GOING TO MISS EVA'S BIRTHDAY.
DON'T START, ERIC.
FOR WHAT? TO FIGHT FOR HIS CAUSE?
EVA DESERVES BETTER.
AND SO DO YOU.
KSHH!
KSHH!
KSHH!
LUKE ALWAYS COMES HOME.

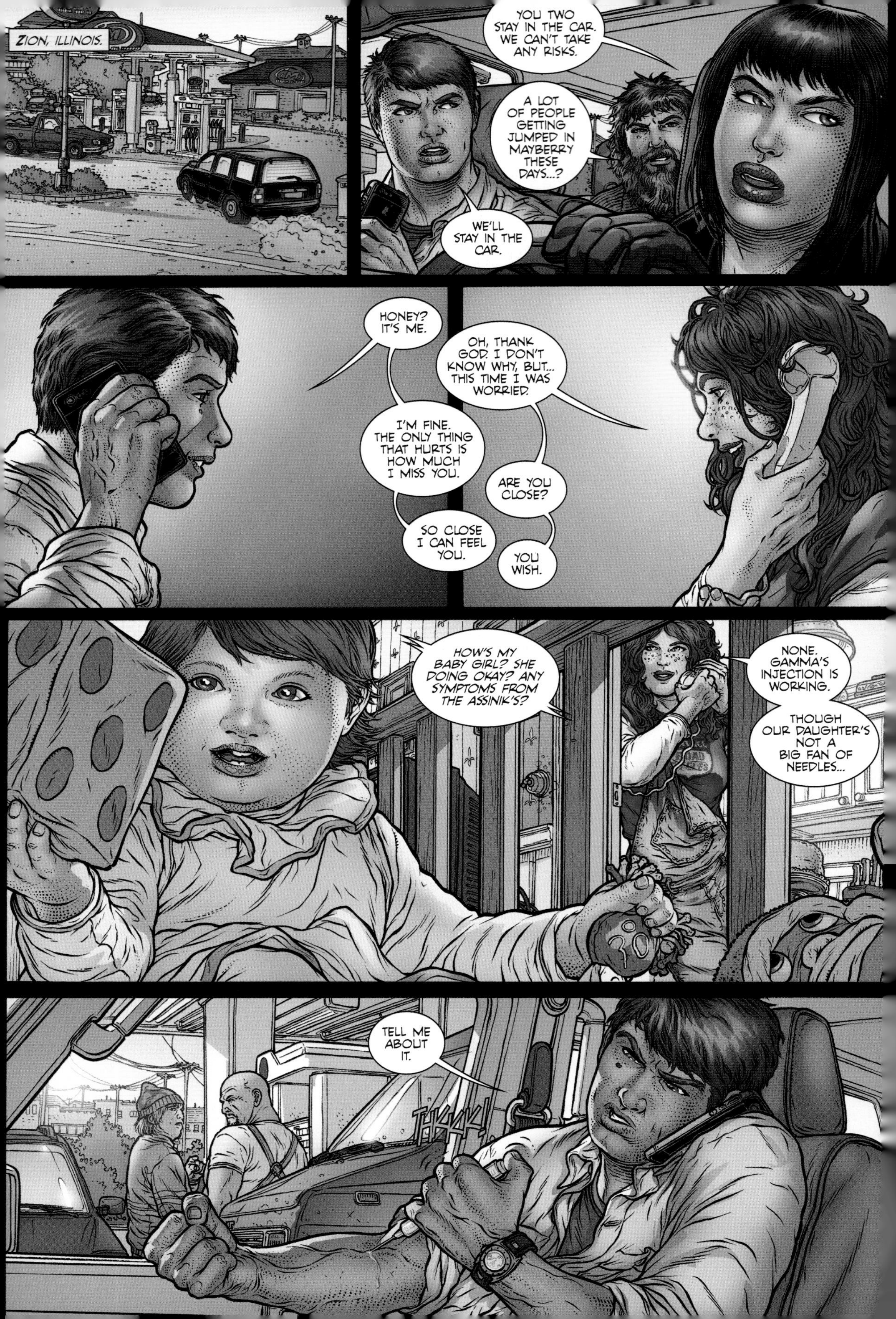
ZION, ILLINOIS.
YOU TWO STAY IN THE CAR. WE CAN'T TAKE ANY RISKS.
A LOT OF PEOPLE GETTING JUMPED IN MAYBERRY THESE DAYS...?
WE'LL STAY IN THE CAR.
HONEY? IT'S ME.
OH, THANK GOD. I DON'T KNOW WHY, BUT... THIS TIME I WAS WORRIED.
I'M FINE. THE ONLY THING THAT HURTS IS HOW MUCH I MISS YOU.
ARE YOU CLOSE?
SO CLOSE I CAN FEEL YOU.
YOU WISH.
HOW'S MY BABY GIRL? SHE DOING OKAY? ANY SYMPTOMS FROM THE ASSINIK'S?
NONE. GAMMA'S INJECTION IS WORKING.
THOUGH OUR DAUGHTER'S NOT A BIG FAN OF NEEDLES...
TELL ME ABOUT IT.
THUK!

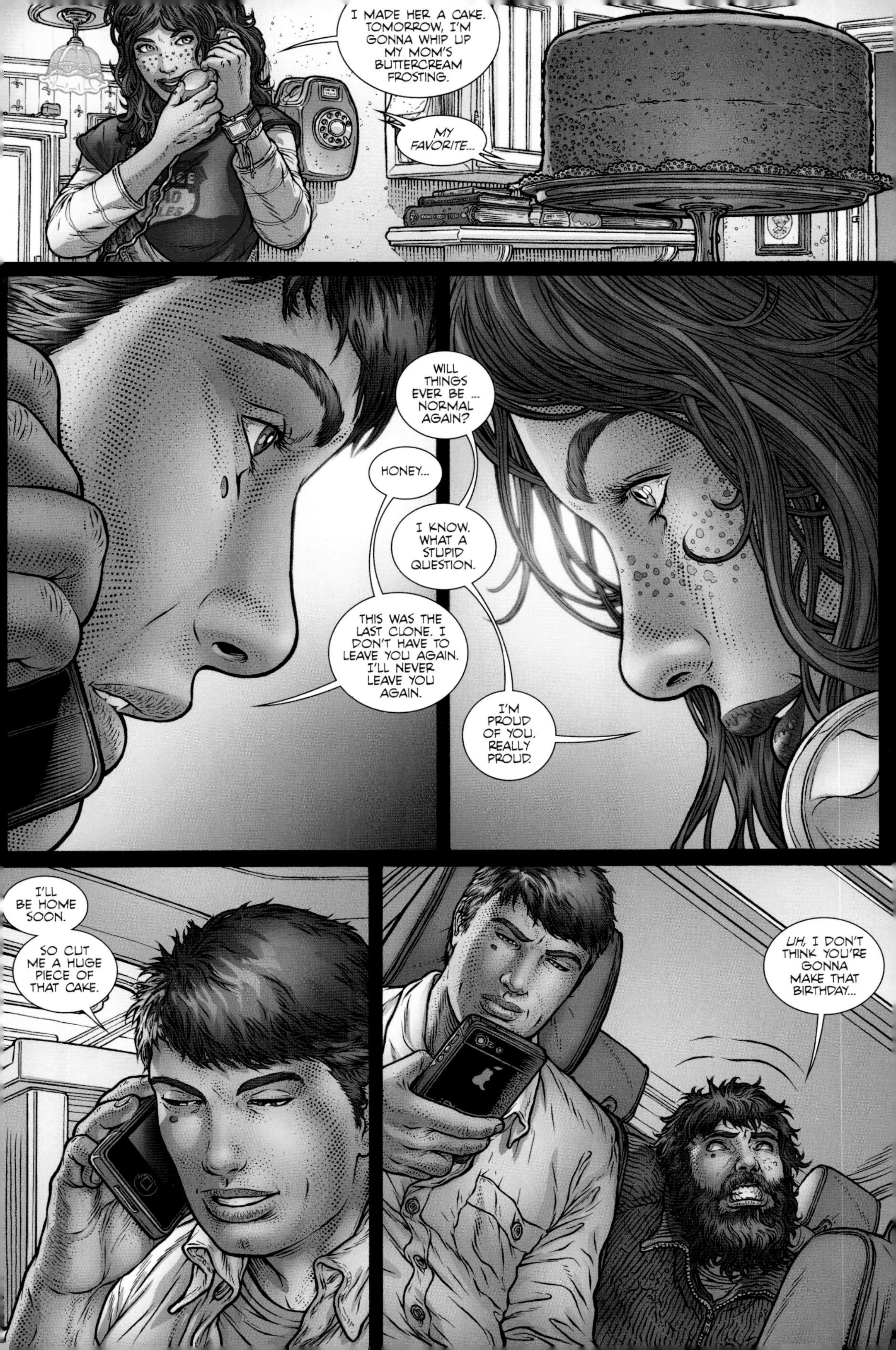
I MADE HER A CAKE. TOMORROW, I'M GONNA WHIP UP MY MOM'S BUTTERCREAM FROSTING.
MY FAVORITE...
WILL THINGS EVER BE ... NORMAL AGAIN?
HONEY...
I KNOW. WHAT A STUPID QUESTION.
THIS WAS THE LAST CLONE. I DON'T HAVE TO LEAVE YOU AGAIN. I'LL NEVER LEAVE YOU AGAIN.
I'M PROUD OF YOU. REALLY PROUD.
I'LL BE HOME SOON.
SO CUT ME A HUGE PIECE OF THAT CAKE.
UH, I DON'T THINK YOU'RE GONNA MAKE THAT BIRTHDAY...

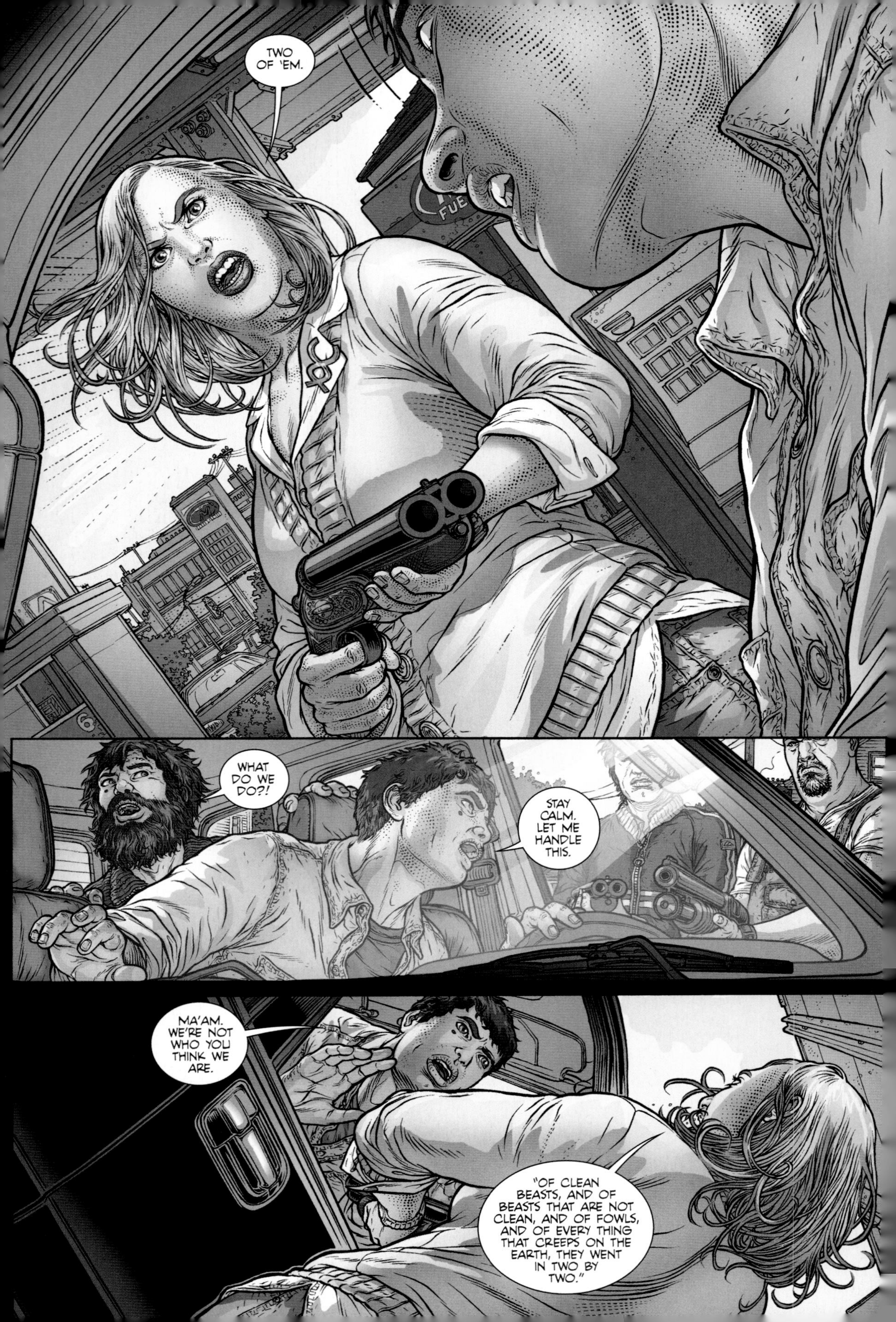
TWO OF 'EM.
WHAT DO WE DO?!
STAY CALM. LET ME HANDLE THIS.
MA'AM. WE'RE NOT WHO YOU THINK WE ARE.
"OF CLEAN BEASTS, AND OF BEASTS THAT ARE NOT CLEAN, AND OF FOWLS, AND OF EVERY THING THAT CREEPS ON THE EARTH, THEY WENT IN TWO BY TWO."

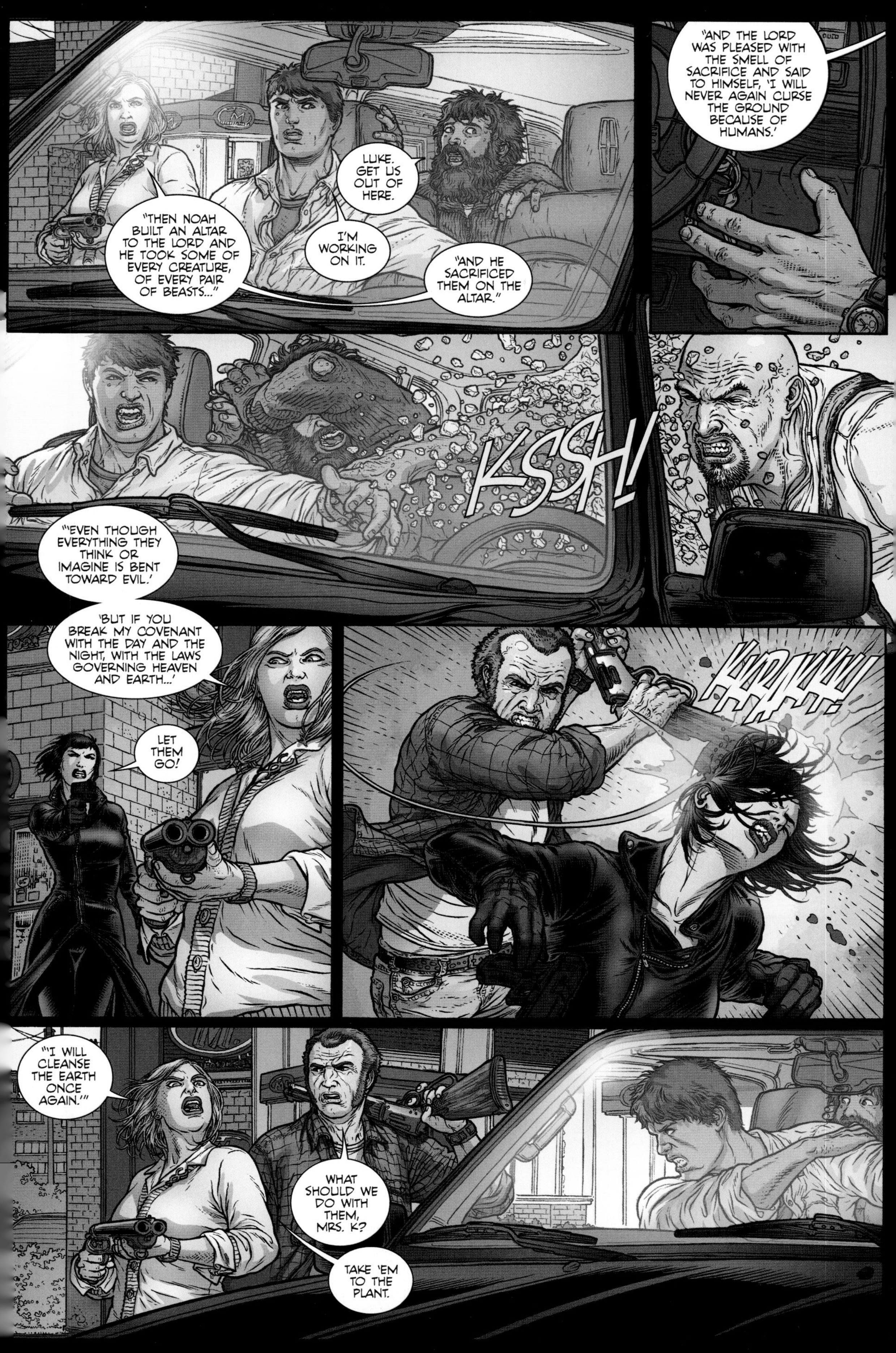
LUKE. GET US OUT OF HERE.
I'M WORKING ON IT.
"THEN NOAH BUILT AN ALTAR TO THE LORD AND HE TOOK SOME OF EVERY CREATURE, OF EVERY PAIR OF BEASTS..."
"AND HE SACRIFICED THEM ON THE ALTAR."
"AND THE LORD WAS PLEASED WITH THE SMELL OF SACRIFICE AND SAID TO HIMSELF, 'I WILL NEVER AGAIN CURSE THE GROUND BECAUSE OF HUMANS.'
KSSH!
"EVEN THOUGH EVERYTHING THEY THINK OR IMAGINE IS BENT TOWARD EVIL.'
'BUT IF YOU BREAK MY COVENANT WITH THE DAY AND THE NIGHT, WITH THE LAWS GOVERNING HEAVEN AND EARTH...'
LET THEM GO!
KRAKK!
"I WILL CLEANSE THE EARTH ONCE AGAIN.'"
WHAT SHOULD WE DO WITH THEM, MRS. K?
TAKE 'EM TO THE PLANT.

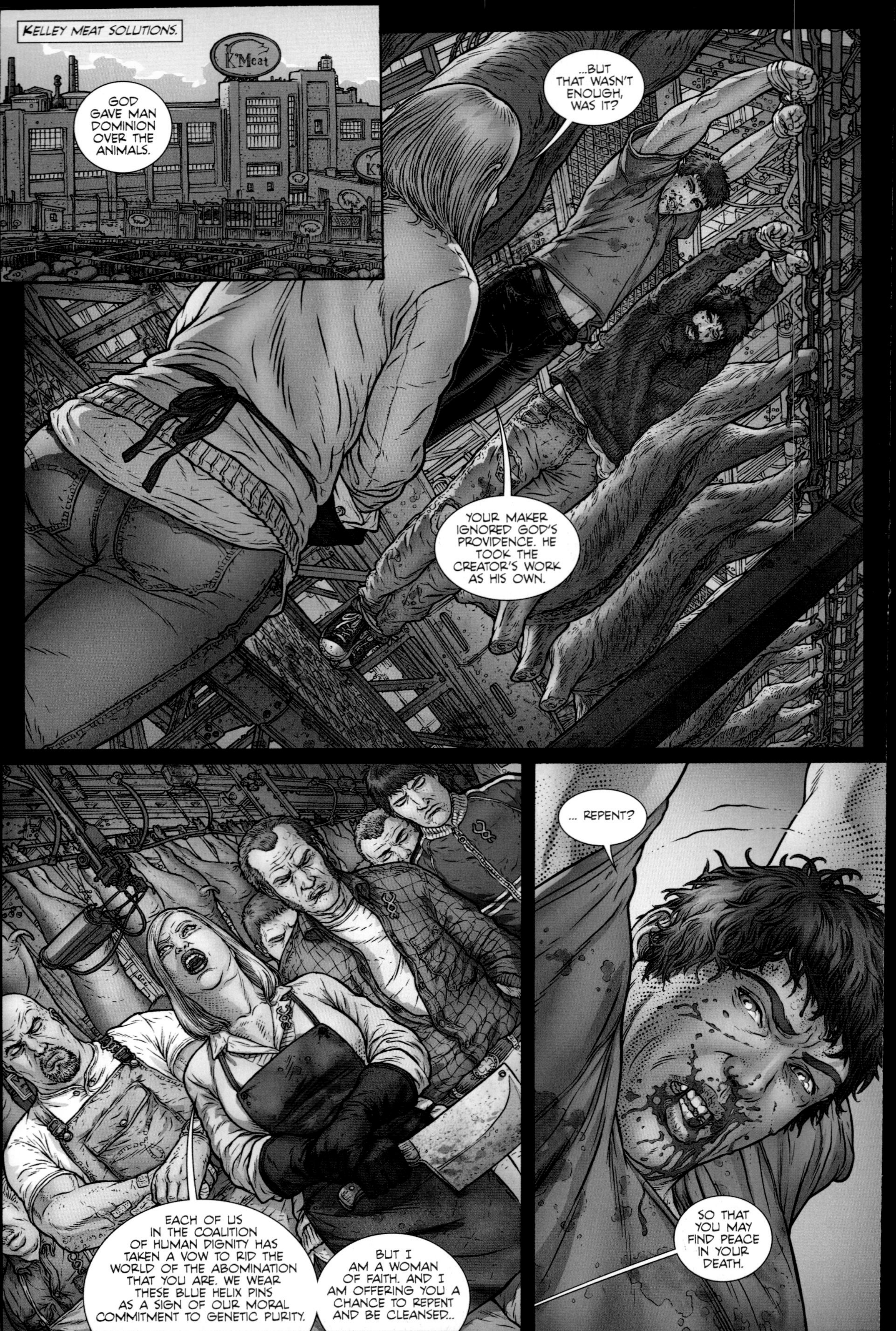
KELLEY MEAT SOLUTIONS.
K'Meat
GOD GAVE MAN DOMINION OVER THE ANIMALS.
...BUT THAT WASN'T ENOUGH, WAS IT?
YOUR MAKER IGNORED GOD'S PROVIDENCE. HE TOOK THE CREATOR'S WORK AS HIS OWN.
EACH OF US IN THE COALITION OF HUMAN DIGNITY HAS TAKEN A VOW TO RID THE WORLD OF THE ABOMINATION THAT YOU ARE. WE WEAR THESE BLUE HELIX PINS AS A SIGN OF OUR MORAL COMMITMENT TO GENETIC PURITY.
BUT I AM A WOMAN OF FAITH. AND I AM OFFERING YOU A CHANCE TO REPENT AND BE CLEANSED...
... REPENT?
SO THAT YOU MAY FIND PEACE IN YOUR DEATH.

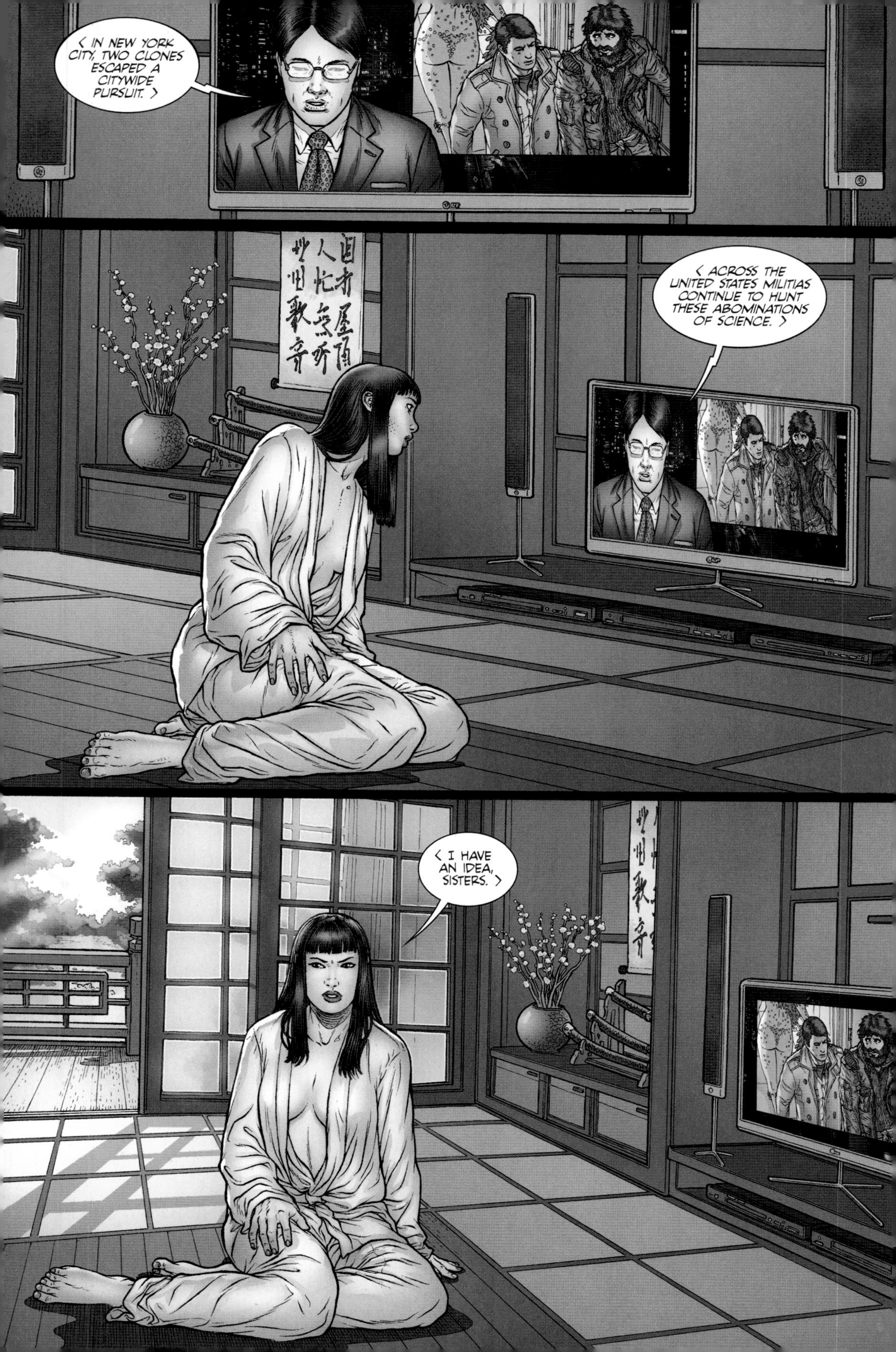
< IN NEW YORK CITY, TWO CLONES ESCAPED A CITYWIDE PURSUIT. >
< ACROSS THE UNITED STATES MILITIAS CONTINUE TO HUNT THESE ABOMINATIONS OF SCIENCE. >
< I HAVE AN IDEA, SISTERS. >

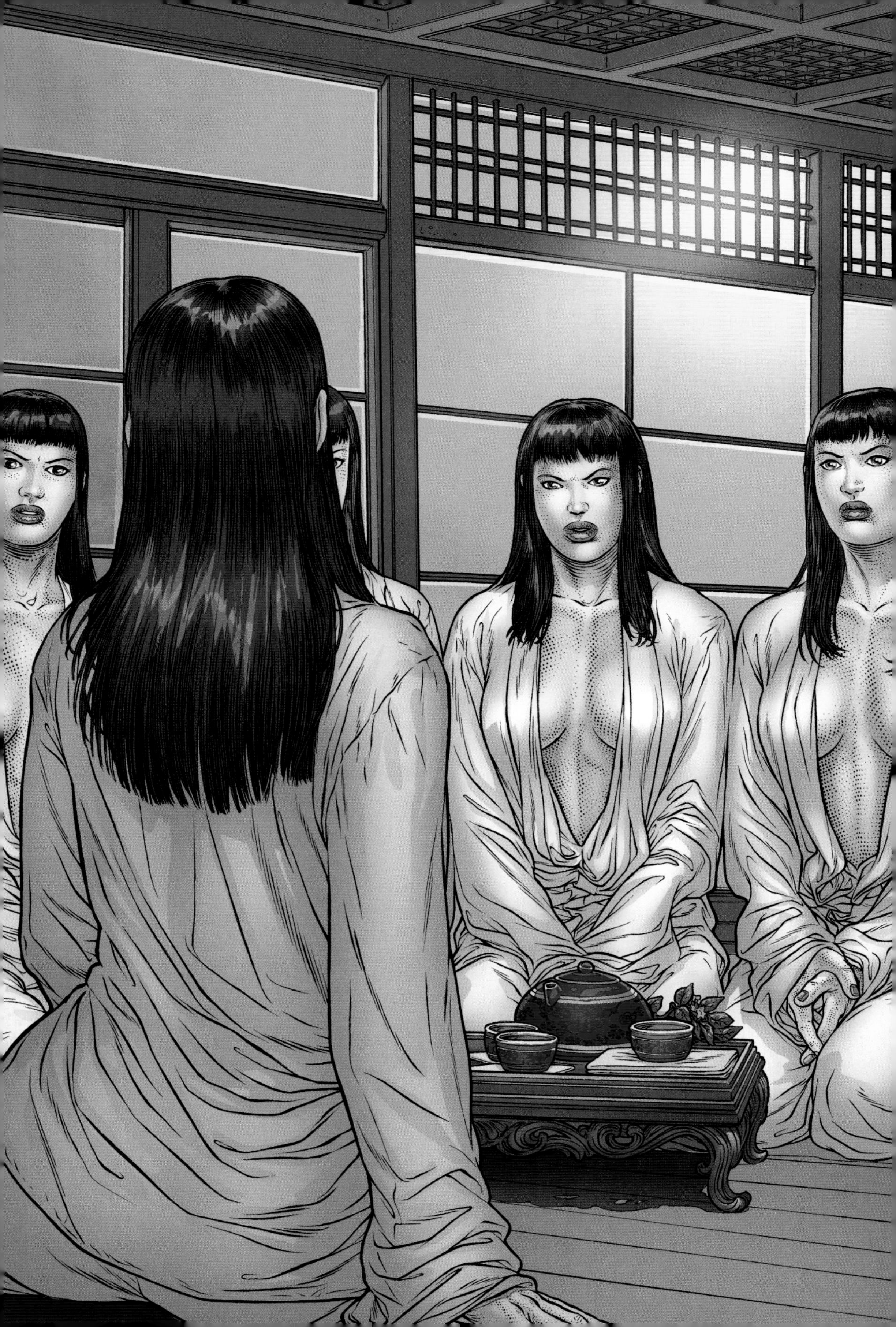

CHAPTER 12

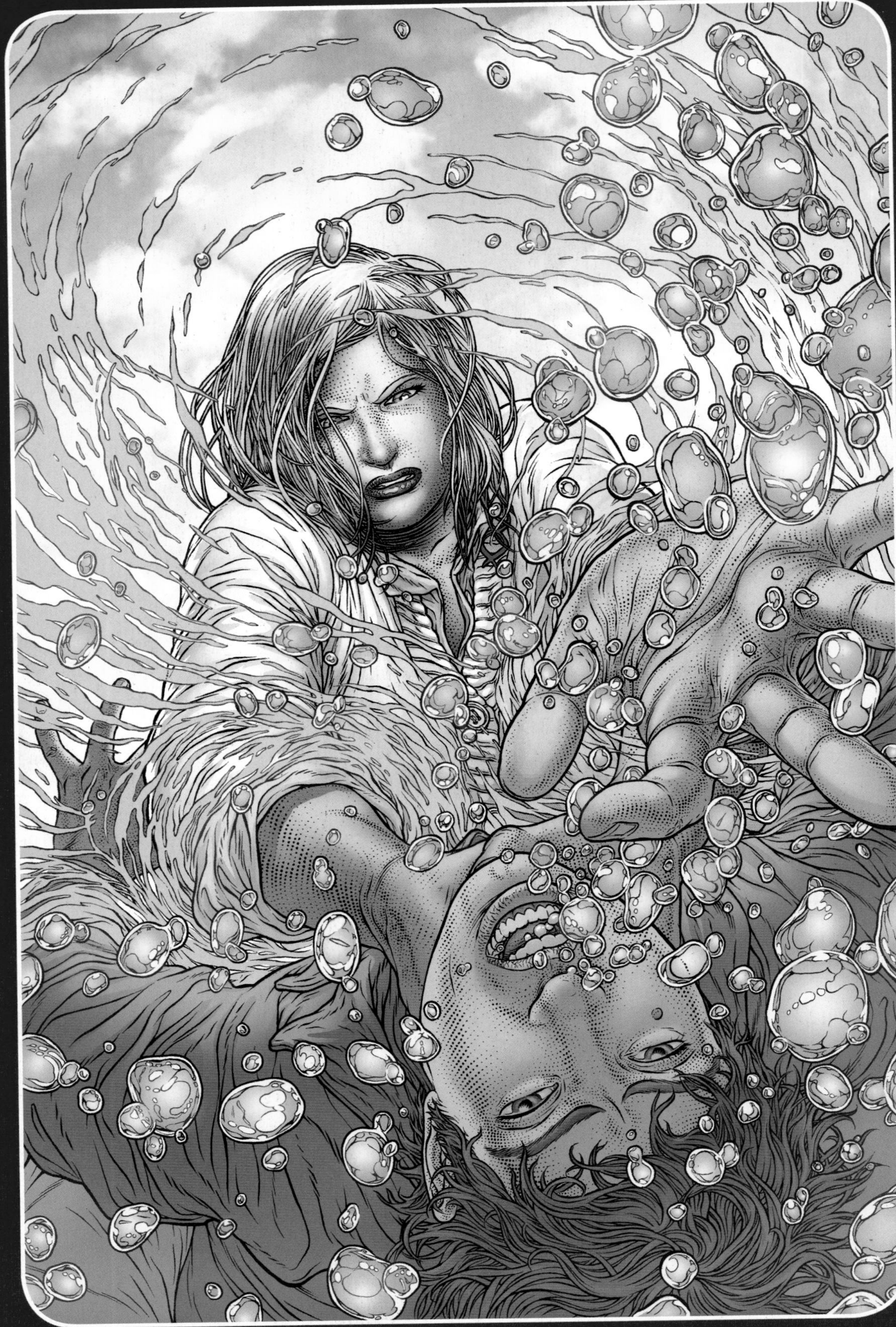

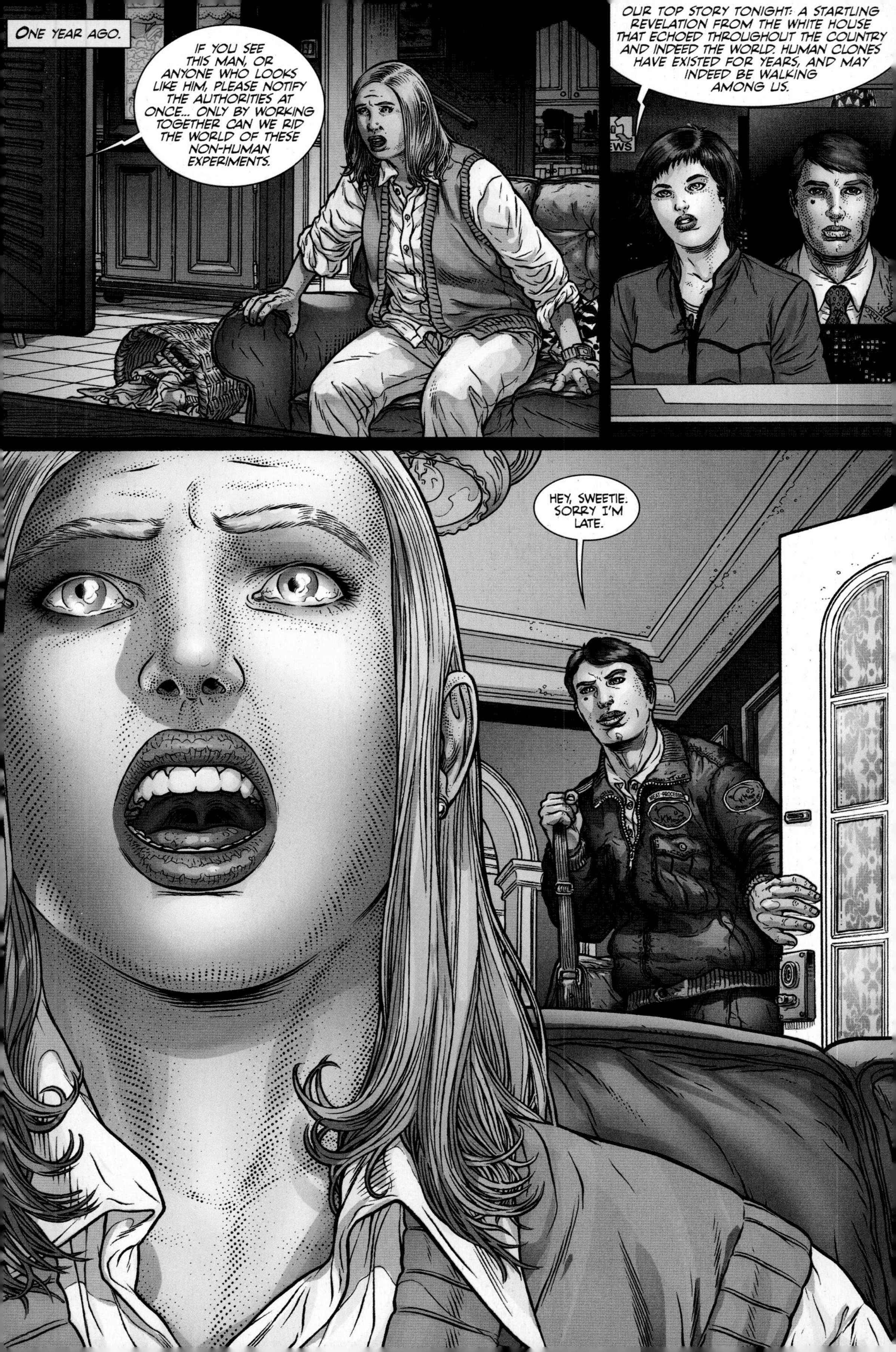
ONE YEAR AGO.
IF YOU SEE THIS MAN, OR ANYONE WHO LOOKS LIKE HIM, PLEASE NOTIFY THE AUTHORITIES AT ONCE... ONLY BY WORKING TOGETHER CAN WE RID THE WORLD OF THESE NON-HUMAN EXPERIMENTS.
OUR TOP STORY TONIGHT: A STARTLING REVELATION FROM THE WHITE HOUSE THAT ECHOED THROUGHOUT THE COUNTRY AND INDEED THE WORLD. HUMAN CLONES HAVE EXISTED FOR YEARS, AND MAY INDEED BE WALKING AMONG US.
HEY, SWEETIE. SORRY I'M LATE.

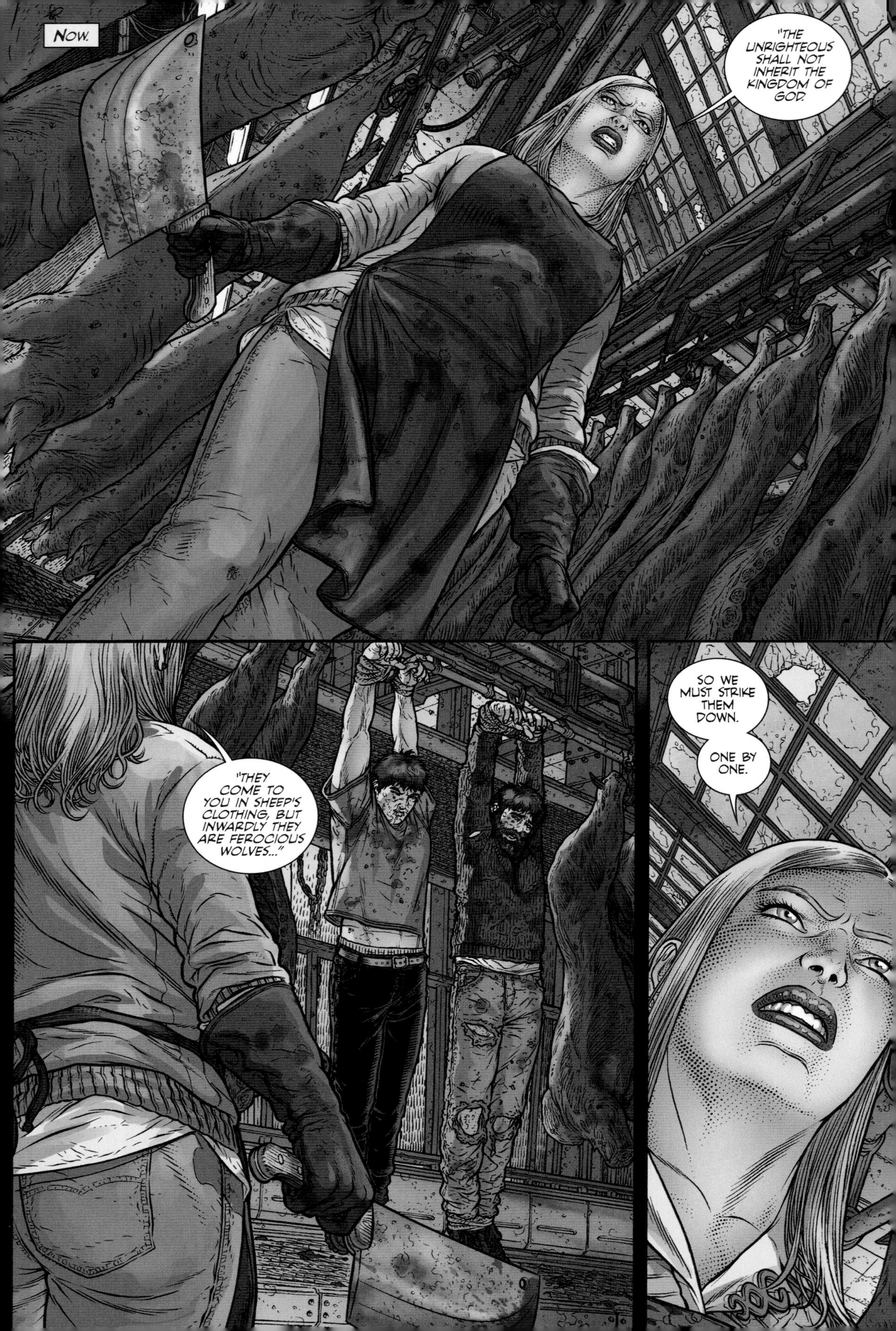
NOW.
"THE UNRIGHTEOUS SHALL NOT INHERIT THE KINGDOM OF GOD.
"THEY COME TO YOU IN SHEEP'S CLOTHING, BUT INWARDLY THEY ARE FEROCIOUS WOLVES..."
SO WE MUST STRIKE THEM DOWN.
ONE BY ONE.

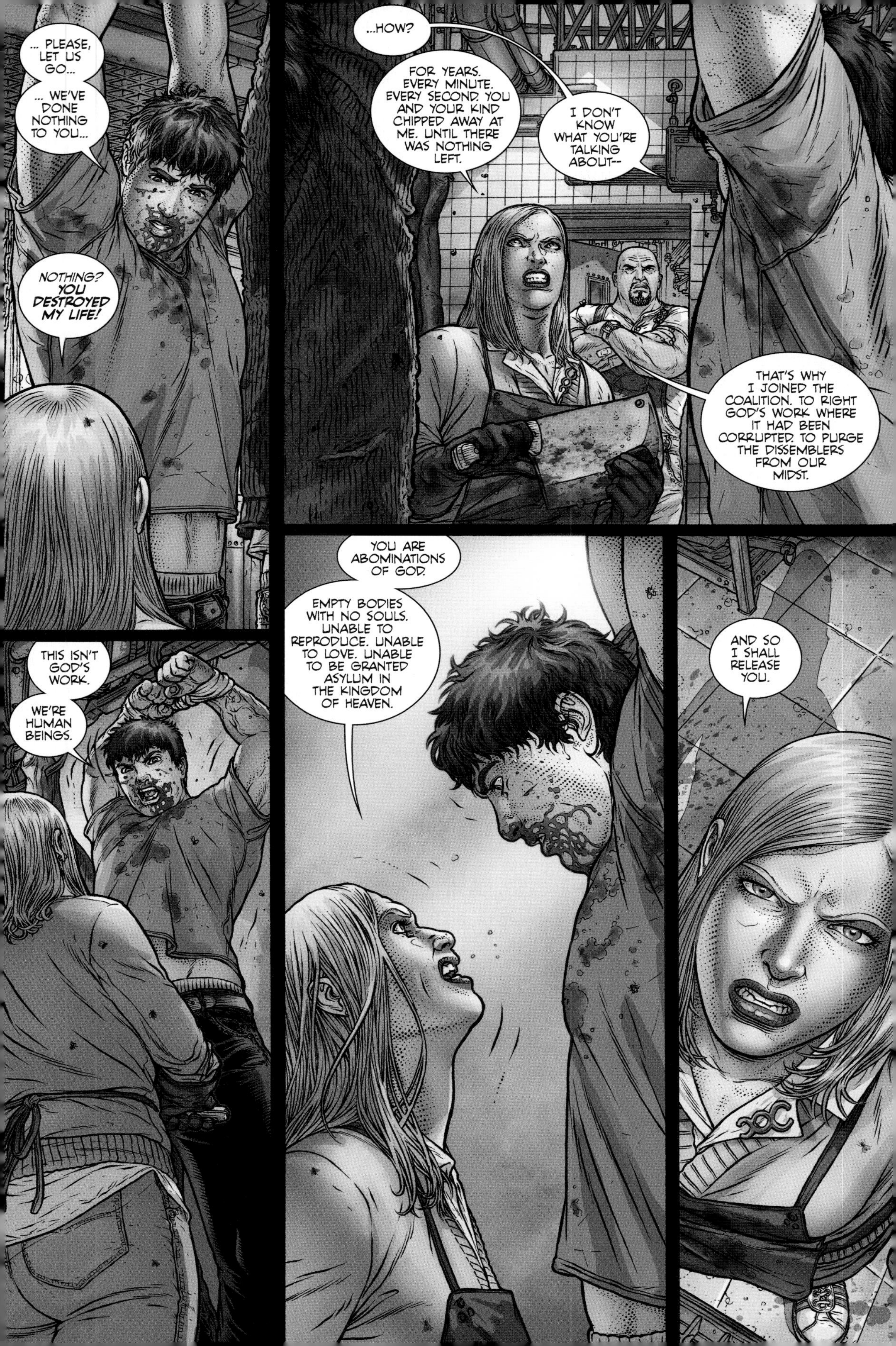

... PLEASE, LET US GO...
... WE'VE DONE NOTHING TO YOU...
NOTHING? *YOU DESTROYED MY LIFE!*
...HOW?
FOR YEARS. EVERY MINUTE. EVERY SECOND. YOU AND YOUR KIND CHIPPED AWAY AT ME. UNTIL THERE WAS NOTHING LEFT.
I DON'T KNOW WHAT YOU'RE TALKING ABOUT--
THAT'S WHY I JOINED THE COALITION. TO RIGHT GOD'S WORK WHERE IT HAD BEEN CORRUPTED. TO PURGE THE DISSEMBLERS FROM OUR MIDST.
THIS ISN'T GOD'S WORK.
WE'RE HUMAN BEINGS.
YOU ARE ABOMINATIONS OF GOD.
EMPTY BODIES WITH NO SOULS. UNABLE TO REPRODUCE. UNABLE TO LOVE. UNABLE TO BE GRANTED ASYLUM IN THE KINGDOM OF HEAVEN.
AND SO I SHALL RELEASE YOU.

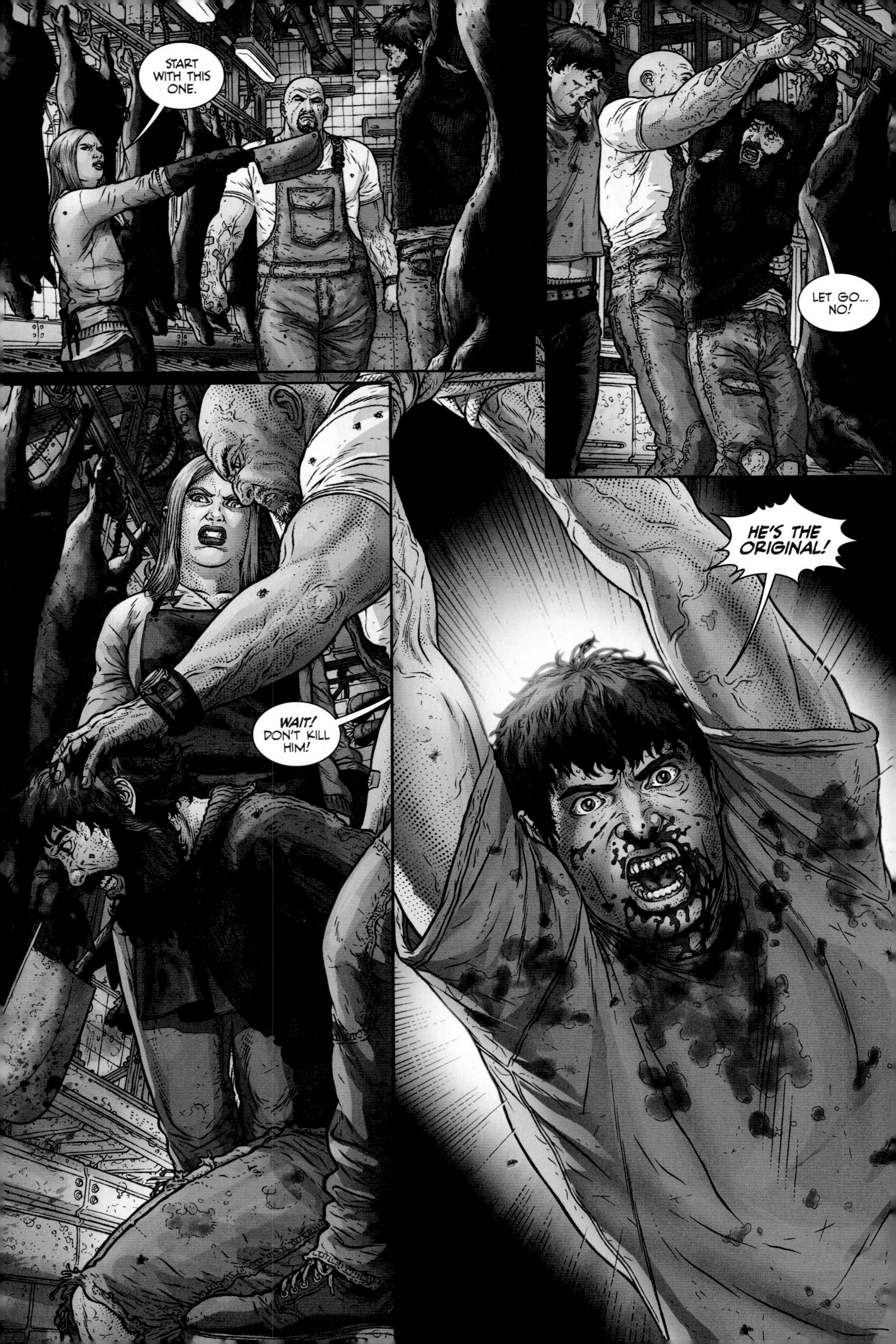
START WITH THIS ONE.
LET GO... NO!
WAIT! DON'T KILL HIM!
HE'S THE ORIGINAL!

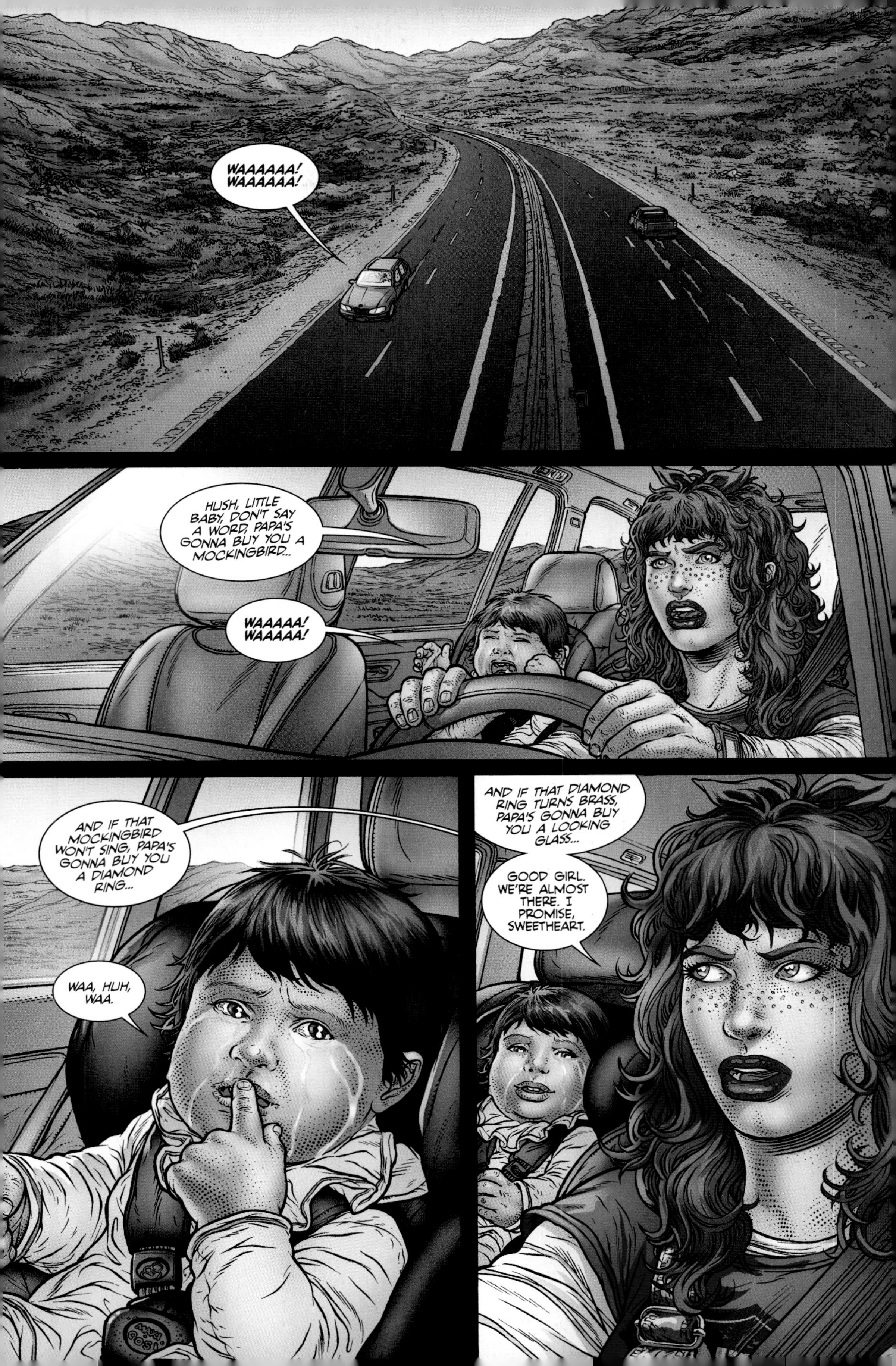
WAAAAAA! WAAAAAA!
HUSH, LITTLE BABY, DON'T SAY A WORD, PAPA'S GONNA BUY YOU A MOCKINGBIRD...
WAAAAA! WAAAAA!
AND IF THAT MOCKINGBIRD WON'T SING, PAPA'S GONNA BUY YOU A DIAMOND RING...
WAA, HUH, WAA.
AND IF THAT DIAMOND RING TURNS BRASS, PAPA'S GONNA BUY YOU A LOOKING GLASS...
GOOD GIRL. WE'RE ALMOST THERE. I PROMISE, SWEETHEART.

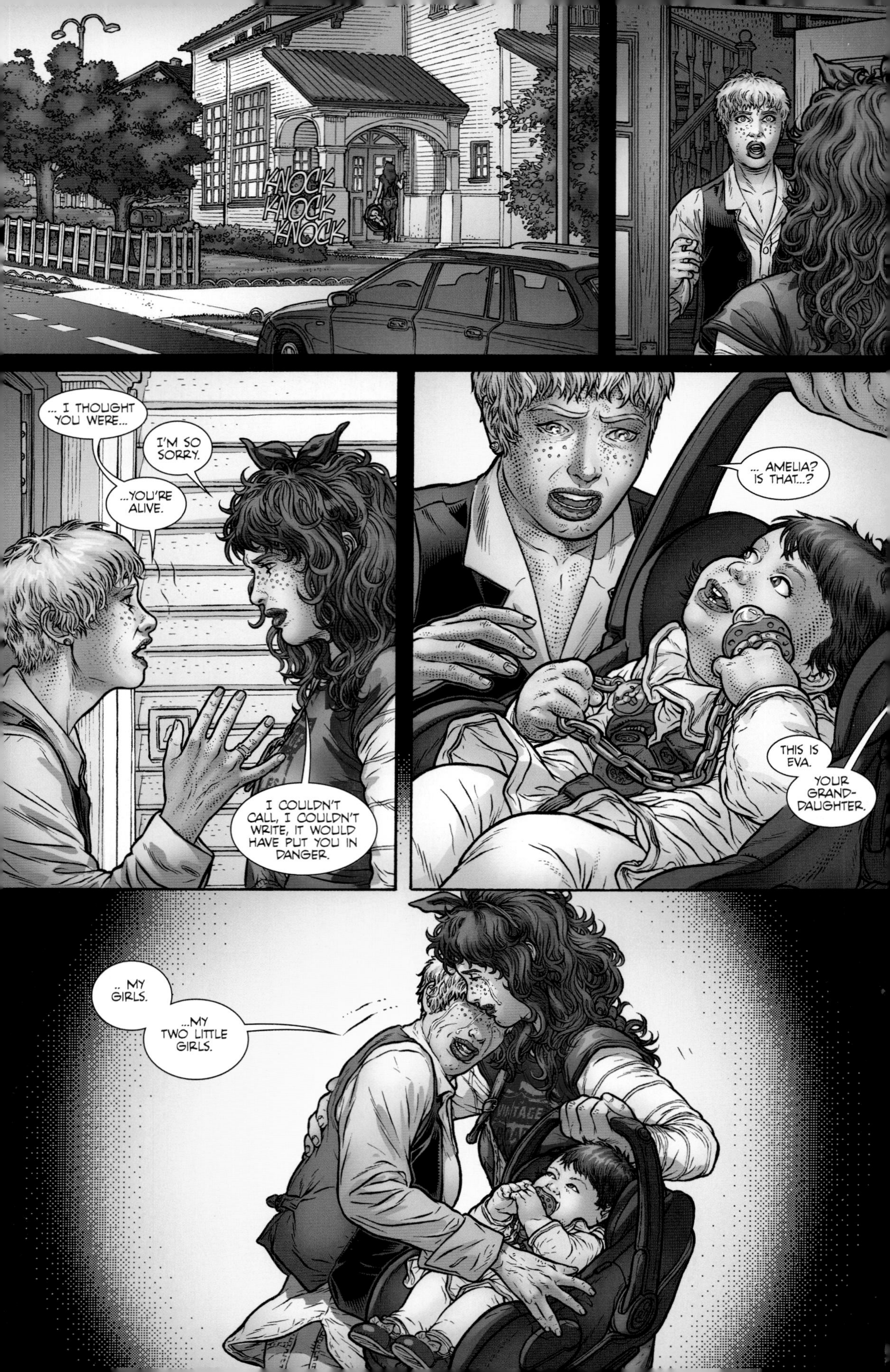
KNOCK
KNOCK
KNOCK
... I THOUGHT YOU WERE...
...YOU'RE ALIVE.
I'M SO SORRY.
I COULDN'T CALL, I COULDN'T WRITE, IT WOULD HAVE PUT YOU IN DANGER.
... AMELIA? IS THAT...?
THIS IS EVA.
YOUR GRAND-DAUGHTER.
.. MY GIRLS.
...MY TWO LITTLE GIRLS.

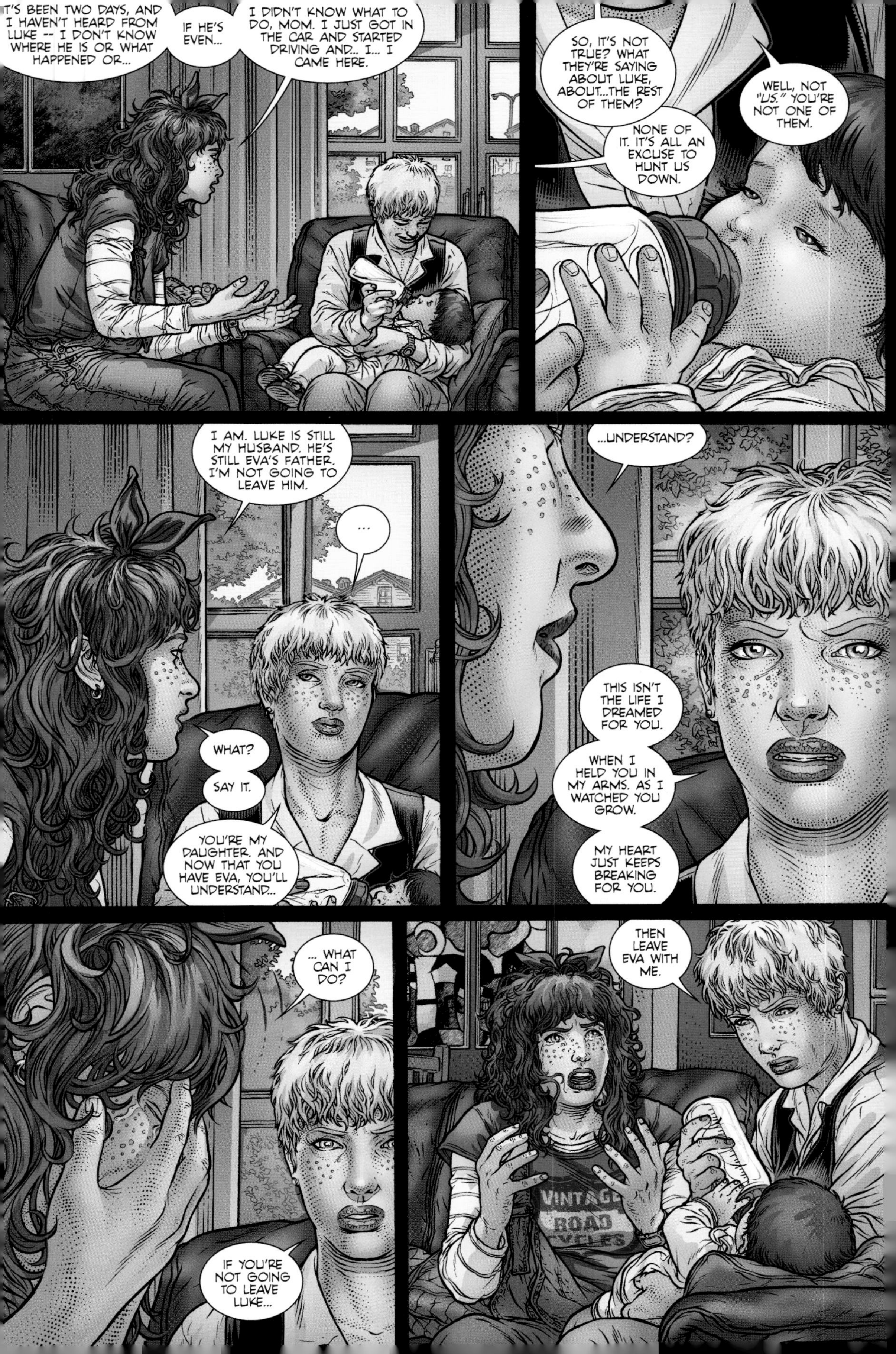
T'S BEEN TWO DAYS, AND I HAVEN'T HEARD FROM LUKE -- I DON'T KNOW WHERE HE IS OR WHAT HAPPENED OR...
IF HE'S EVEN...
I DIDN'T KNOW WHAT TO DO, MOM. I JUST GOT IN THE CAR AND STARTED DRIVING AND... I... I CAME HERE.
SO, IT'S NOT TRUE? WHAT THEY'RE SAYING ABOUT LUKE, ABOUT...THE REST OF THEM?
NONE OF IT. IT'S ALL AN EXCUSE TO HUNT US DOWN.
WELL, NOT "US." YOU'RE NOT ONE OF THEM.
I AM. LUKE IS STILL MY HUSBAND. HE'S STILL EVA'S FATHER. I'M NOT GOING TO LEAVE HIM.
...
WHAT?
SAY IT.
YOU'RE MY DAUGHTER. AND NOW THAT YOU HAVE EVA, YOU'LL UNDERSTAND...
...UNDERSTAND?
THIS ISN'T THE LIFE I DREAMED FOR YOU.
WHEN I HELD YOU IN MY ARMS. AS I WATCHED YOU GROW.
MY HEART JUST KEEPS BREAKING FOR YOU.
... WHAT CAN I DO?
IF YOU'RE NOT GOING TO LEAVE LUKE...
THEN LEAVE EVA WITH ME.
VINTAGE ROAD CYCLES

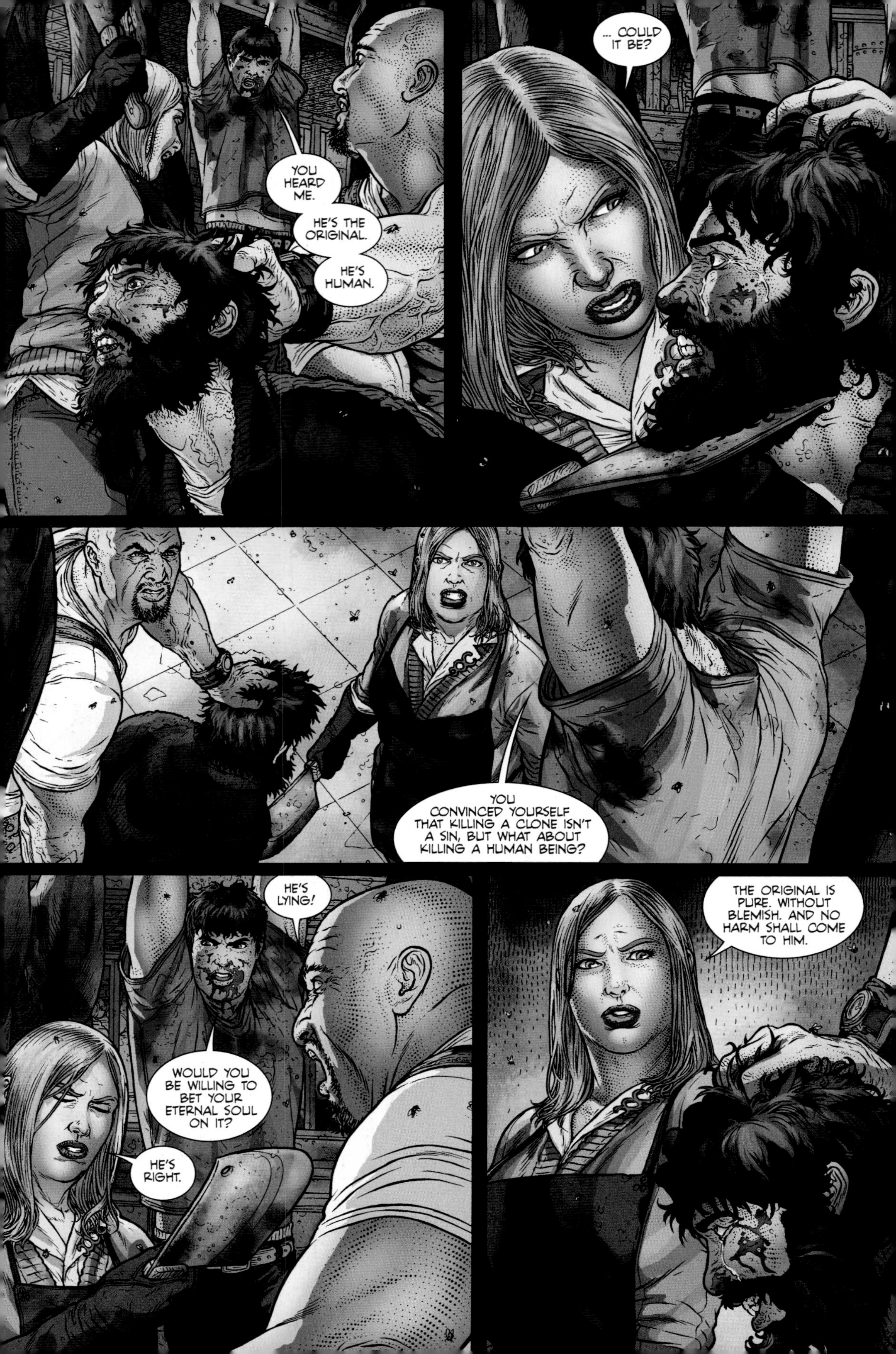
YOU HEARD ME.
HE'S THE ORIGINAL.
HE'S HUMAN.
... COULD IT BE?
YOU CONVINCED YOURSELF THAT KILLING A CLONE ISN'T A SIN, BUT WHAT ABOUT KILLING A HUMAN BEING?
HE'S LYING!
WOULD YOU BE WILLING TO BET YOUR ETERNAL SOUL ON IT?
HE'S RIGHT.
THE ORIGINAL IS PURE. WITHOUT BLEMISH. AND NO HARM SHALL COME TO HIM.

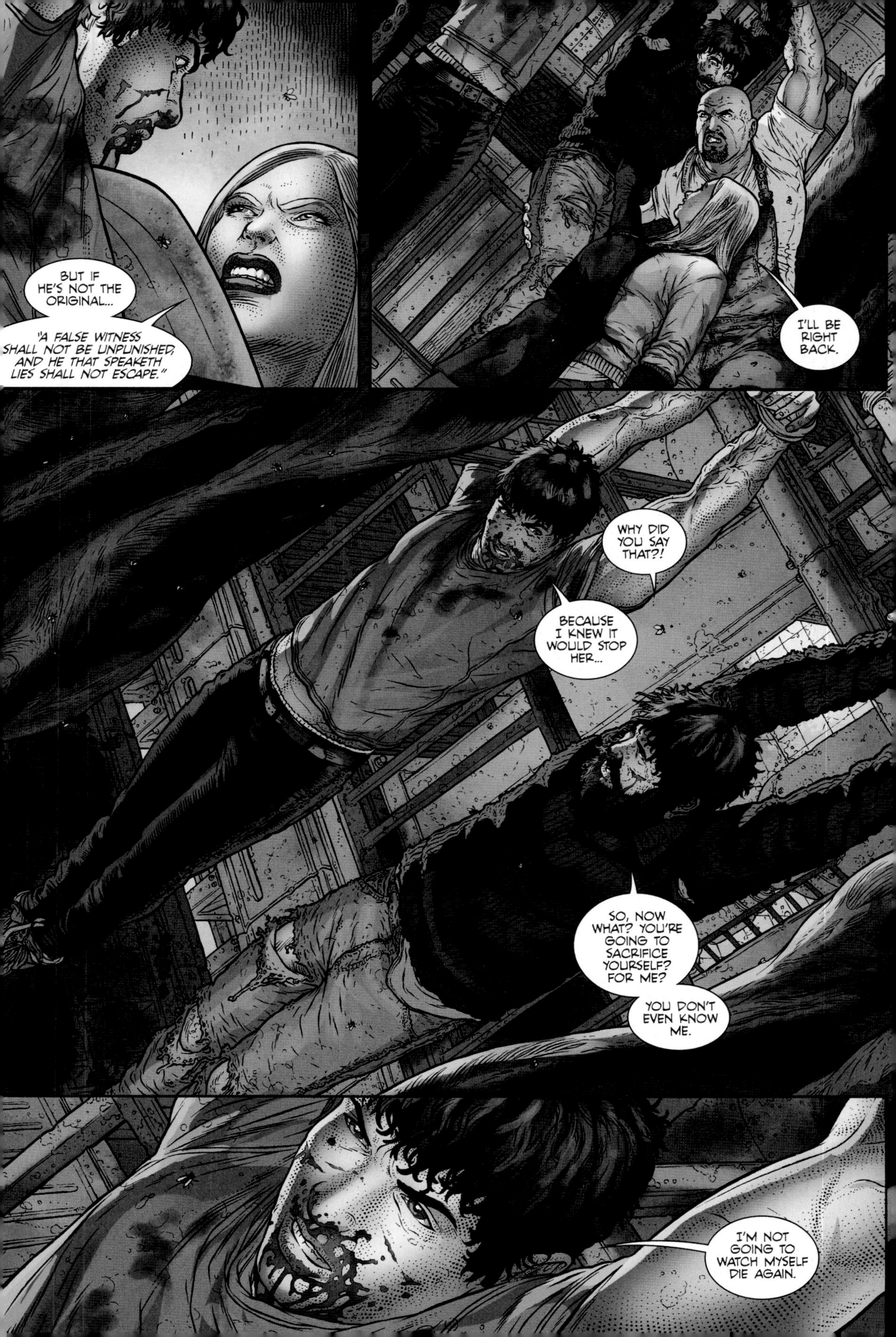
BUT IF HE'S NOT THE ORIGINAL...
"A FALSE WITNESS SHALL NOT BE UNPUNISHED, AND HE THAT SPEAKETH LIES SHALL NOT ESCAPE."
I'LL BE RIGHT BACK.
WHY DID YOU SAY THAT?!
BECAUSE I KNEW IT WOULD STOP HER...
SO, NOW WHAT? YOU'RE GOING TO SACRIFICE YOURSELF? FOR ME?
YOU DON'T EVEN KNOW ME.
I'M NOT GOING TO WATCH MYSELF DIE AGAIN.

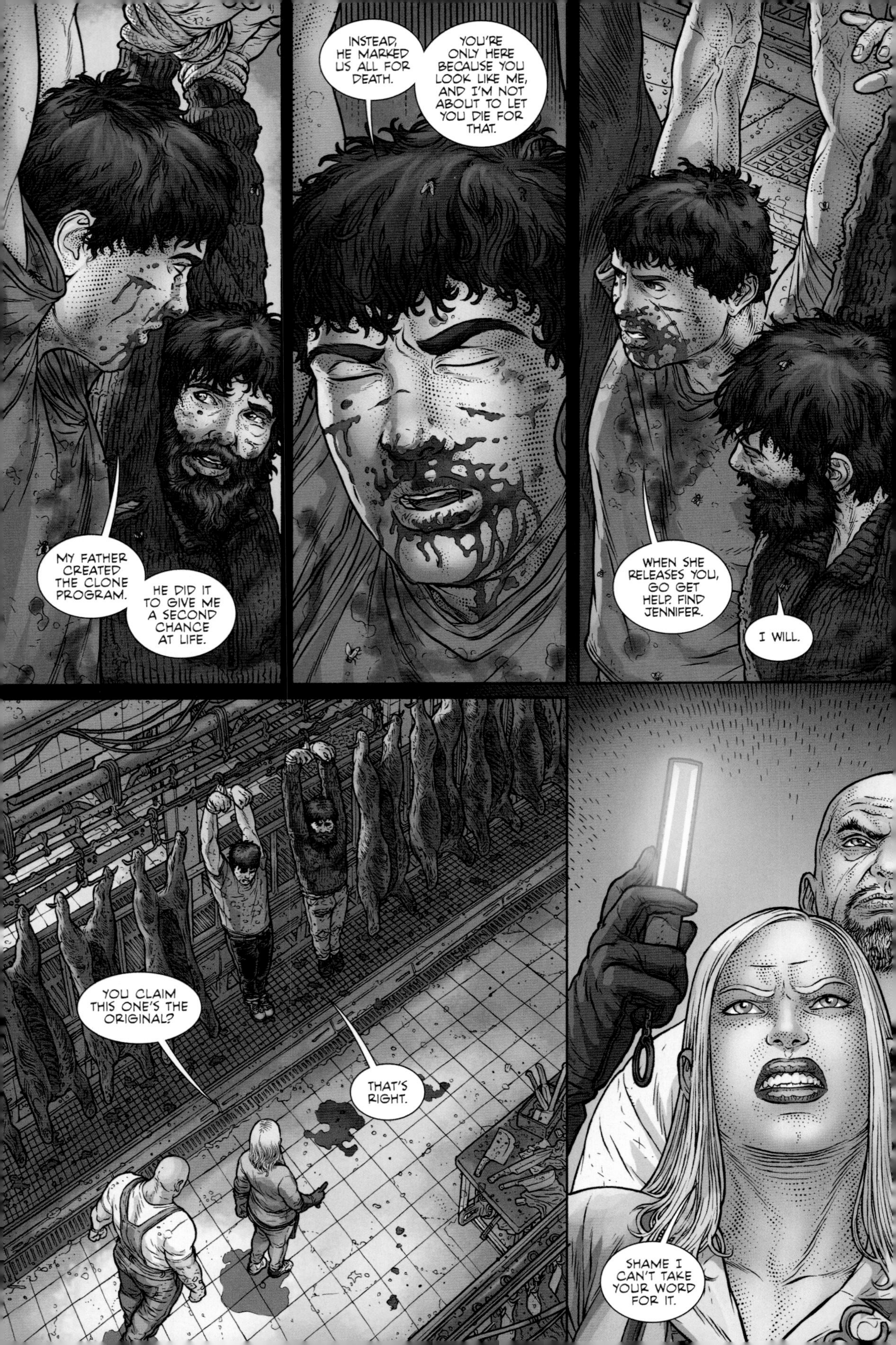
MY FATHER CREATED THE CLONE PROGRAM.
HE DID IT TO GIVE ME A SECOND CHANCE AT LIFE.
INSTEAD, HE MARKED US ALL FOR DEATH.
YOU'RE ONLY HERE BECAUSE YOU LOOK LIKE ME, AND I'M NOT ABOUT TO LET YOU DIE FOR THAT.
WHEN SHE RELEASES YOU, GO GET HELP. FIND JENNIFER.
I WILL.
YOU CLAIM THIS ONE'S THE ORIGINAL?
THAT'S RIGHT.
SHAME I CAN'T TAKE YOUR WORD FOR IT.

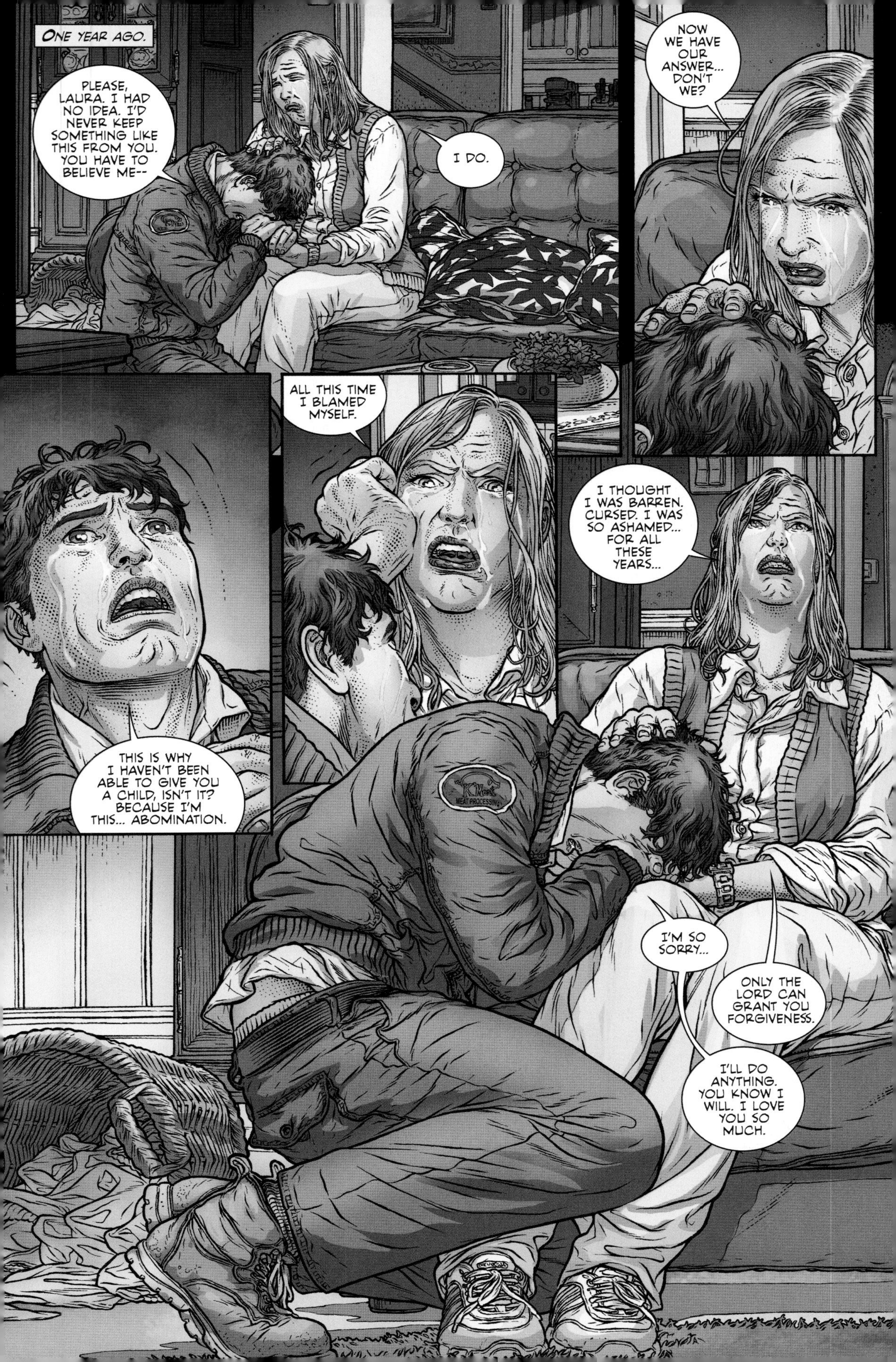
ONE YEAR AGO.
PLEASE, LAURA. I HAD NO IDEA. I'D NEVER KEEP SOMETHING LIKE THIS FROM YOU. YOU HAVE TO BELIEVE ME--
I DO.
NOW WE HAVE OUR ANSWER... DON'T WE?
ALL THIS TIME I BLAMED MYSELF.
I THOUGHT I WAS BARREN. CURSED. I WAS SO ASHAMED... FOR ALL THESE YEARS...
THIS IS WHY I HAVEN'T BEEN ABLE TO GIVE YOU A CHILD, ISN'T IT? BECAUSE I'M THIS... ABOMINATION.
MEAT PROCESSING
I'M SO SORRY...
ONLY THE LORD CAN GRANT YOU FORGIVENESS.
I'LL DO ANYTHING. YOU KNOW I WILL. I LOVE YOU SO MUCH.

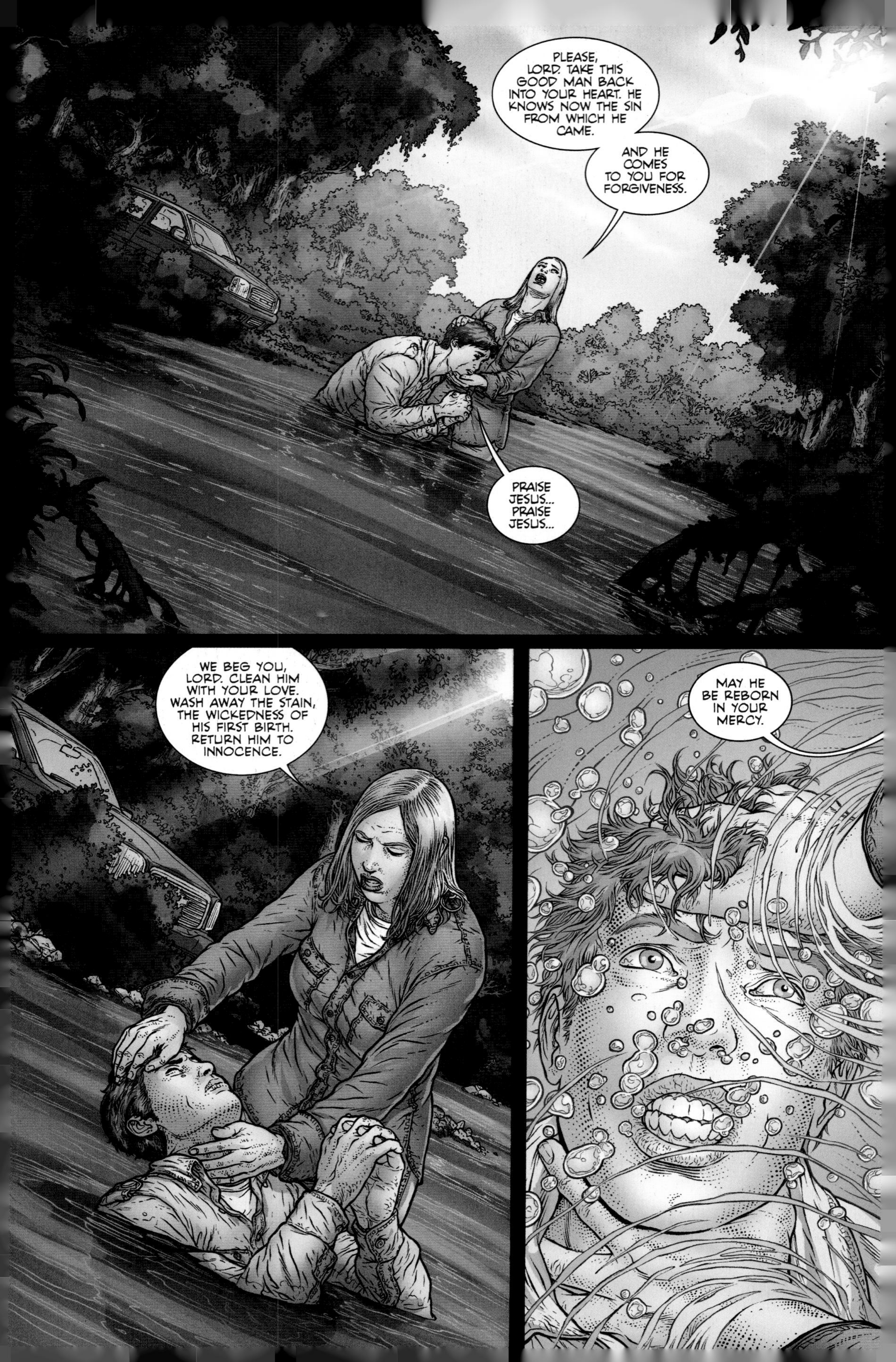
PLEASE, LORD. TAKE THIS GOOD MAN BACK INTO YOUR HEART. HE KNOWS NOW THE SIN FROM WHICH HE CAME.
AND HE COMES TO YOU FOR FORGIVENESS.
PRAISE JESUS... PRAISE JESUS...
WE BEG YOU, LORD. CLEAN HIM WITH YOUR LOVE. WASH AWAY THE STAIN, THE WICKEDNESS OF HIS FIRST BIRTH. RETURN HIM TO INNOCENCE.
MAY HE BE REBORN IN YOUR MERCY.

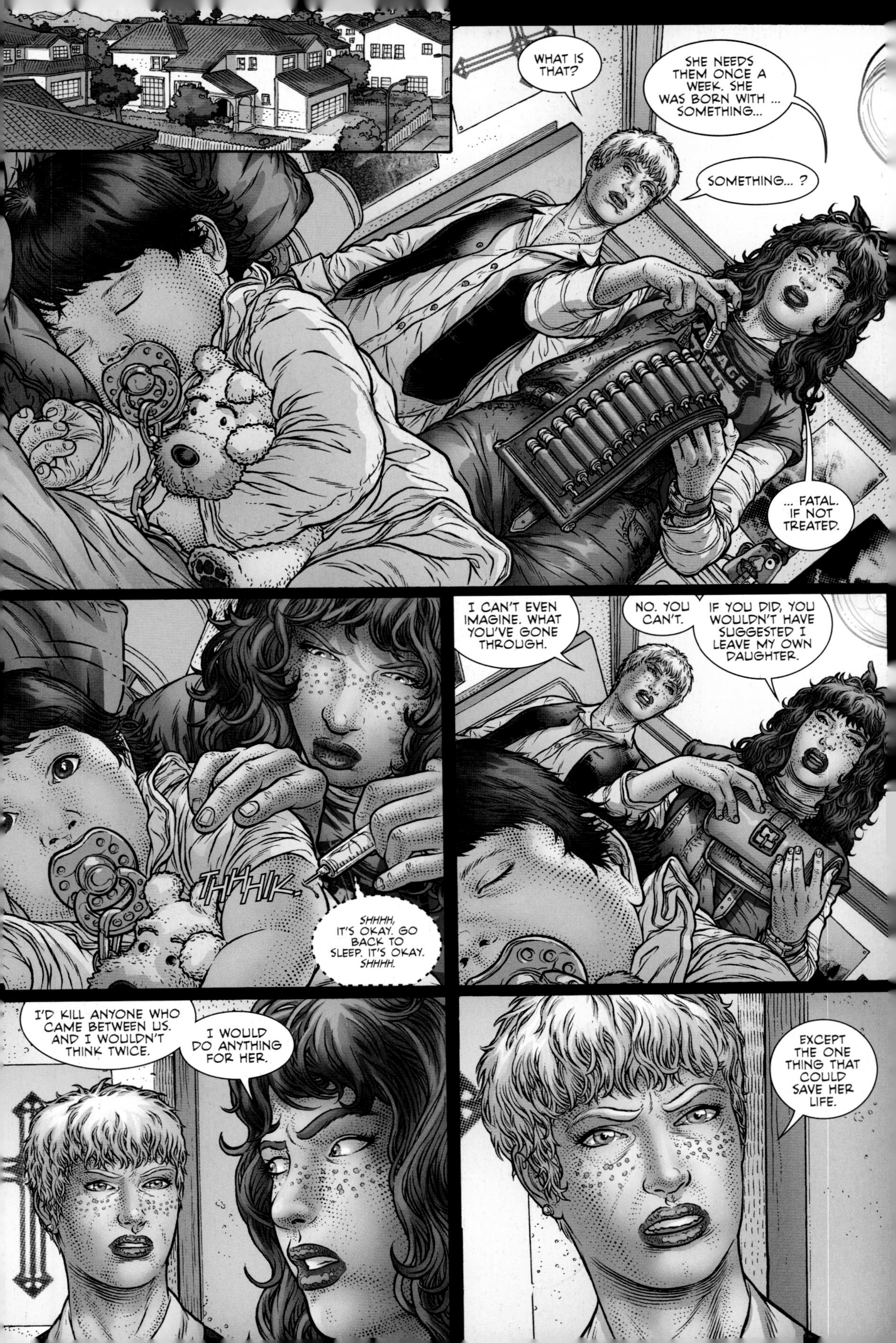
WHAT IS THAT?
SHE NEEDS THEM ONCE A WEEK. SHE WAS BORN WITH ... SOMETHING...
SOMETHING... ?
... FATAL. IF NOT TREATED.
THHHK.
SHHHH, IT'S OKAY. GO BACK TO SLEEP. IT'S OKAY. SHHHH.
I CAN'T EVEN IMAGINE. WHAT YOU'VE GONE THROUGH.
NO. YOU CAN'T.
IF YOU DID, YOU WOULDN'T HAVE SUGGESTED I LEAVE MY OWN DAUGHTER.
I'D KILL ANYONE WHO CAME BETWEEN US. AND I WOULDN'T THINK TWICE.
I WOULD DO ANYTHING FOR HER.
EXCEPT THE ONE THING THAT COULD SAVE HER LIFE.

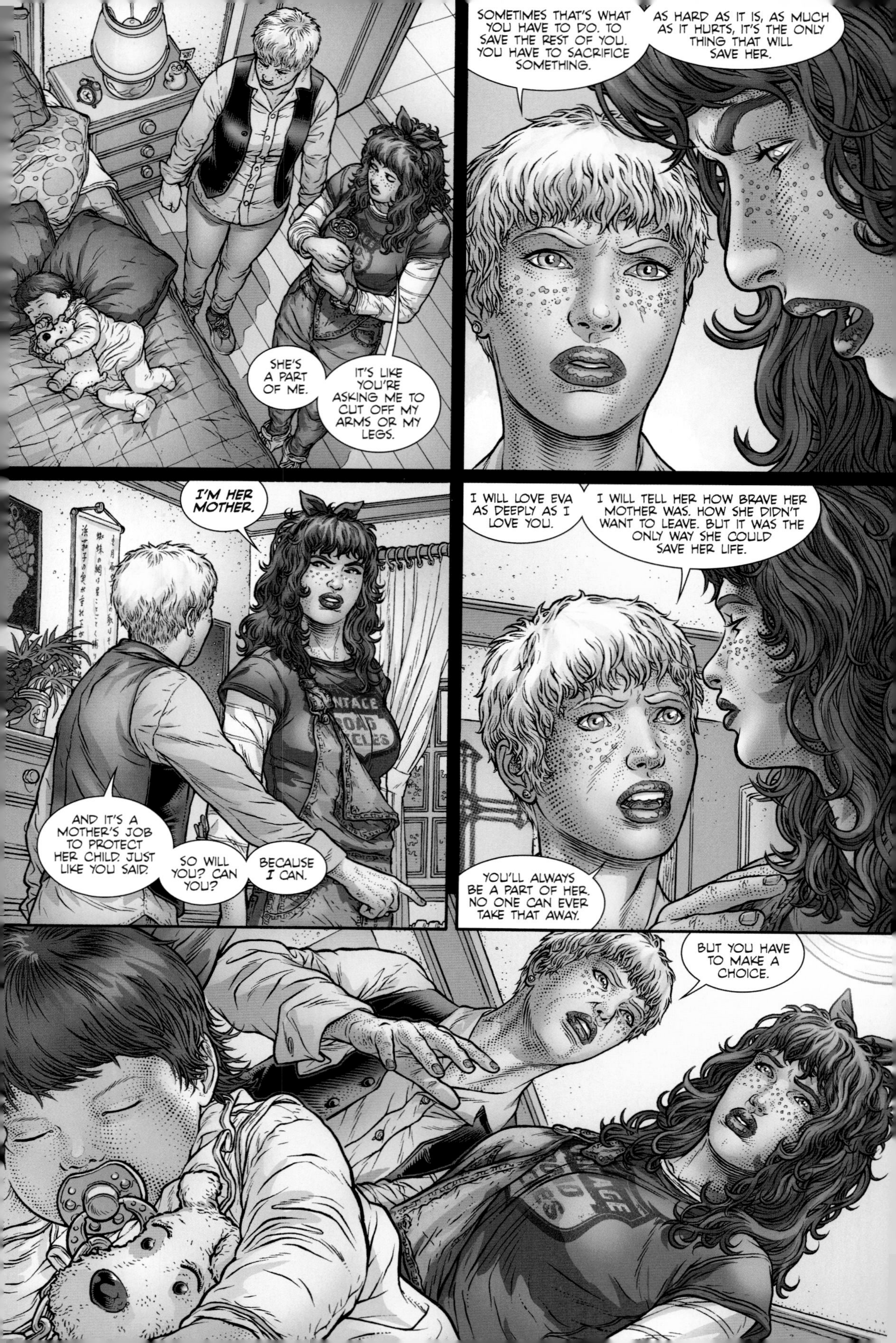
SHE'S A PART OF ME.
IT'S LIKE YOU'RE ASKING ME TO CUT OFF MY ARMS OR MY LEGS.
SOMETIMES THAT'S WHAT YOU HAVE TO DO. TO SAVE THE REST OF YOU. YOU HAVE TO SACRIFICE SOMETHING.
AS HARD AS IT IS, AS MUCH AS IT HURTS, IT'S THE ONLY THING THAT WILL SAVE HER.
I'M HER MOTHER.
AND IT'S A MOTHER'S JOB TO PROTECT HER CHILD. JUST LIKE YOU SAID.
SO WILL YOU? CAN YOU?
BECAUSE I CAN.
I WILL LOVE EVA AS DEEPLY AS I LOVE YOU.
I WILL TELL HER HOW BRAVE HER MOTHER WAS. HOW SHE DIDN'T WANT TO LEAVE. BUT IT WAS THE ONLY WAY SHE COULD SAVE HER LIFE.
YOU'LL ALWAYS BE A PART OF HER. NO ONE CAN EVER TAKE THAT AWAY.
BUT YOU HAVE TO MAKE A CHOICE.

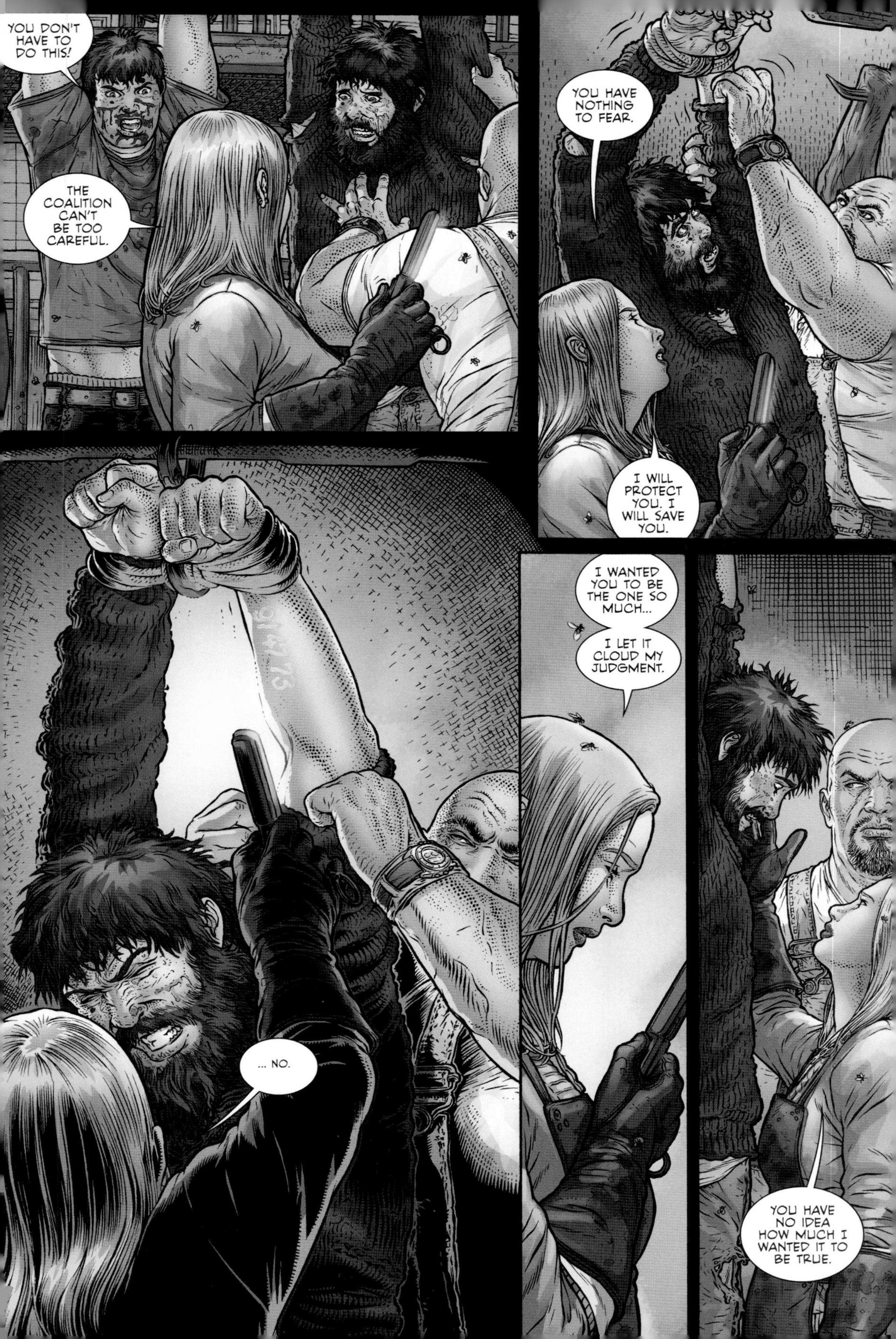
YOU DON'T HAVE TO DO THIS!
THE COALITION CAN'T BE TOO CAREFUL.
YOU HAVE NOTHING TO FEAR.
I WILL PROTECT YOU. I WILL SAVE YOU.
... NO.
I WANTED YOU TO BE THE ONE SO MUCH...
I LET IT CLOUD MY JUDGMENT.
YOU HAVE NO IDEA HOW MUCH I WANTED IT TO BE TRUE.

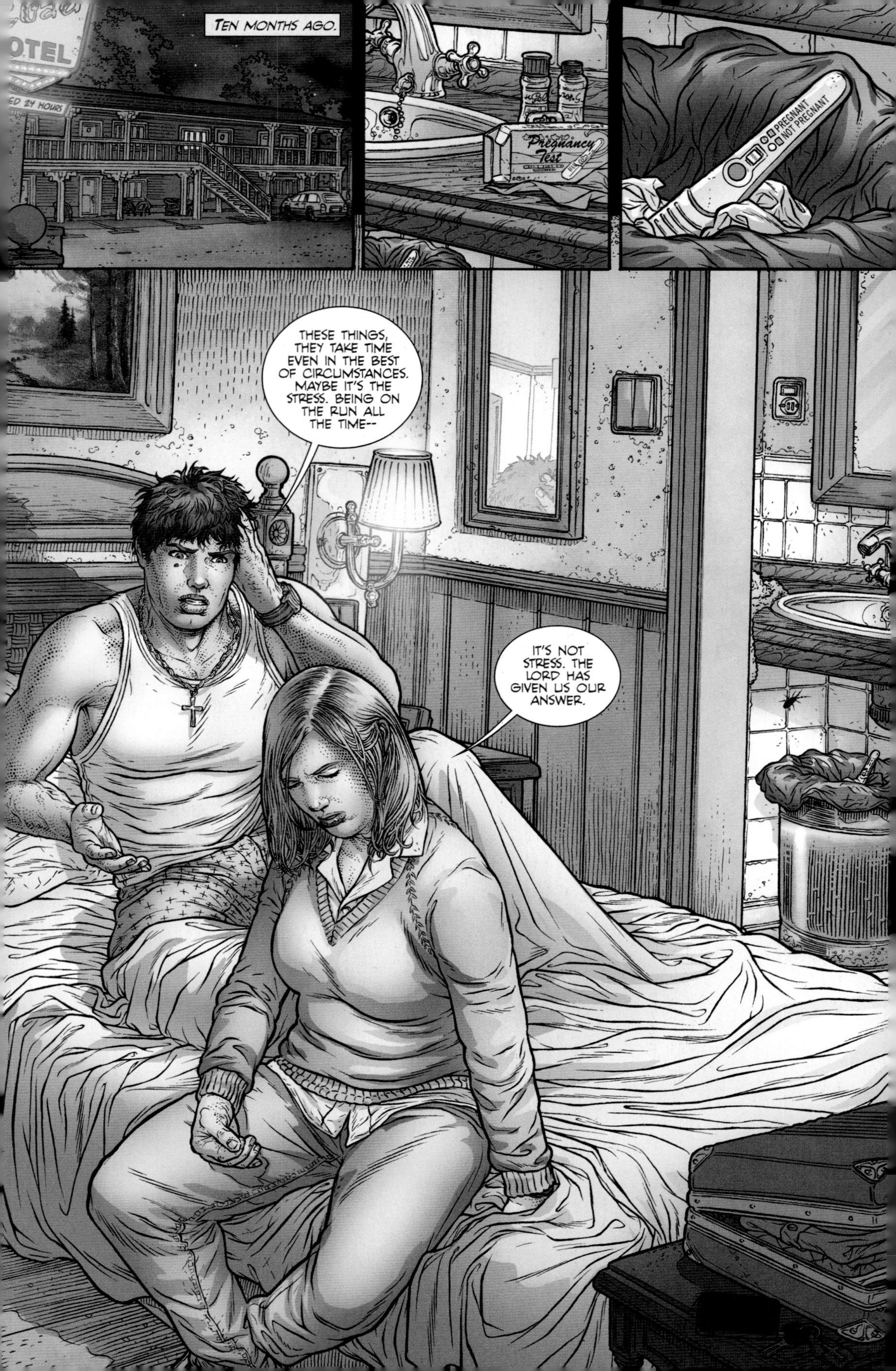
TEN MONTHS AGO.
OTEL
ED 24 HOURS
Pregnancy Test
PREGNANT
NOT PREGNANT
THESE THINGS, THEY TAKE TIME EVEN IN THE BEST OF CIRCUMSTANCES. MAYBE IT'S THE STRESS. BEING ON THE RUN ALL THE TIME--
IT'S NOT STRESS. THE LORD HAS GIVEN US OUR ANSWER.

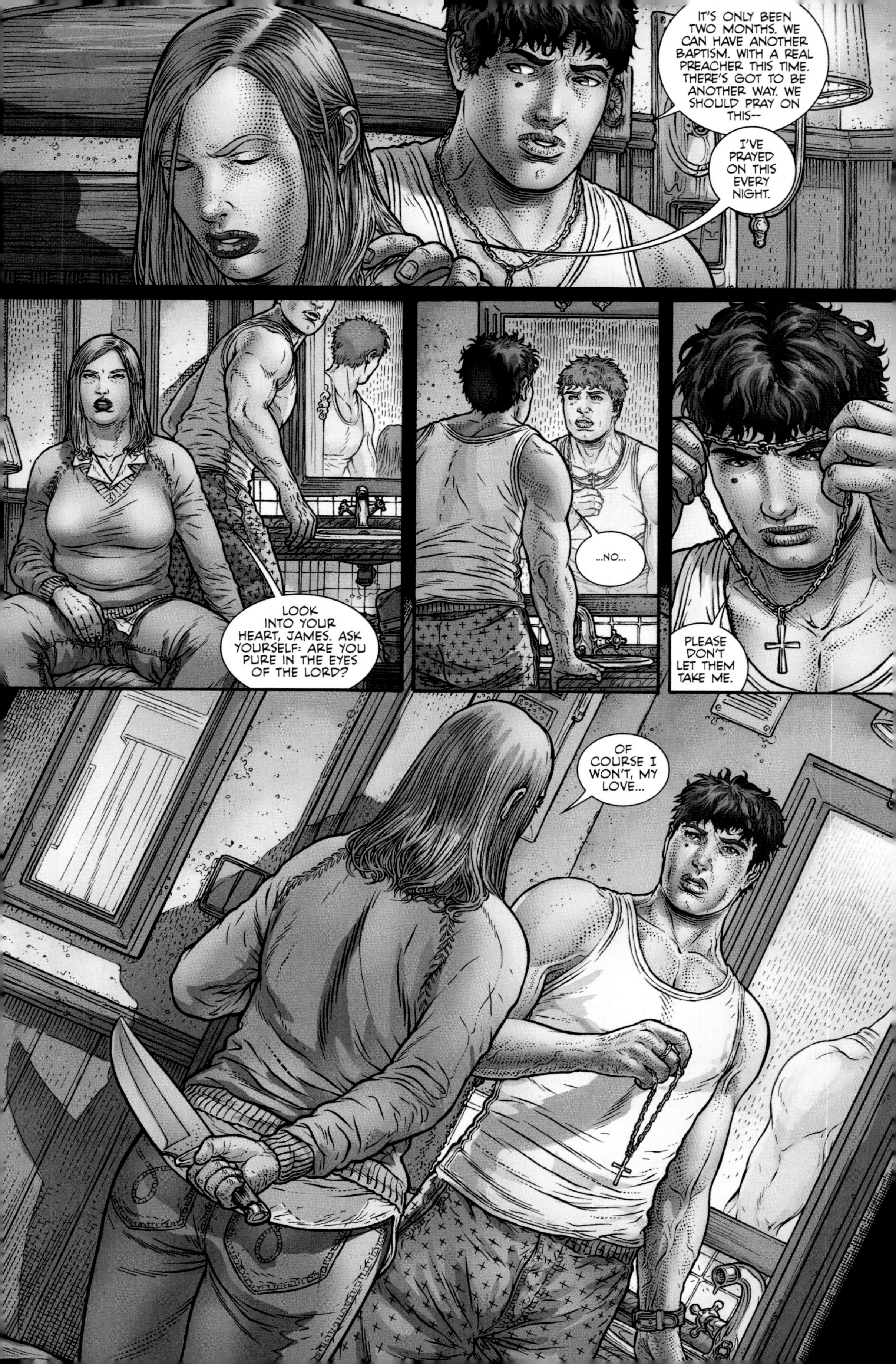
IT'S ONLY BEEN TWO MONTHS. WE CAN HAVE ANOTHER BAPTISM. WITH A REAL PREACHER THIS TIME. THERE'S GOT TO BE ANOTHER WAY. WE SHOULD PRAY ON THIS--
I'VE PRAYED ON THIS EVERY NIGHT.
LOOK INTO YOUR HEART, JAMES. ASK YOURSELF: ARE YOU PURE IN THE EYES OF THE LORD?
...NO...
PLEASE DON'T LET THEM TAKE ME.
OF COURSE I WON'T, MY LOVE...

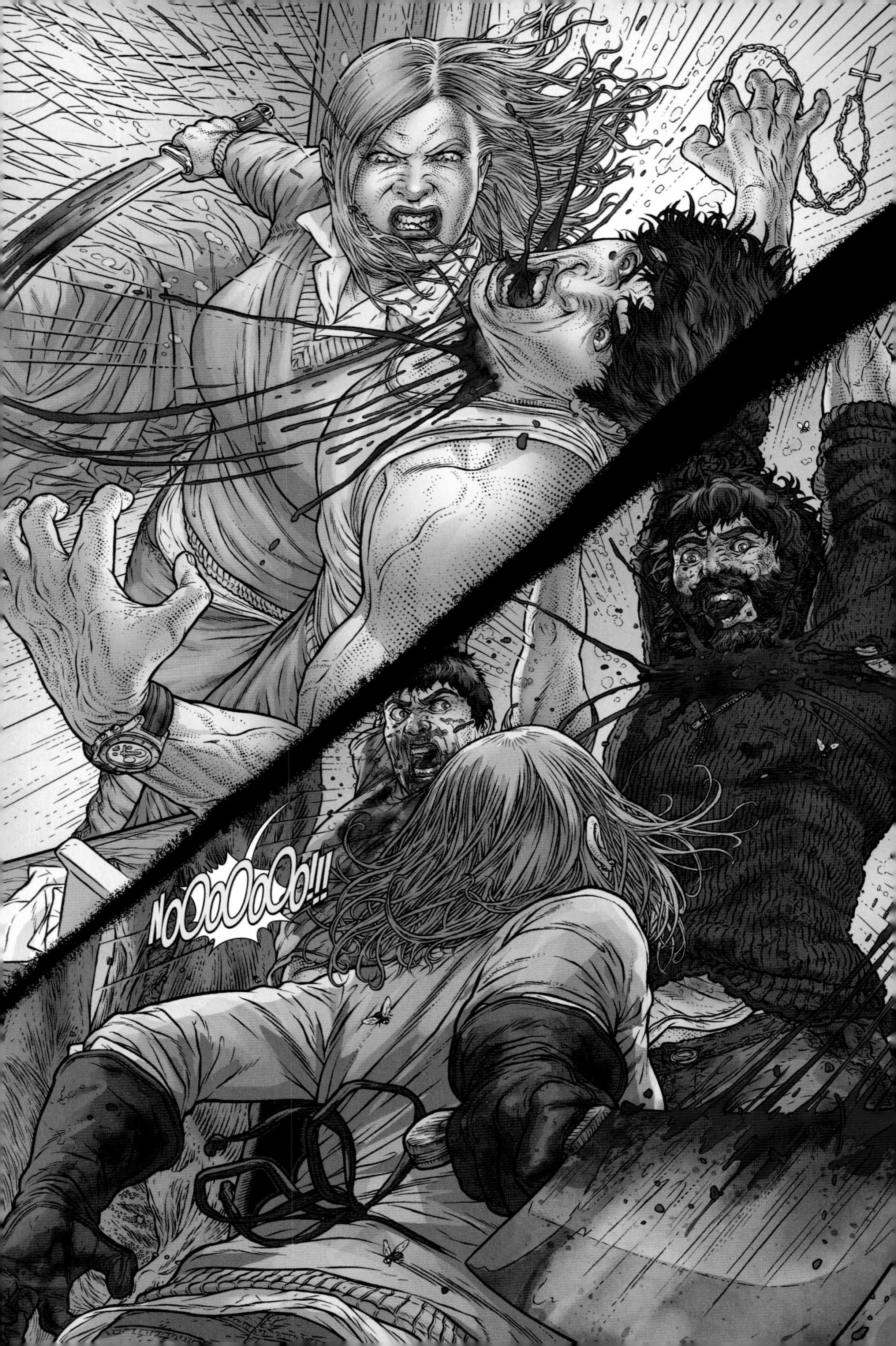
NOOoOoOOo!!!

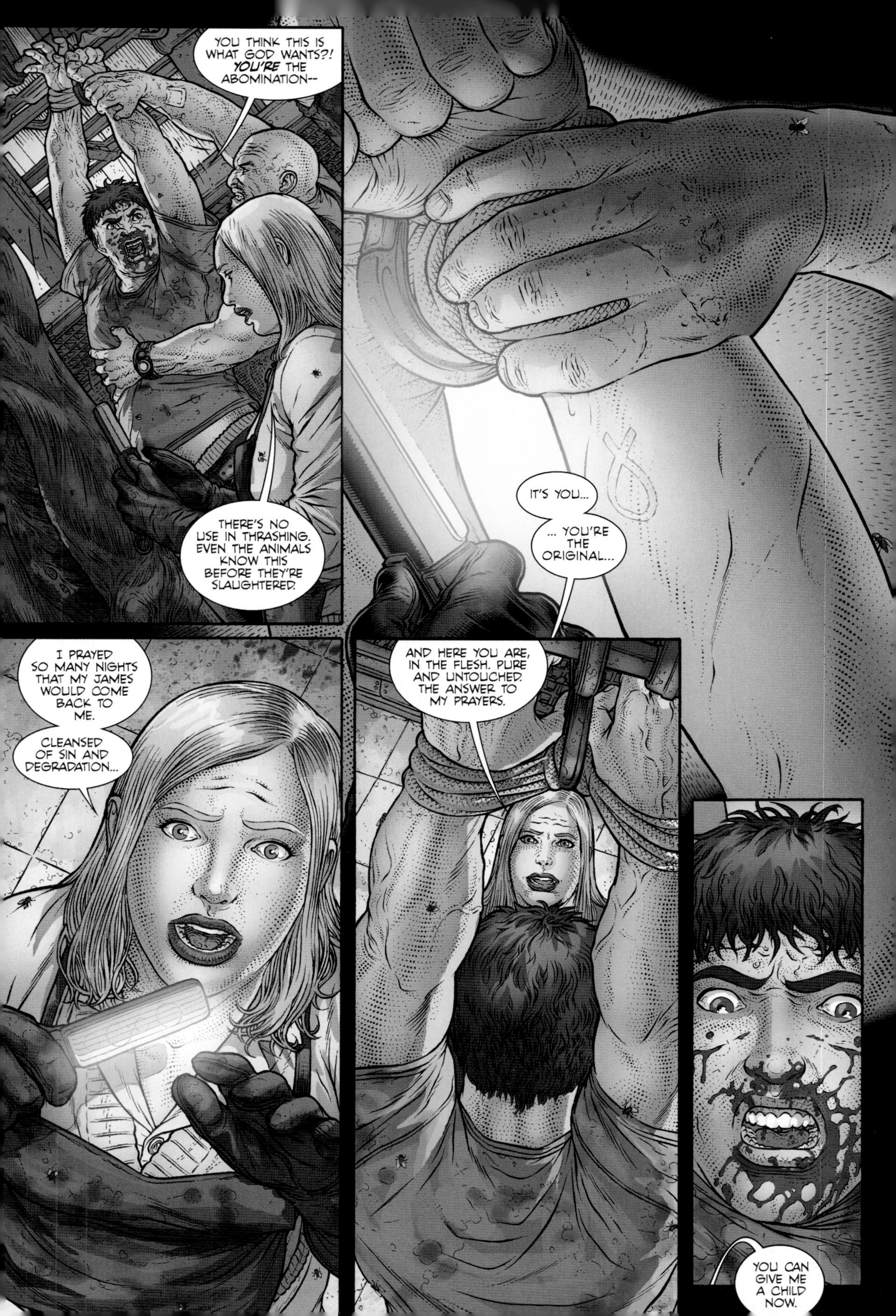
YOU THINK THIS IS WHAT GOD WANTS?! YOU'RE THE ABOMINATION--
THERE'S NO USE IN THRASHING. EVEN THE ANIMALS KNOW THIS BEFORE THEY'RE SLAUGHTERED.
IT'S YOU...
... YOU'RE THE ORIGINAL...
I PRAYED SO MANY NIGHTS THAT MY JAMES WOULD COME BACK TO ME.
CLEANSED OF SIN AND DEGRADATION...
AND HERE YOU ARE, IN THE FLESH. PURE AND UNTOUCHED. THE ANSWER TO MY PRAYERS.
YOU CAN GIVE ME A CHILD NOW.

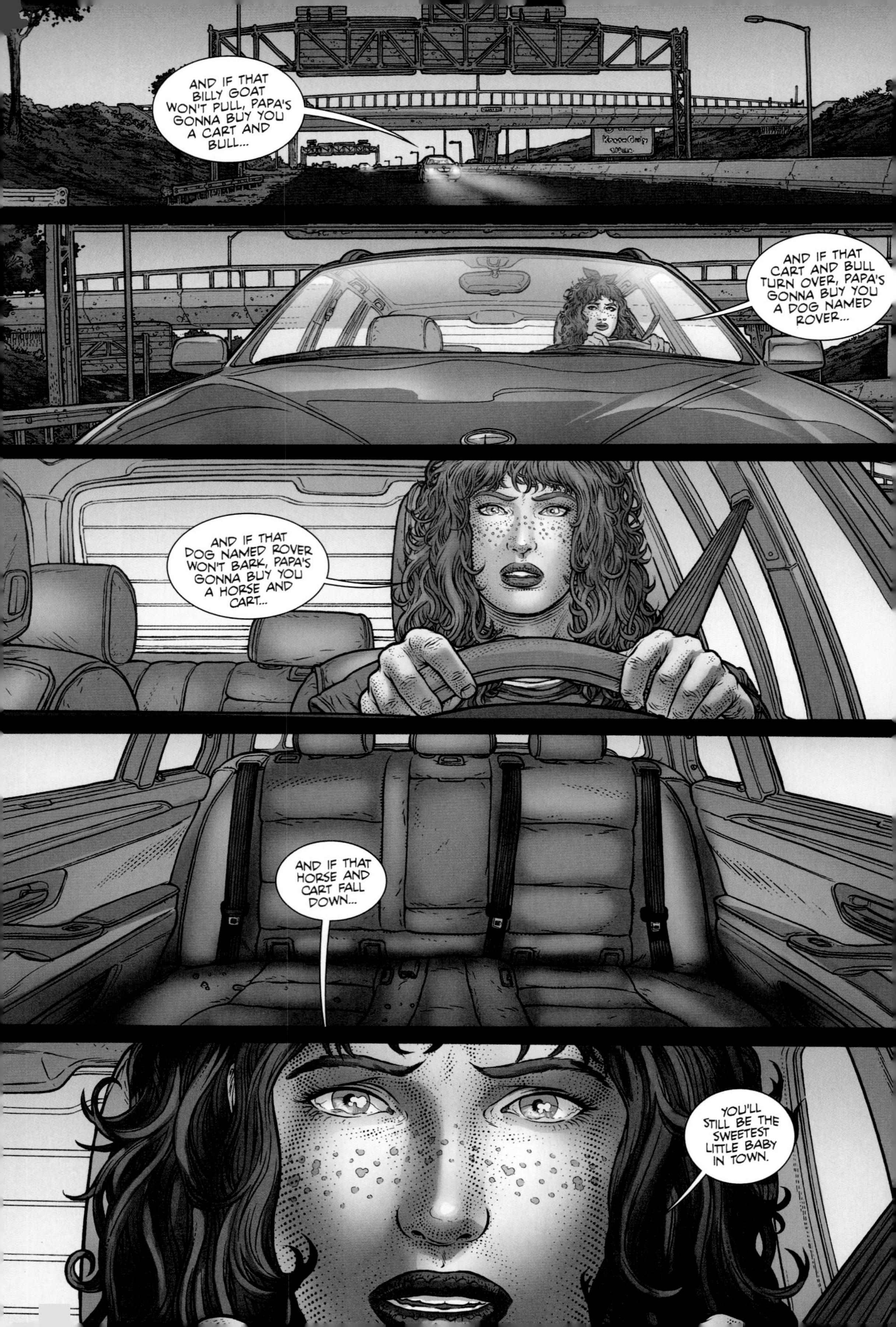
AND IF THAT BILLY GOAT WON'T PULL, PAPA'S GONNA BUY YOU A CART AND BULL...
AND IF THAT CART AND BULL TURN OVER, PAPA'S GONNA BUY YOU A DOG NAMED ROVER...
AND IF THAT DOG NAMED ROVER WON'T BARK, PAPA'S GONNA BUY YOU A HORSE AND CART...
AND IF THAT HORSE AND CART FALL DOWN...
YOU'LL STILL BE THE SWEETEST LITTLE BABY IN TOWN.

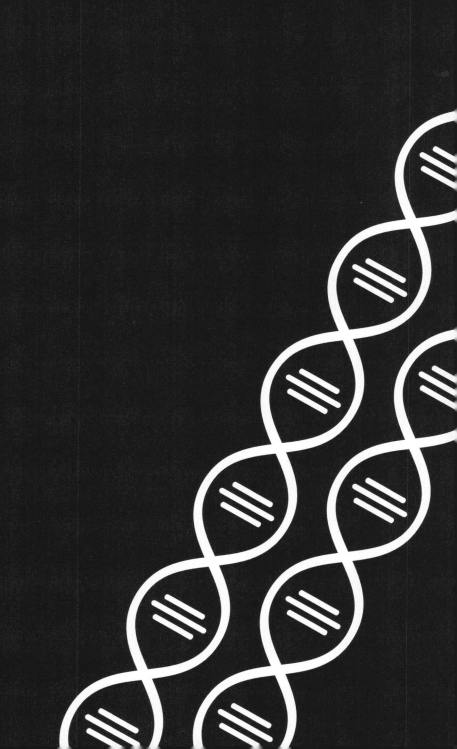

CHAPTER 13

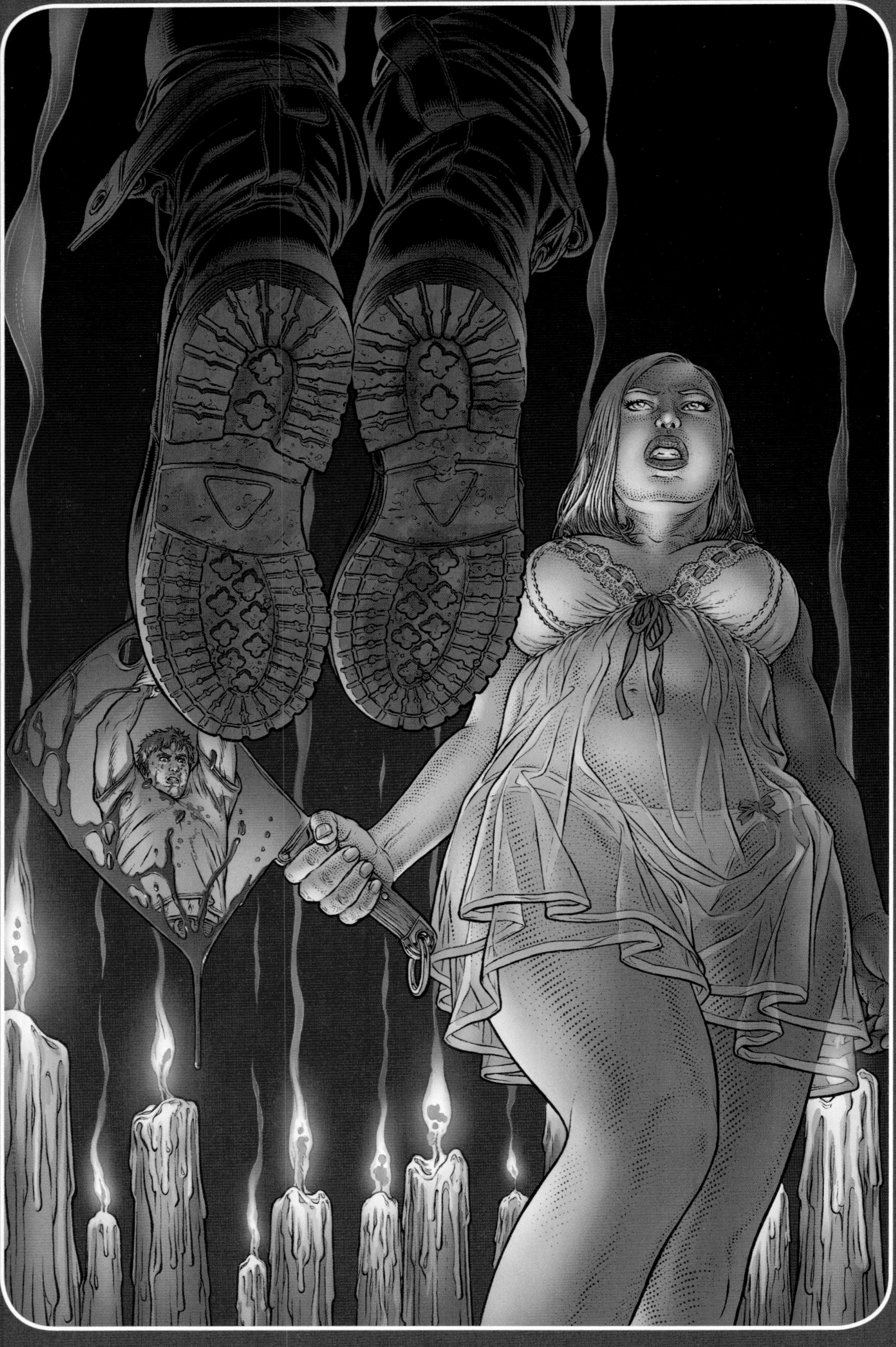

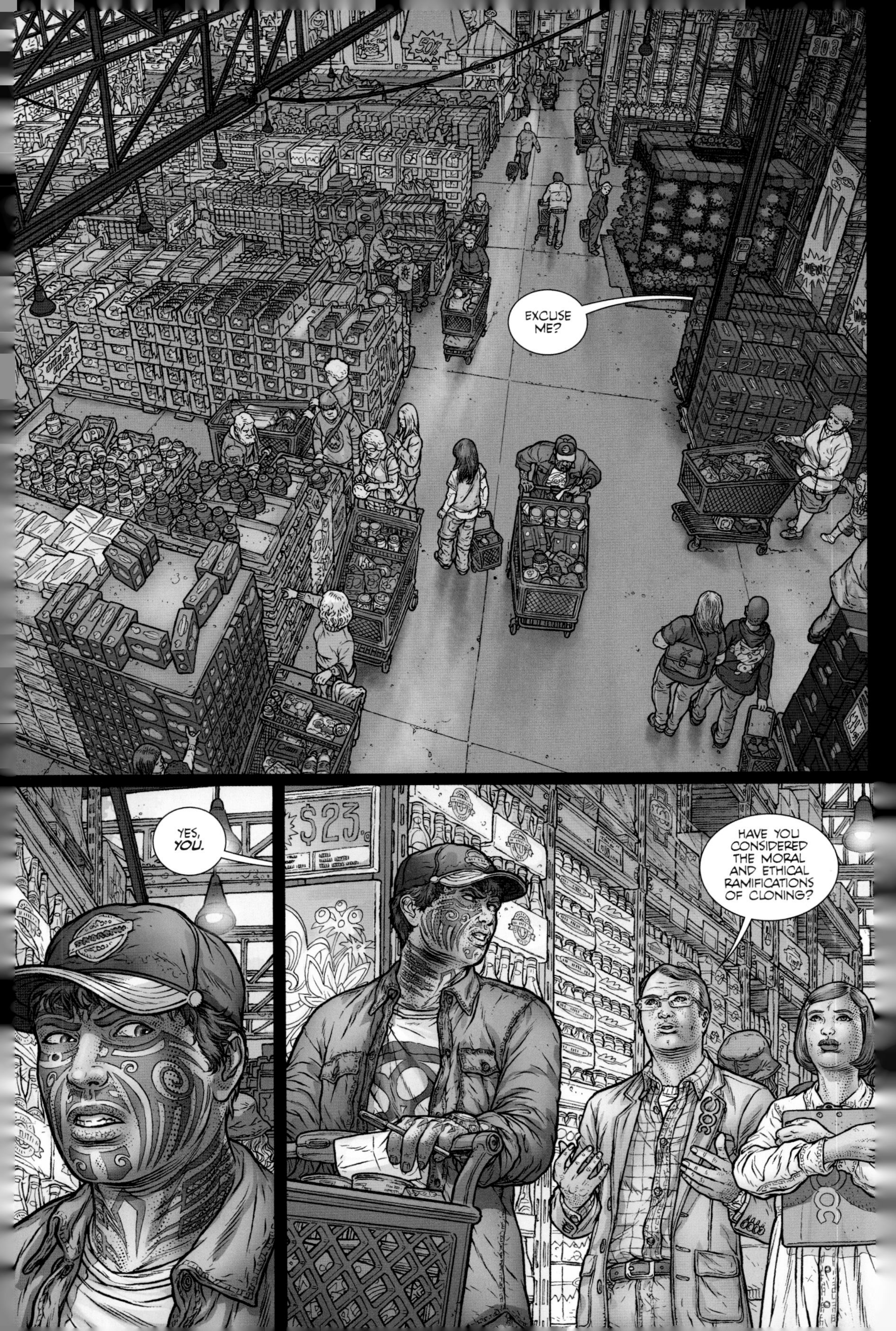
EXCUSE ME?
YES, *YOU.*
HAVE YOU CONSIDERED THE MORAL AND ETHICAL RAMIFICATIONS OF CLONING?

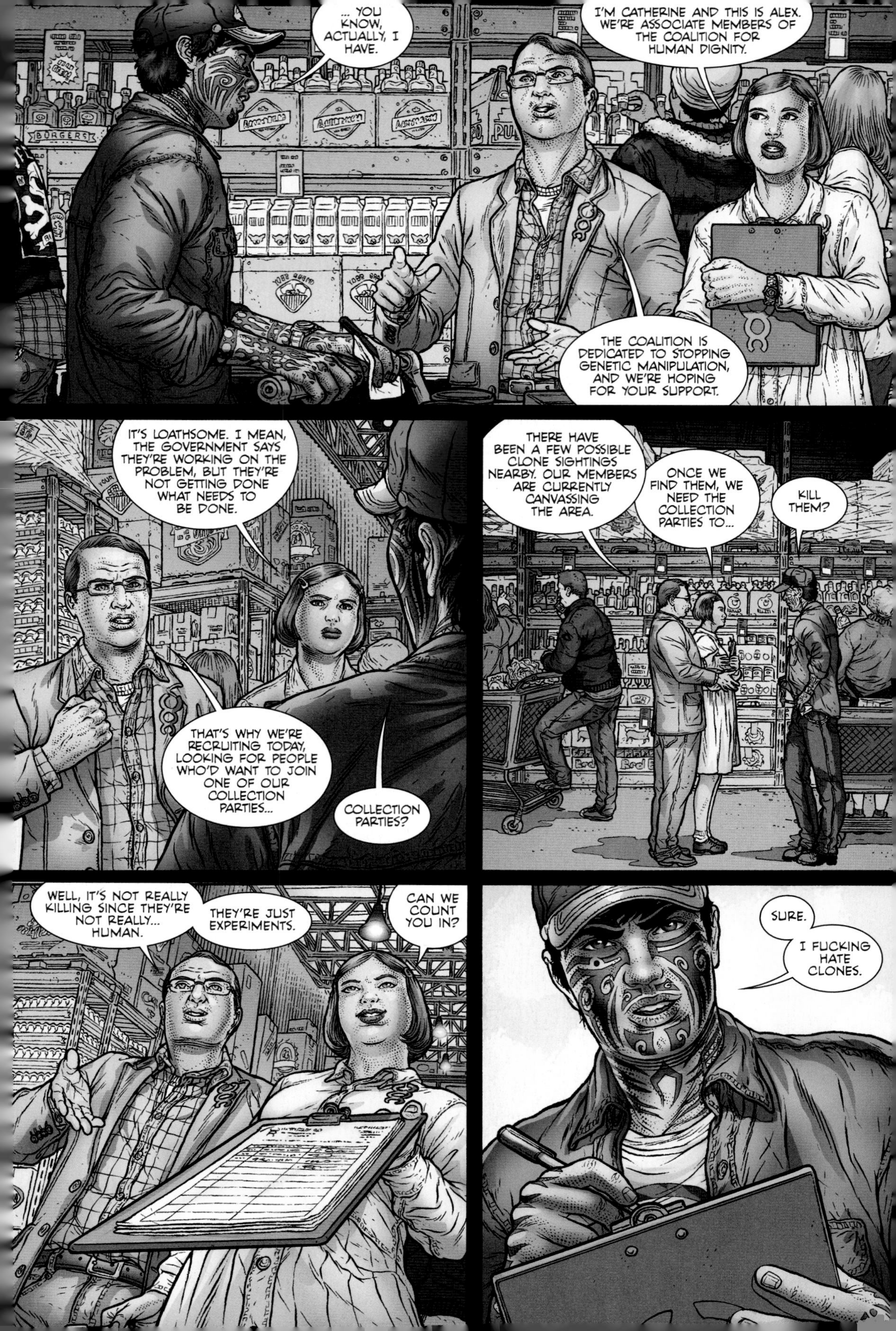
... YOU KNOW, ACTUALLY, I HAVE.
I'M CATHERINE AND THIS IS ALEX. WE'RE ASSOCIATE MEMBERS OF THE COALITION FOR HUMAN DIGNITY.
THE COALITION IS DEDICATED TO STOPPING GENETIC MANIPULATION, AND WE'RE HOPING FOR YOUR SUPPORT.
IT'S LOATHSOME. I MEAN, THE GOVERNMENT SAYS THEY'RE WORKING ON THE PROBLEM, BUT THEY'RE NOT GETTING DONE WHAT NEEDS TO BE DONE.
THAT'S WHY WE'RE RECRUITING TODAY, LOOKING FOR PEOPLE WHO'D WANT TO JOIN ONE OF OUR COLLECTION PARTIES...
COLLECTION PARTIES?
THERE HAVE BEEN A FEW POSSIBLE CLONE SIGHTINGS NEARBY. OUR MEMBERS ARE CURRENTLY CANVASSING THE AREA.
ONCE WE FIND THEM, WE NEED THE COLLECTION PARTIES TO...
KILL THEM?
WELL, IT'S NOT REALLY KILLING SINCE THEY'RE NOT REALLY... HUMAN.
THEY'RE JUST EXPERIMENTS.
CAN WE COUNT YOU IN?
SURE.
I FUCKING HATE CLONES.

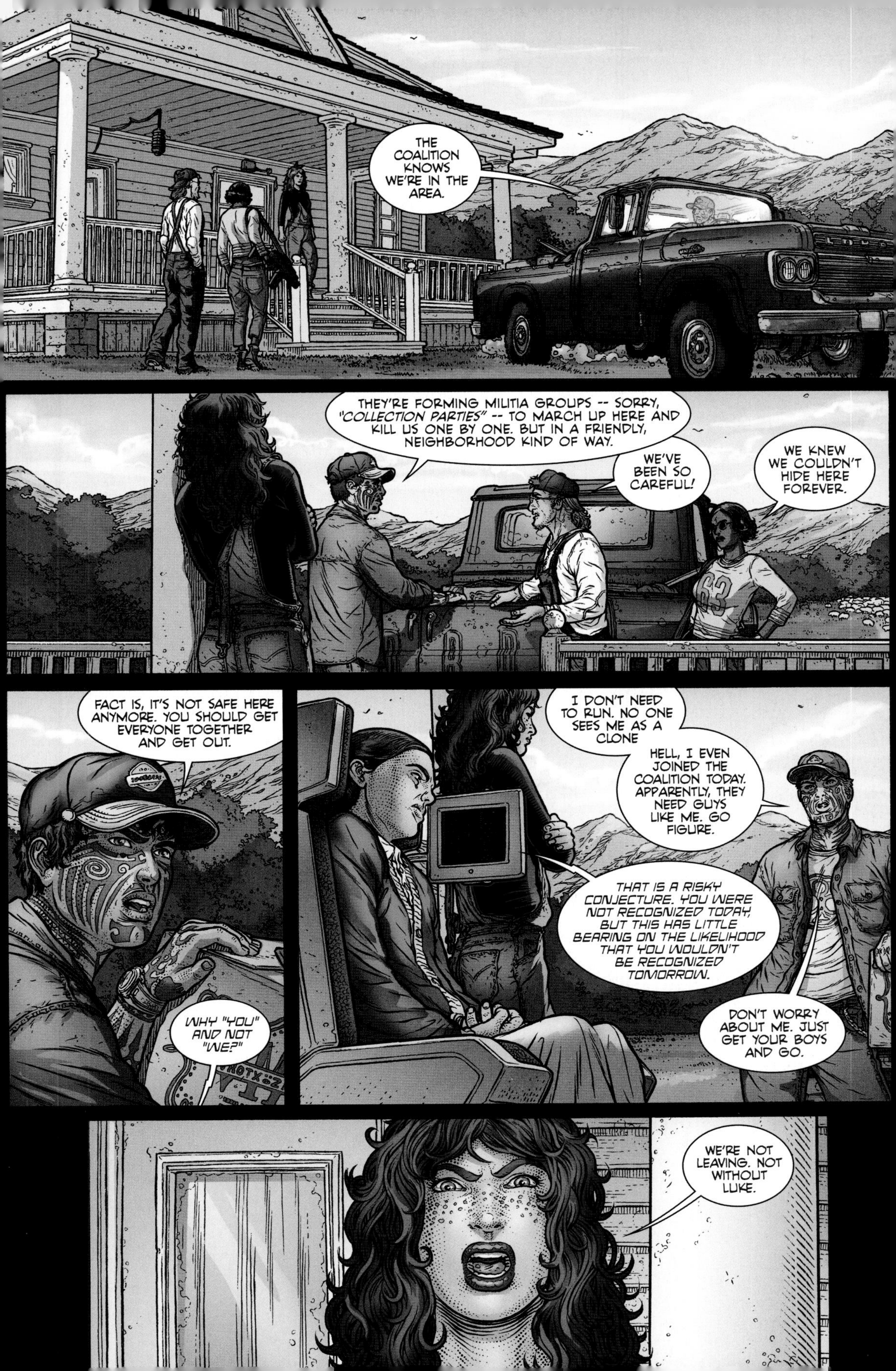
THE COALITION KNOWS WE'RE IN THE AREA.
THEY'RE FORMING MILITIA GROUPS -- SORRY, "COLLECTION PARTIES" -- TO MARCH UP HERE AND KILL US ONE BY ONE. BUT IN A FRIENDLY, NEIGHBORHOOD KIND OF WAY.
WE'VE BEEN SO CAREFUL!
WE KNEW WE COULDN'T HIDE HERE FOREVER.
FACT IS, IT'S NOT SAFE HERE ANYMORE. YOU SHOULD GET EVERYONE TOGETHER AND GET OUT.
WHY "YOU" AND NOT "WE?"
I DON'T NEED TO RUN. NO ONE SEES ME AS A CLONE
HELL, I EVEN JOINED THE COALITION TODAY. APPARENTLY, THEY NEED GUYS LIKE ME. GO FIGURE.
THAT IS A RISKY CONJECTURE. YOU WERE NOT RECOGNIZED TODAY, BUT THIS HAS LITTLE BEARING ON THE LIKELIHOOD THAT YOU WOULDN'T BE RECOGNIZED TOMORROW.
DON'T WORRY ABOUT ME. JUST GET YOUR BOYS AND GO.
WE'RE NOT LEAVING. NOT WITHOUT LUKE.

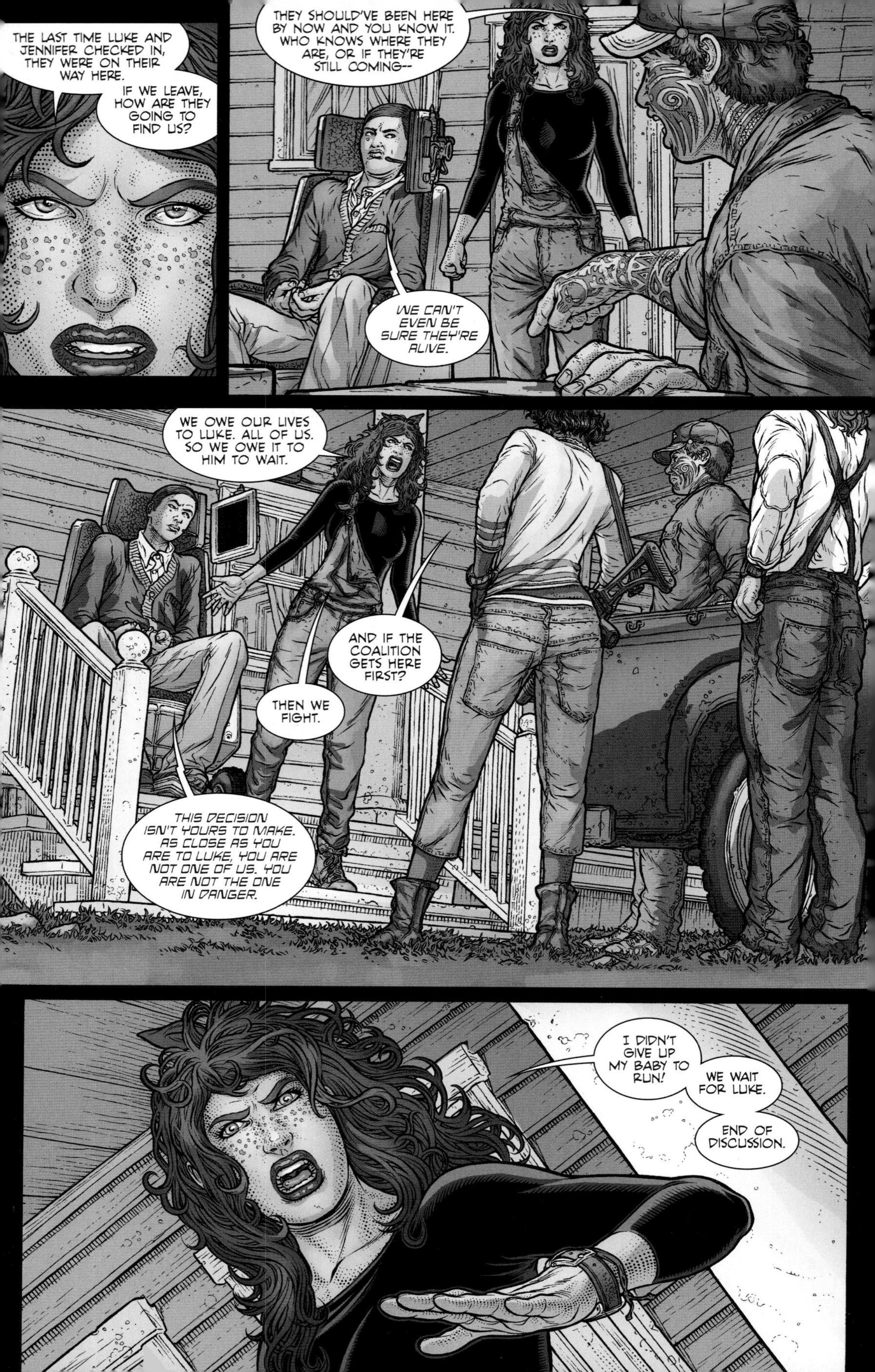
THE LAST TIME LUKE AND JENNIFER CHECKED IN, THEY WERE ON THEIR WAY HERE.
IF WE LEAVE, HOW ARE THEY GOING TO FIND US?
THEY SHOULD'VE BEEN HERE BY NOW AND YOU KNOW IT. WHO KNOWS WHERE THEY ARE, OR IF THEY'RE STILL COMING--
WE CAN'T EVEN BE SURE THEY'RE ALIVE.
WE OWE OUR LIVES TO LUKE. ALL OF US. SO WE OWE IT TO HIM TO WAIT.
AND IF THE COALITION GETS HERE FIRST?
THEN WE FIGHT.
THIS DECISION ISN'T YOURS TO MAKE. AS CLOSE AS YOU ARE TO LUKE, YOU ARE NOT ONE OF US. YOU ARE NOT THE ONE IN DANGER.
I DIDN'T GIVE UP MY BABY TO RUN!
WE WAIT FOR LUKE.
END OF DISCUSSION.

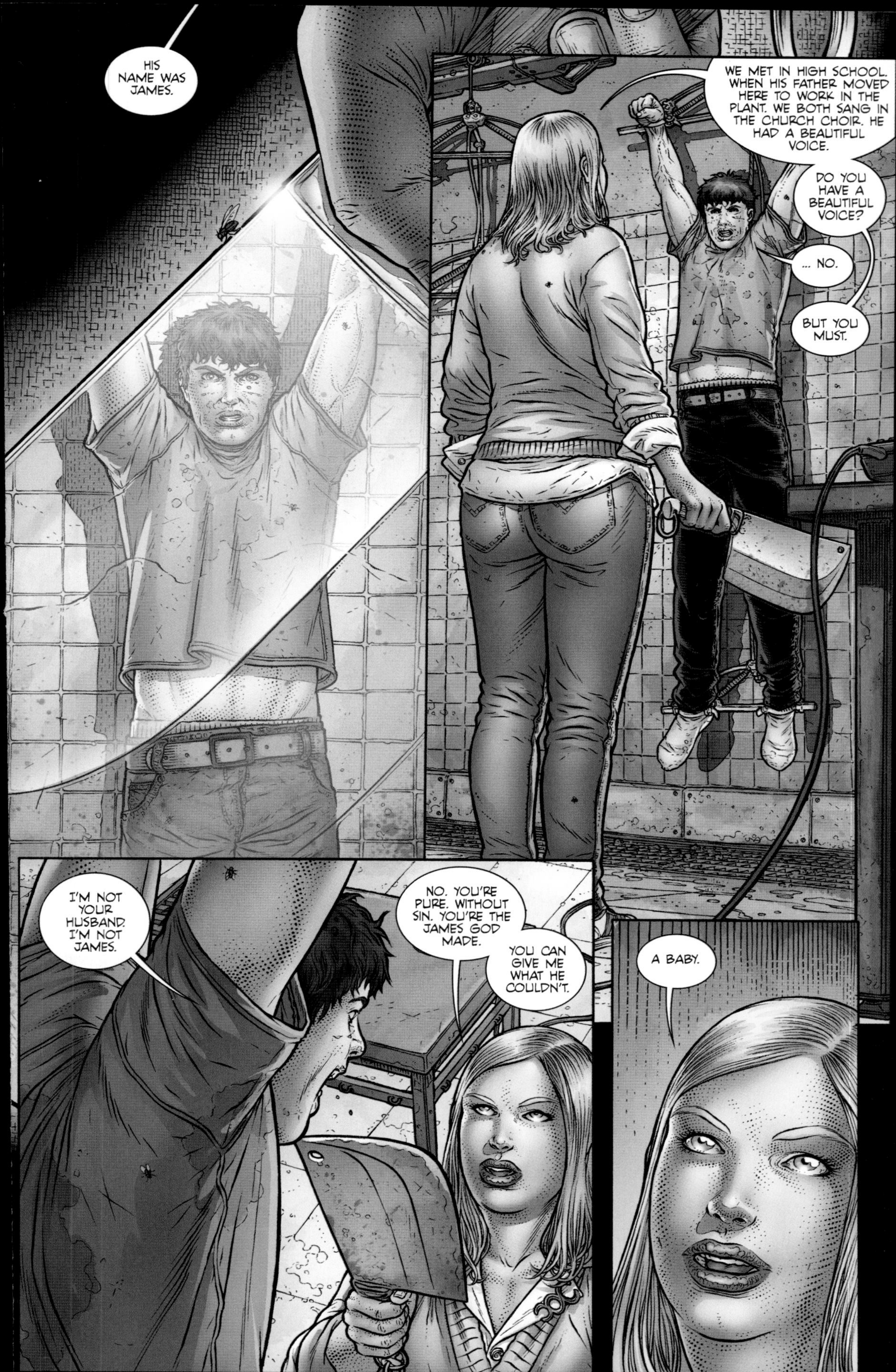
HIS NAME WAS JAMES.
WE MET IN HIGH SCHOOL. WHEN HIS FATHER MOVED HERE TO WORK IN THE PLANT. WE BOTH SANG IN THE CHURCH CHOIR. HE HAD A BEAUTIFUL VOICE.
DO YOU HAVE A BEAUTIFUL VOICE?
... NO.
BUT YOU MUST.
I'M NOT YOUR HUSBAND. I'M NOT JAMES.
NO. YOU'RE PURE. WITHOUT SIN. YOU'RE THE JAMES GOD MADE.
YOU CAN GIVE ME WHAT HE COULDN'T.
A BABY.

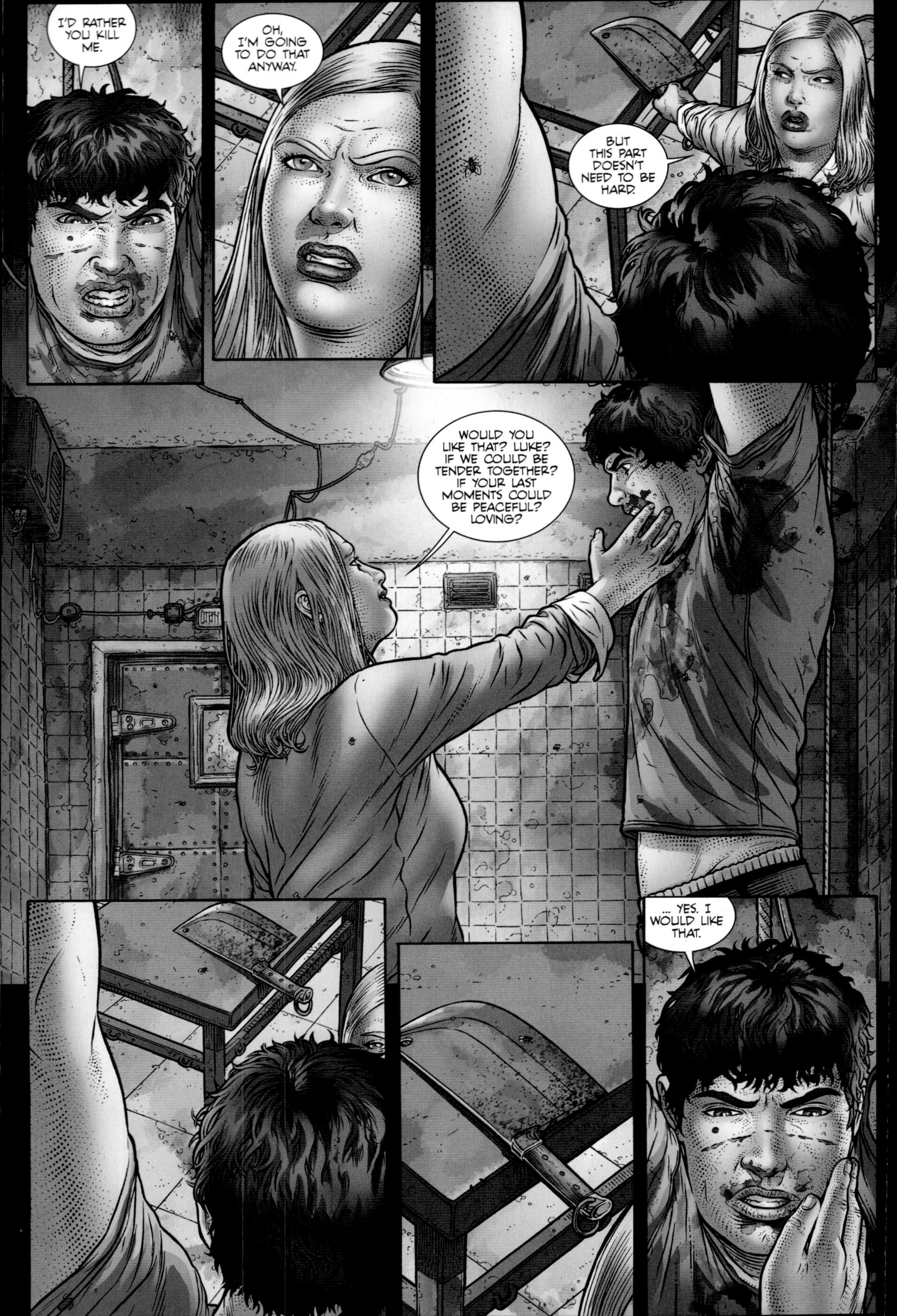
I'D RATHER YOU KILL ME.
OH, I'M GOING TO DO THAT ANYWAY.
BUT THIS PART DOESN'T NEED TO BE HARD.
WOULD YOU LIKE THAT? LUKE? IF WE COULD BE TENDER TOGETHER? IF YOUR LAST MOMENTS COULD BE PEACEFUL? LOVING?
... YES. I WOULD LIKE THAT.

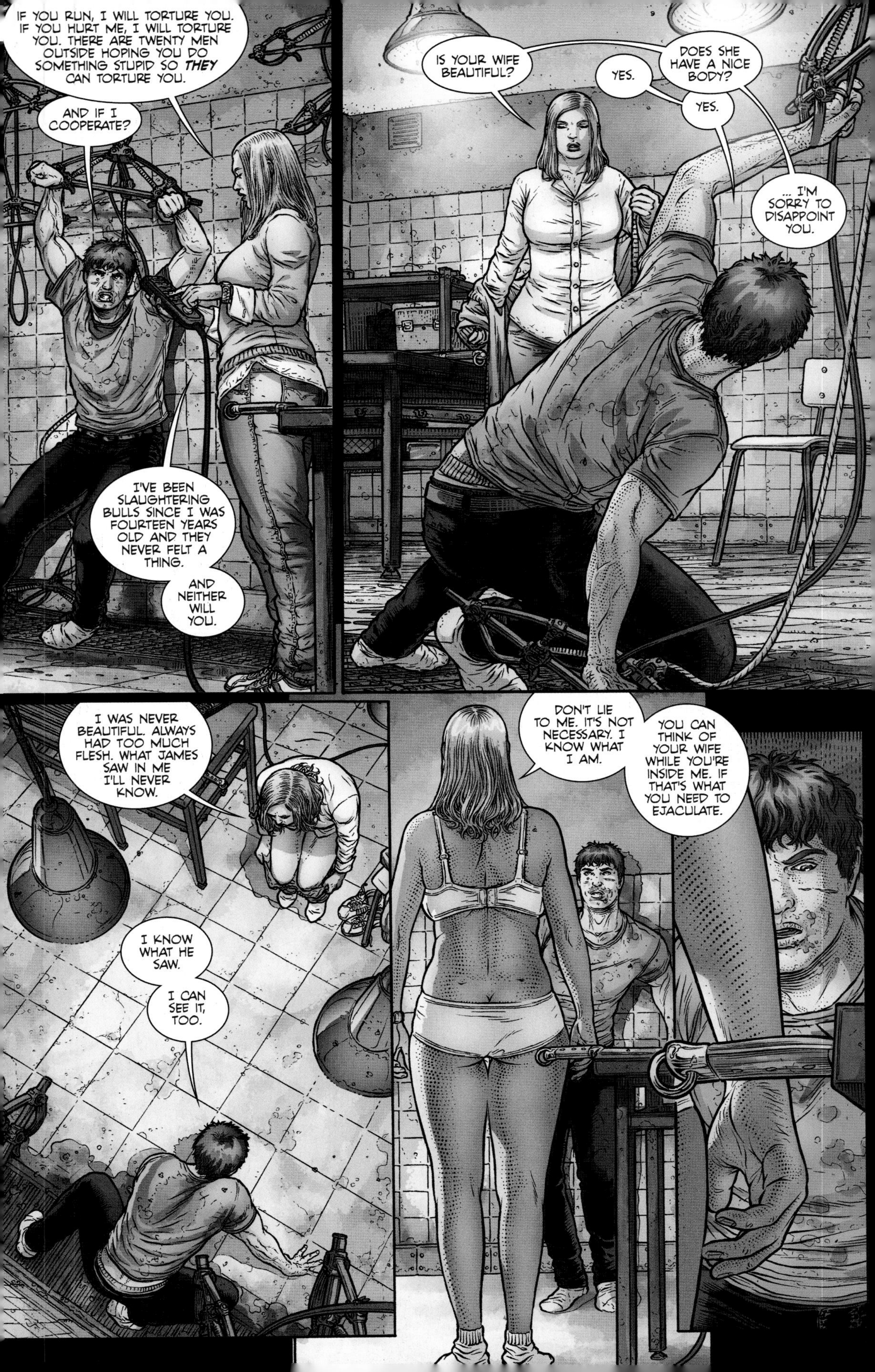
IF YOU RUN, I WILL TORTURE YOU. IF YOU HURT ME, I WILL TORTURE YOU. THERE ARE TWENTY MEN OUTSIDE HOPING YOU DO SOMETHING STUPID SO *THEY* CAN TORTURE YOU.
AND IF I COOPERATE?
I'VE BEEN SLAUGHTERING BULLS SINCE I WAS FOURTEEN YEARS OLD AND THEY NEVER FELT A THING.
AND NEITHER WILL YOU.
IS YOUR WIFE BEAUTIFUL?
YES.
DOES SHE HAVE A NICE BODY?
YES.
... I'M SORRY TO DISAPPOINT YOU.
I WAS NEVER BEAUTIFUL. ALWAYS HAD TOO MUCH FLESH. WHAT JAMES SAW IN ME I'LL NEVER KNOW.
I KNOW WHAT HE SAW.
I CAN SEE IT, TOO.
DON'T LIE TO ME. IT'S NOT NECESSARY. I KNOW WHAT I AM.
YOU CAN THINK OF YOUR WIFE WHILE YOU'RE INSIDE ME. IF THAT'S WHAT YOU NEED TO EJACULATE.

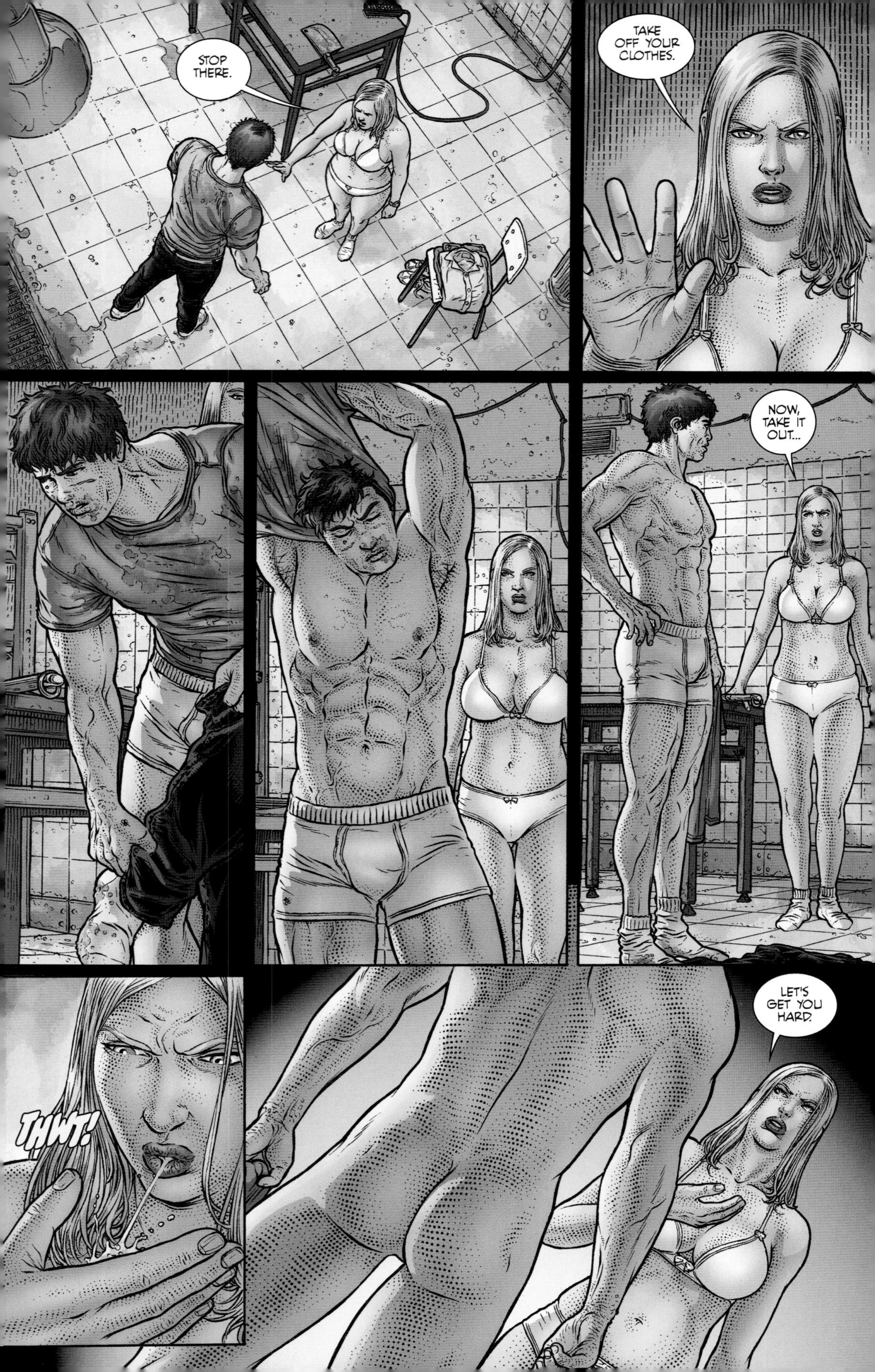
STOP THERE.
TAKE OFF YOUR CLOTHES.
NOW, TAKE IT OUT...
THWT!
LET'S GET YOU HARD.

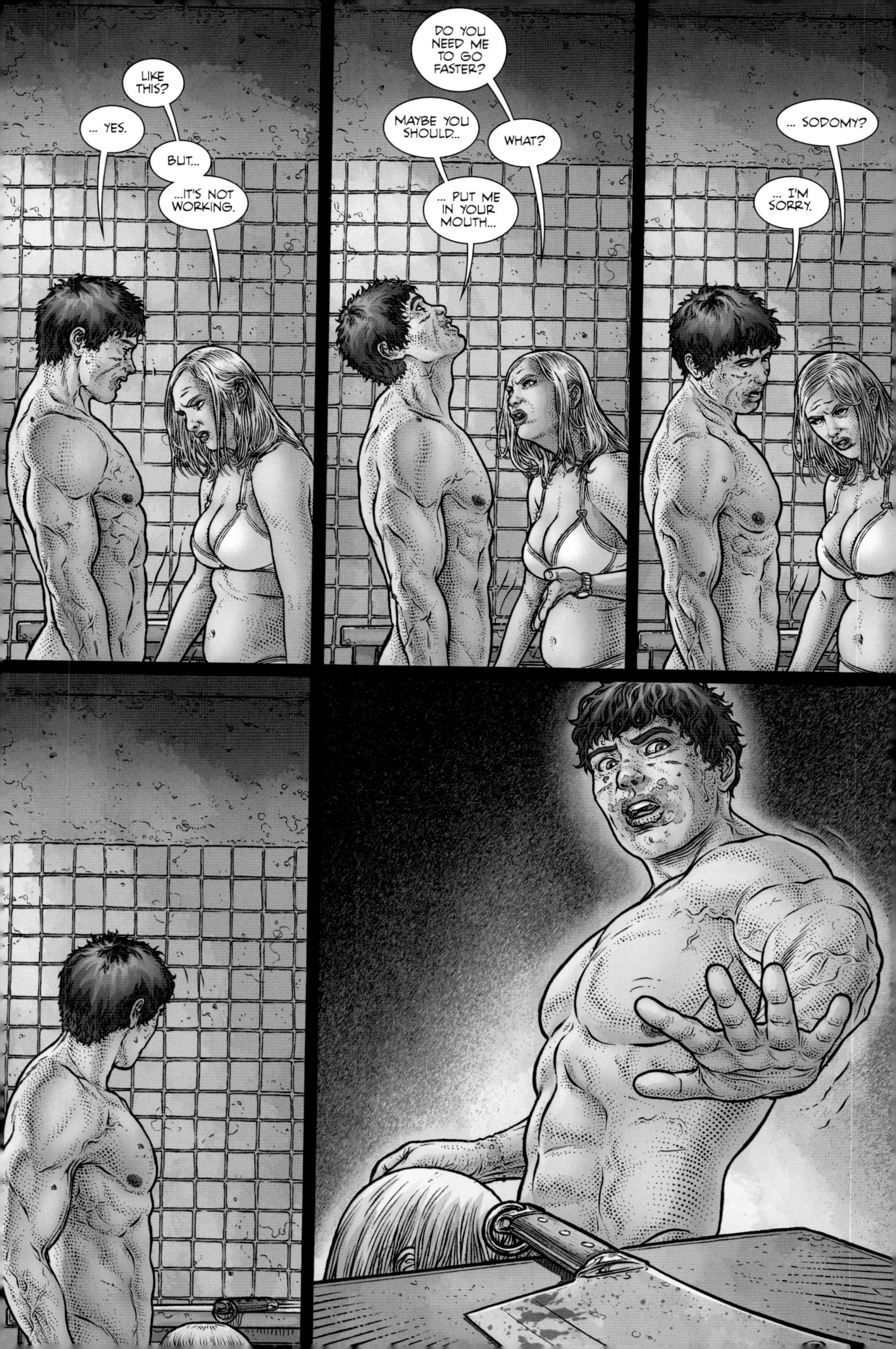
LIKE THIS?
... YES.
BUT...
...IT'S NOT WORKING.
DO YOU NEED ME TO GO FASTER?
MAYBE YOU SHOULD...
WHAT?
... PUT ME IN YOUR MOUTH...
... SODOMY?
... I'M SORRY.

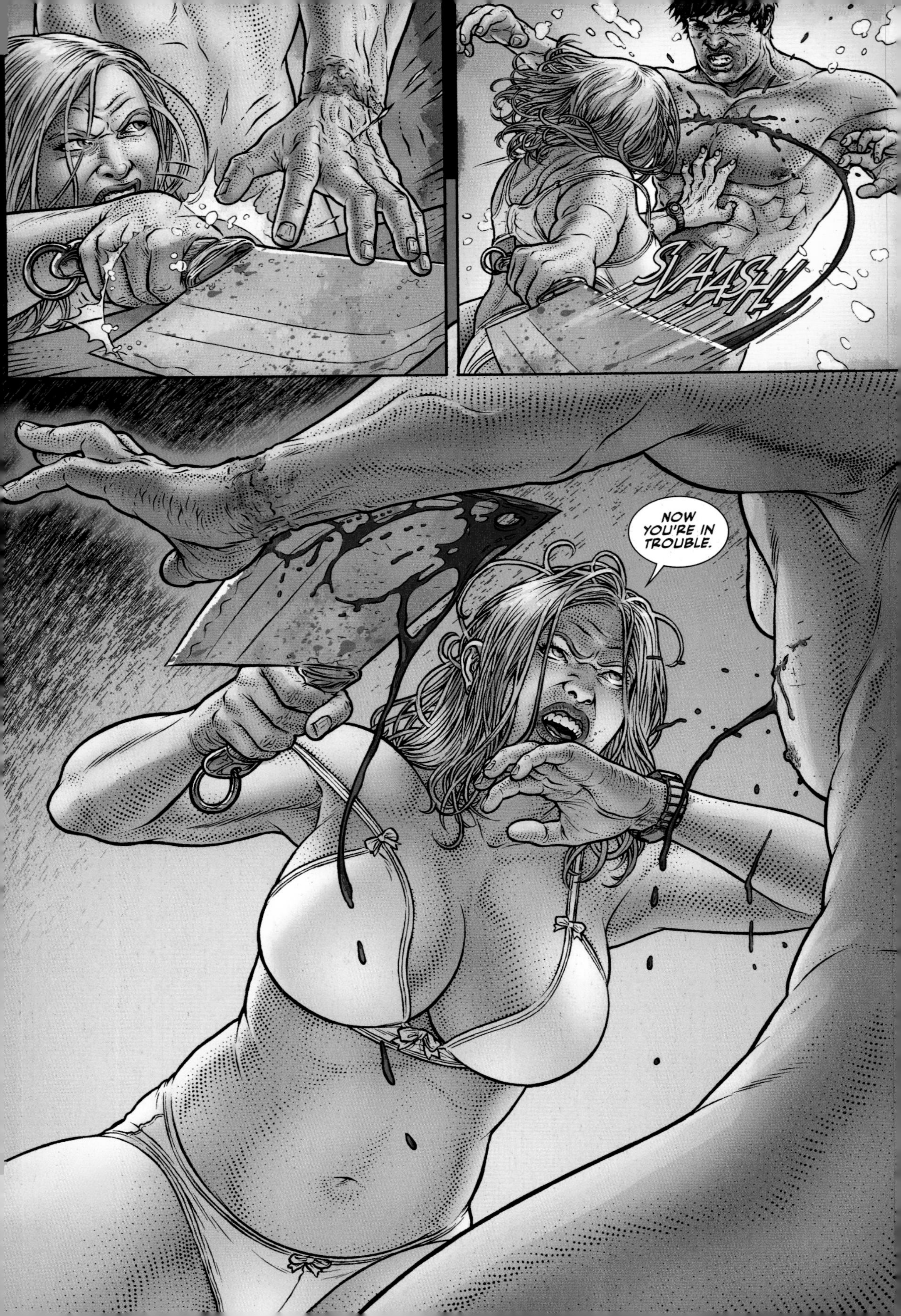
SHAASH!
NOW YOU'RE IN TROUBLE.

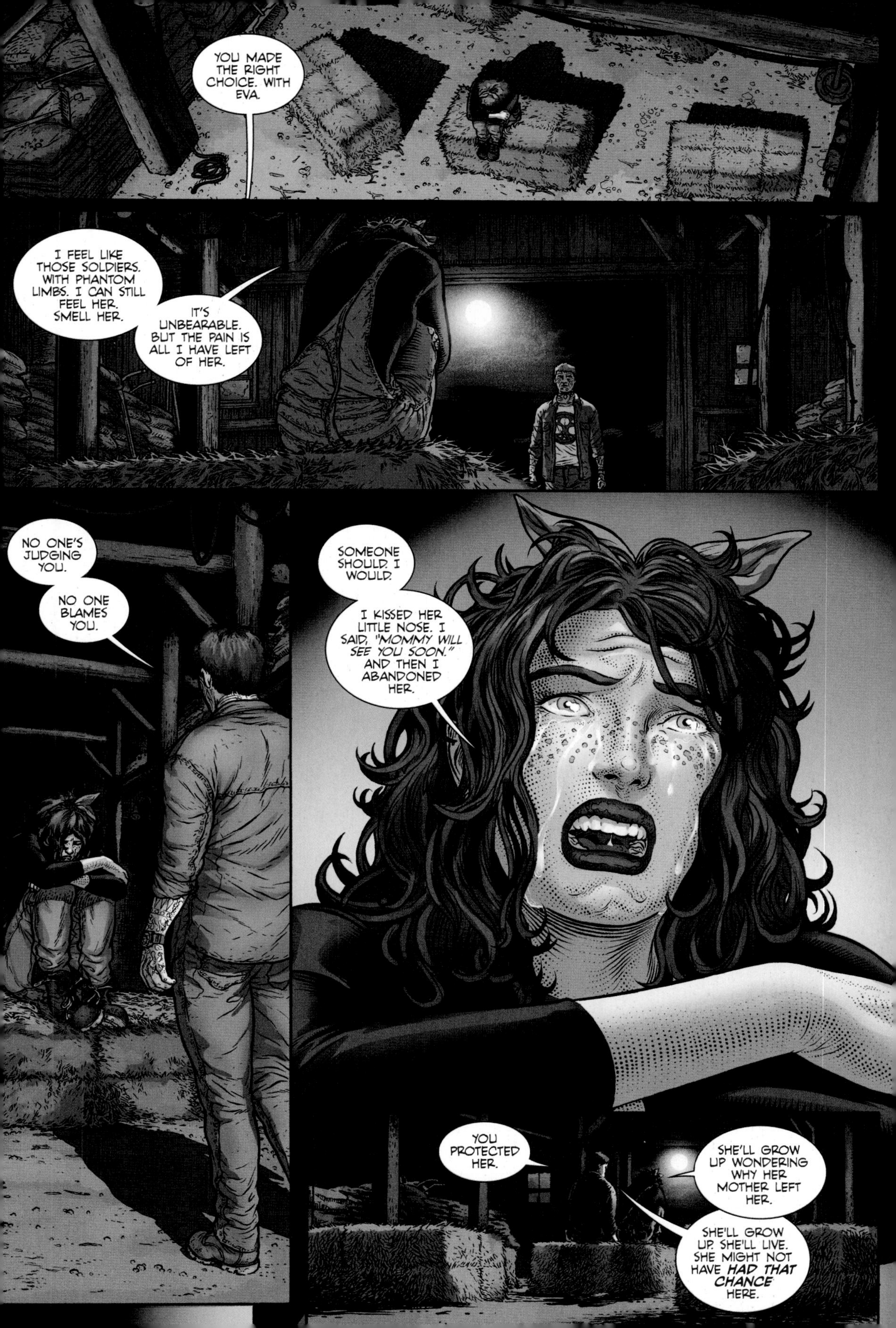
YOU MADE THE RIGHT CHOICE. WITH EVA.
I FEEL LIKE THOSE SOLDIERS. WITH PHANTOM LIMBS. I CAN STILL FEEL HER. SMELL HER.
IT'S UNBEARABLE. BUT THE PAIN IS ALL I HAVE LEFT OF HER.
NO ONE'S JUDGING YOU.
NO ONE BLAMES YOU.
SOMEONE SHOULD. I WOULD.
I KISSED HER LITTLE NOSE. I SAID, "*MOMMY WILL SEE YOU SOON.*" AND THEN I ABANDONED HER.
YOU PROTECTED HER.
SHE'LL GROW UP WONDERING WHY HER MOTHER LEFT HER.
SHE'LL GROW UP. SHE'LL LIVE. SHE MIGHT NOT HAVE ***HAD THAT CHANCE*** HERE.

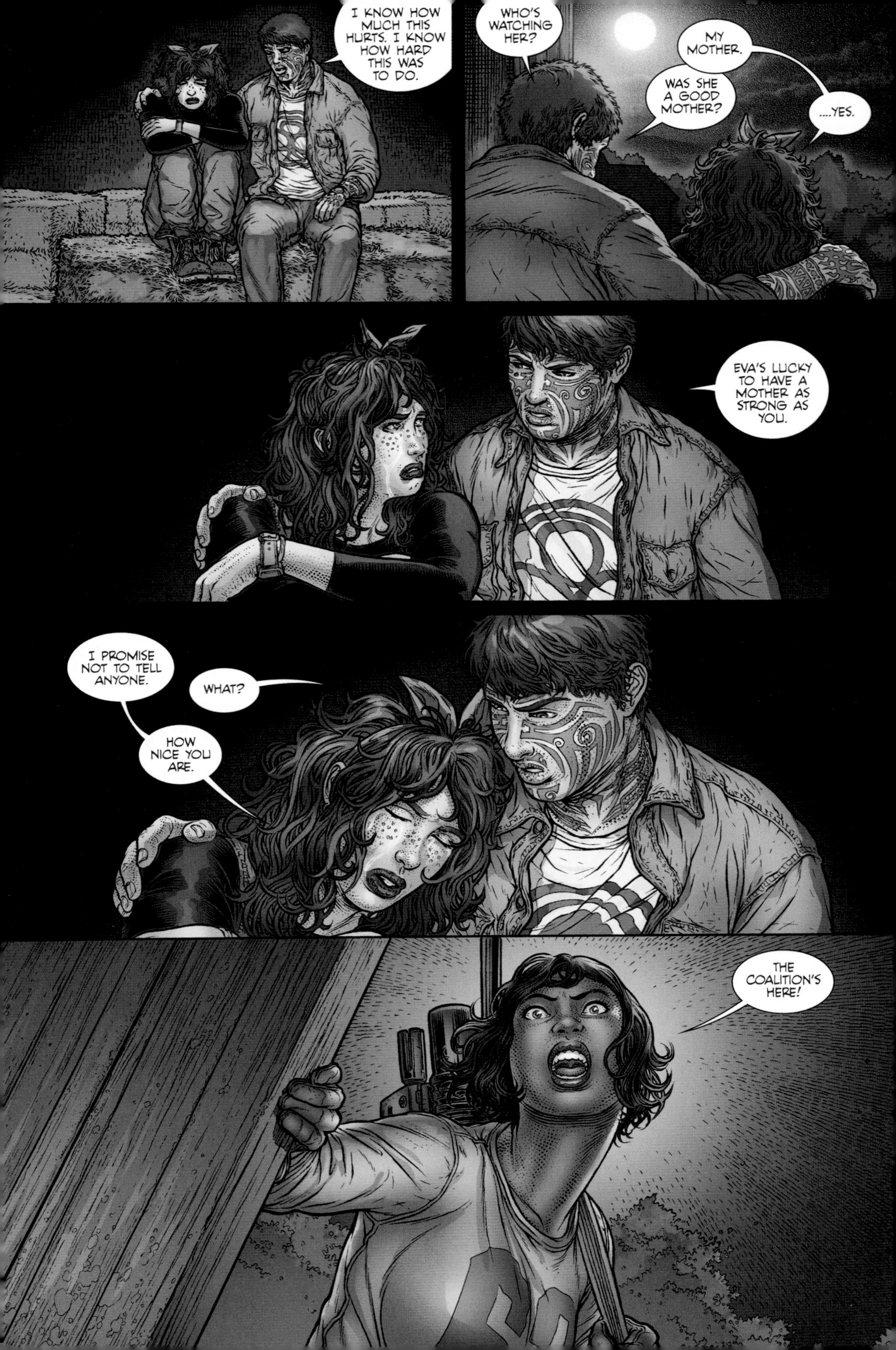
I KNOW HOW MUCH THIS HURTS. I KNOW HOW HARD THIS WAS TO DO.
WHO'S WATCHING HER?
MY MOTHER.
WAS SHE A GOOD MOTHER?
....YES.
EVA'S LUCKY TO HAVE A MOTHER AS STRONG AS YOU.
I PROMISE NOT TO TELL ANYONE.
WHAT?
HOW NICE YOU ARE.
THE COALITION'S HERE!

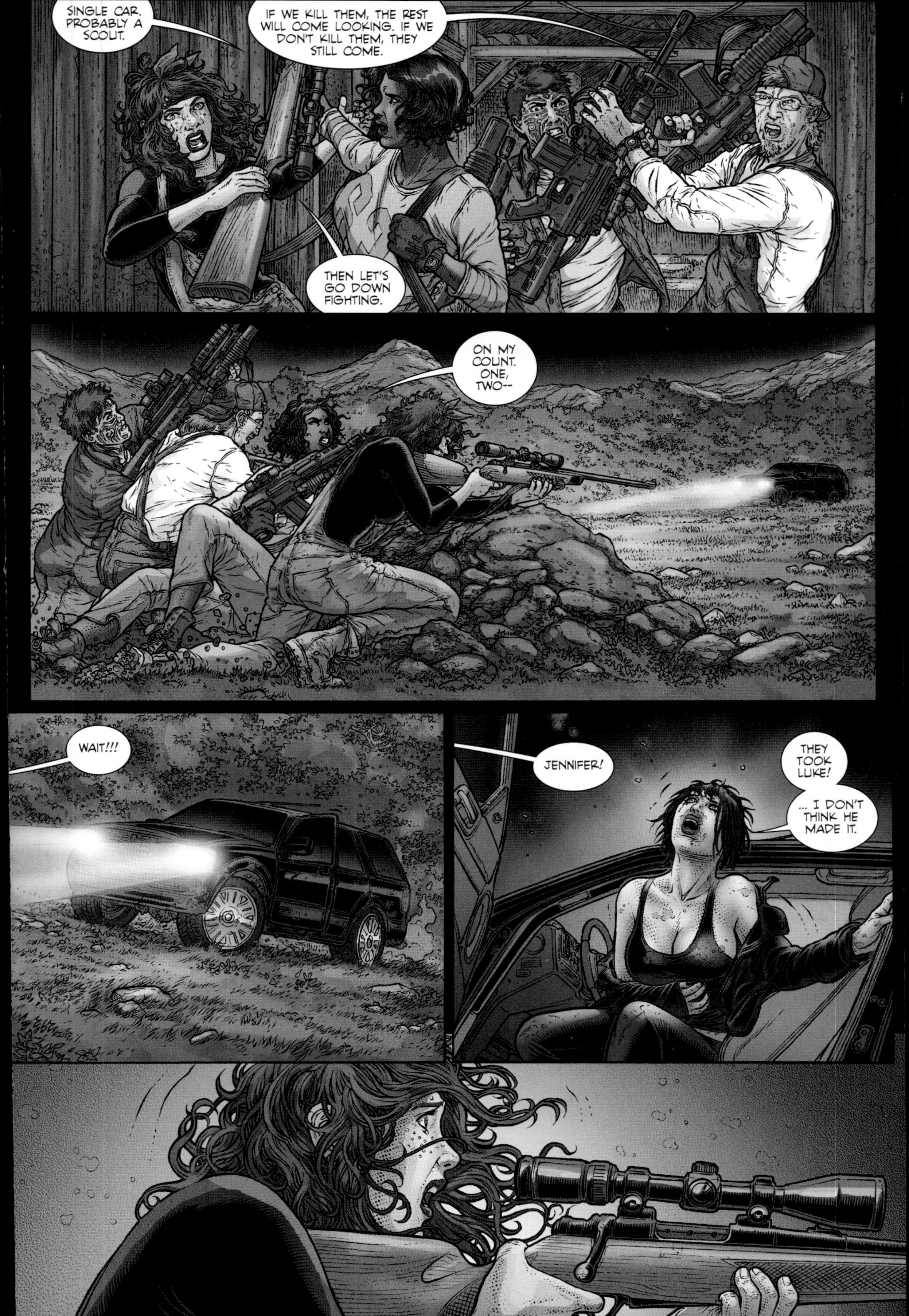
SINGLE CAR. PROBABLY A SCOUT.
IF WE KILL THEM, THE REST WILL COME LOOKING. IF WE DON'T KILL THEM, THEY STILL COME.
THEN LET'S GO DOWN FIGHTING.
ON MY COUNT. ONE, TWO--
WAIT!!!
JENNIFER!
THEY TOOK LUKE!
... I DON'T THINK HE MADE IT.

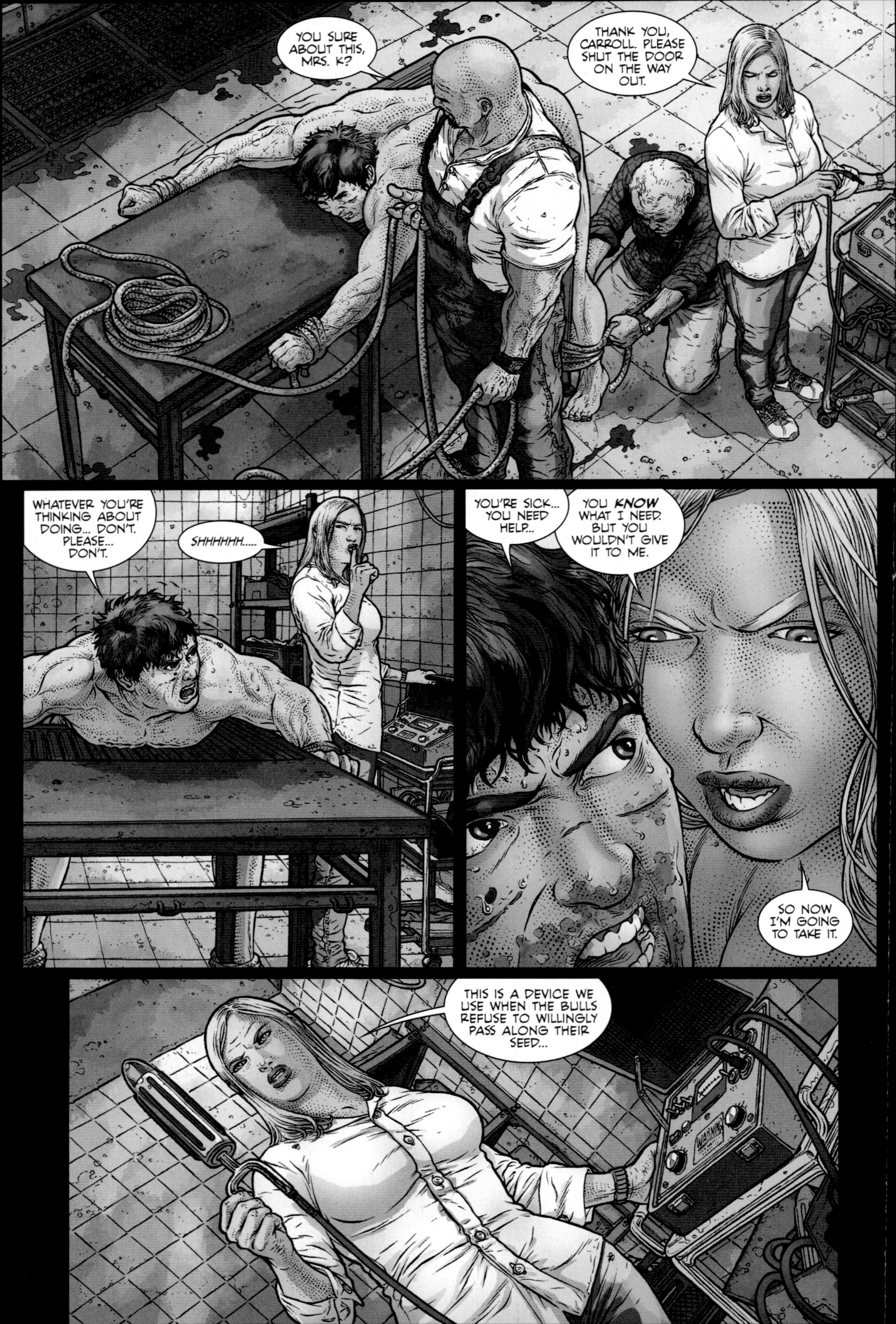
YOU SURE ABOUT THIS, MRS. K?
THANK YOU, CARROLL. PLEASE SHUT THE DOOR ON THE WAY OUT.
WHATEVER YOU'RE THINKING ABOUT DOING... DON'T. PLEASE... DON'T.
SHHHHHH.....
YOU'RE SICK... YOU NEED HELP...
YOU KNOW WHAT I NEED. BUT YOU WOULDN'T GIVE IT TO ME.
SO NOW I'M GOING TO TAKE IT.
THIS IS A DEVICE WE USE WHEN THE BULLS REFUSE TO WILLINGLY PASS ALONG THEIR SEED...
WARNING

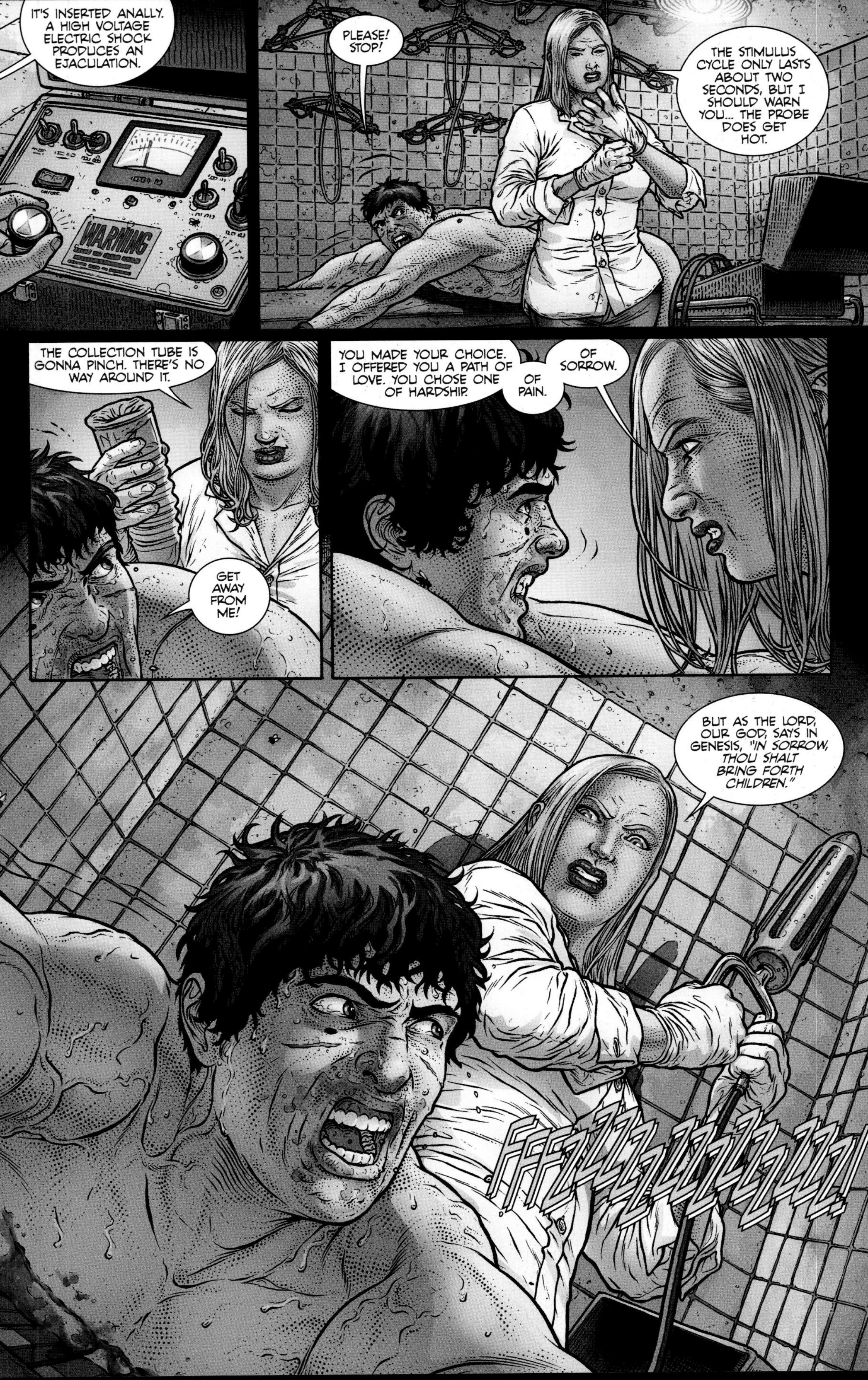
IT'S INSERTED ANALLY. A HIGH VOLTAGE ELECTRIC SHOCK PRODUCES AN EJACULATION.
WARNING
PLEASE! STOP!
THE STIMULUS CYCLE ONLY LASTS ABOUT TWO SECONDS, BUT I SHOULD WARN YOU... THE PROBE DOES GET HOT.
THE COLLECTION TUBE IS GONNA PINCH. THERE'S NO WAY AROUND IT.
GET AWAY FROM ME!
YOU MADE YOUR CHOICE. I OFFERED YOU A PATH OF LOVE. YOU CHOSE ONE OF HARDSHIP.
OF PAIN.
OF SORROW.
BUT AS THE LORD, OUR GOD, SAYS IN GENESIS, "IN SORROW, THOU SHALT BRING FORTH CHILDREN."

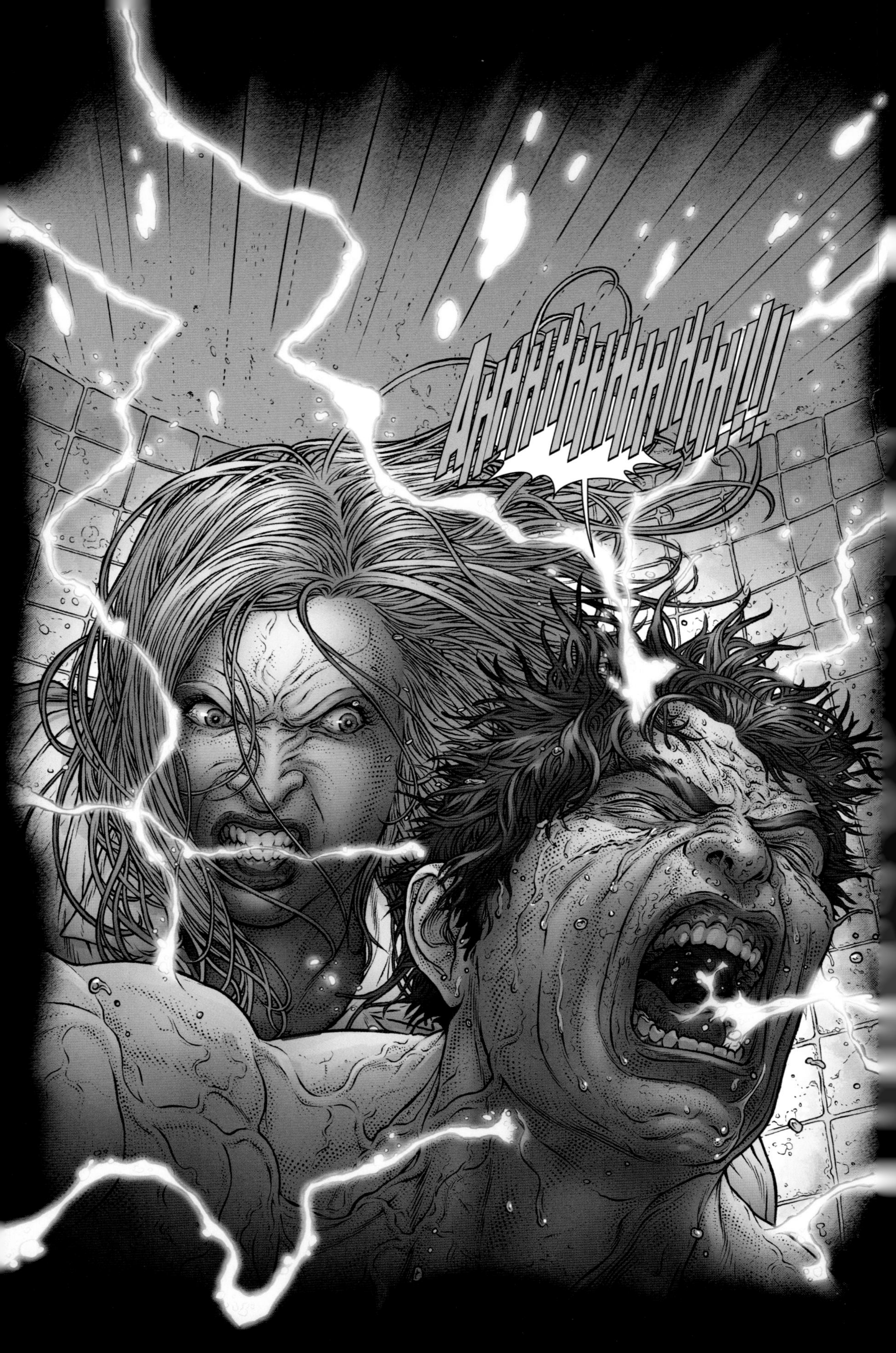
AAAAAAAAAAAAAA!!!

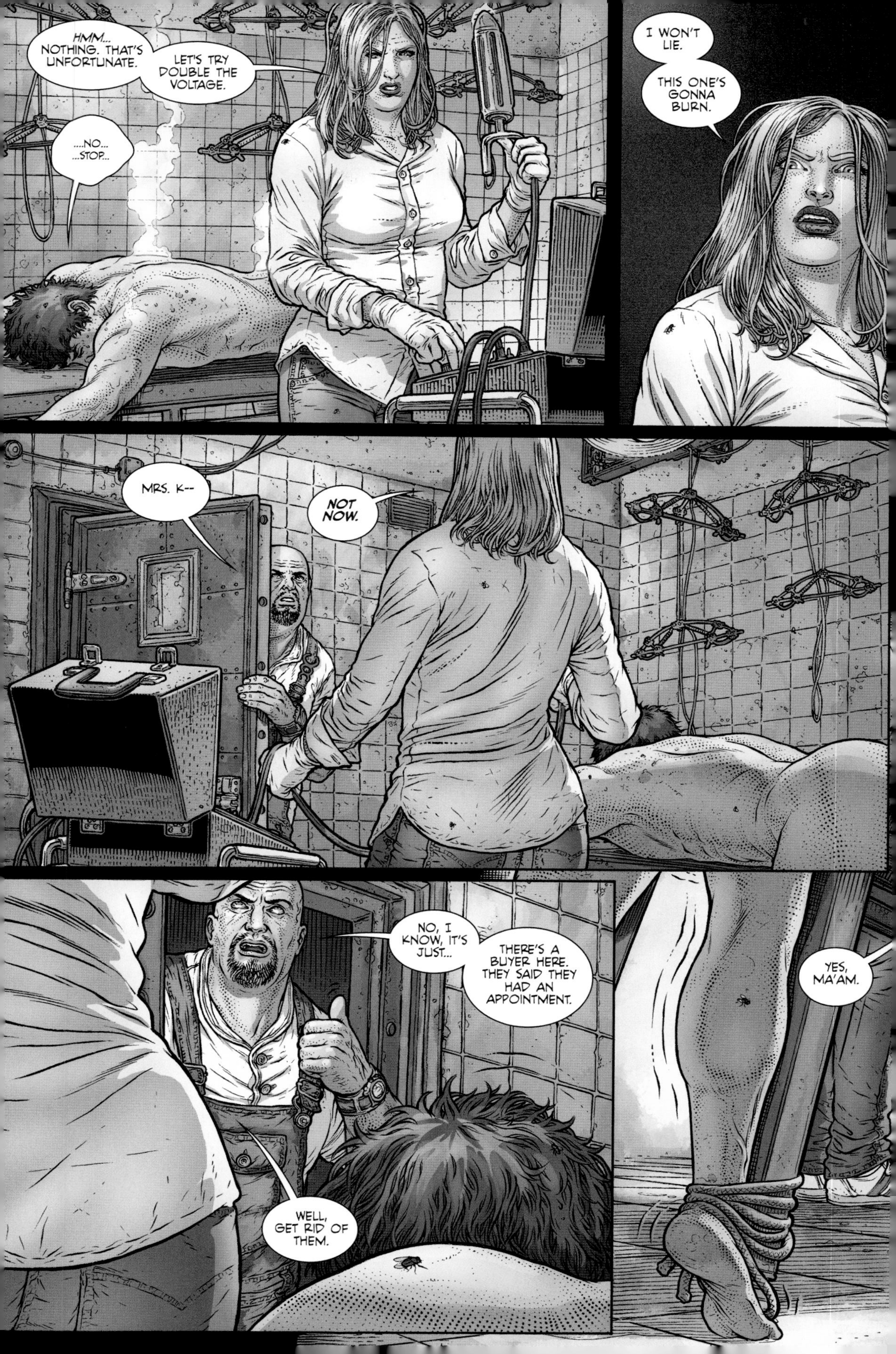
HMM... NOTHING. THAT'S UNFORTUNATE.
LET'S TRY DOUBLE THE VOLTAGE.
...NO... ...STOP...
I WON'T LIE.
THIS ONE'S GONNA BURN.
MRS. K--
NOT NOW.
NO, I KNOW, IT'S JUST...
THERE'S A BUYER HERE. THEY SAID THEY HAD AN APPOINTMENT.
WELL, GET RID OF THEM.
YES, MA'AM.

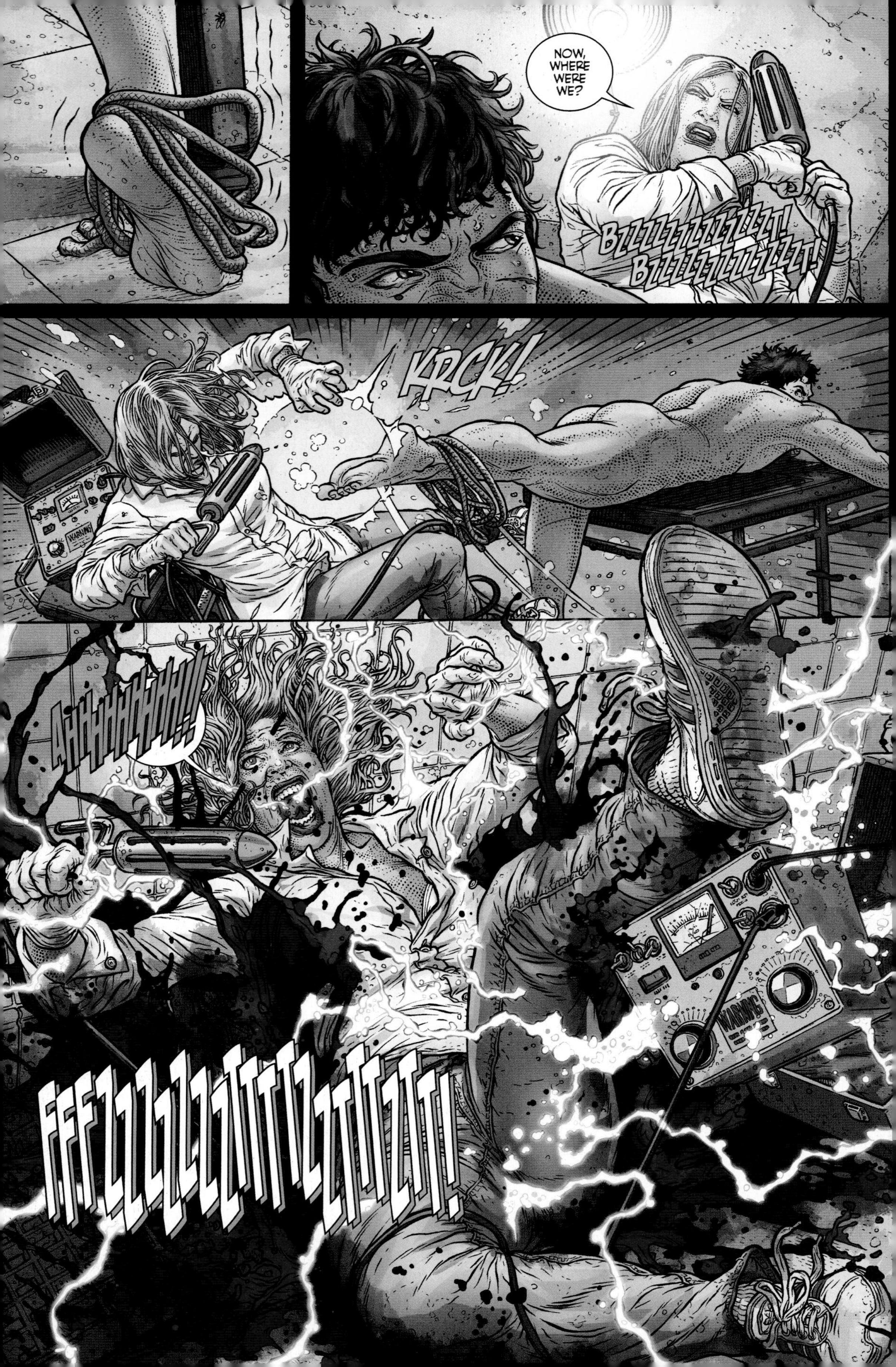
NOW, WHERE WERE WE?
BZZZZZZZZZZZZZT!
BZZZZZZZZZZZZZT!
KRCK!
WARNING
AHHHHHHHH!!!
WARNING
FFFZZZZZZZZTTTTZZTTTZTT!

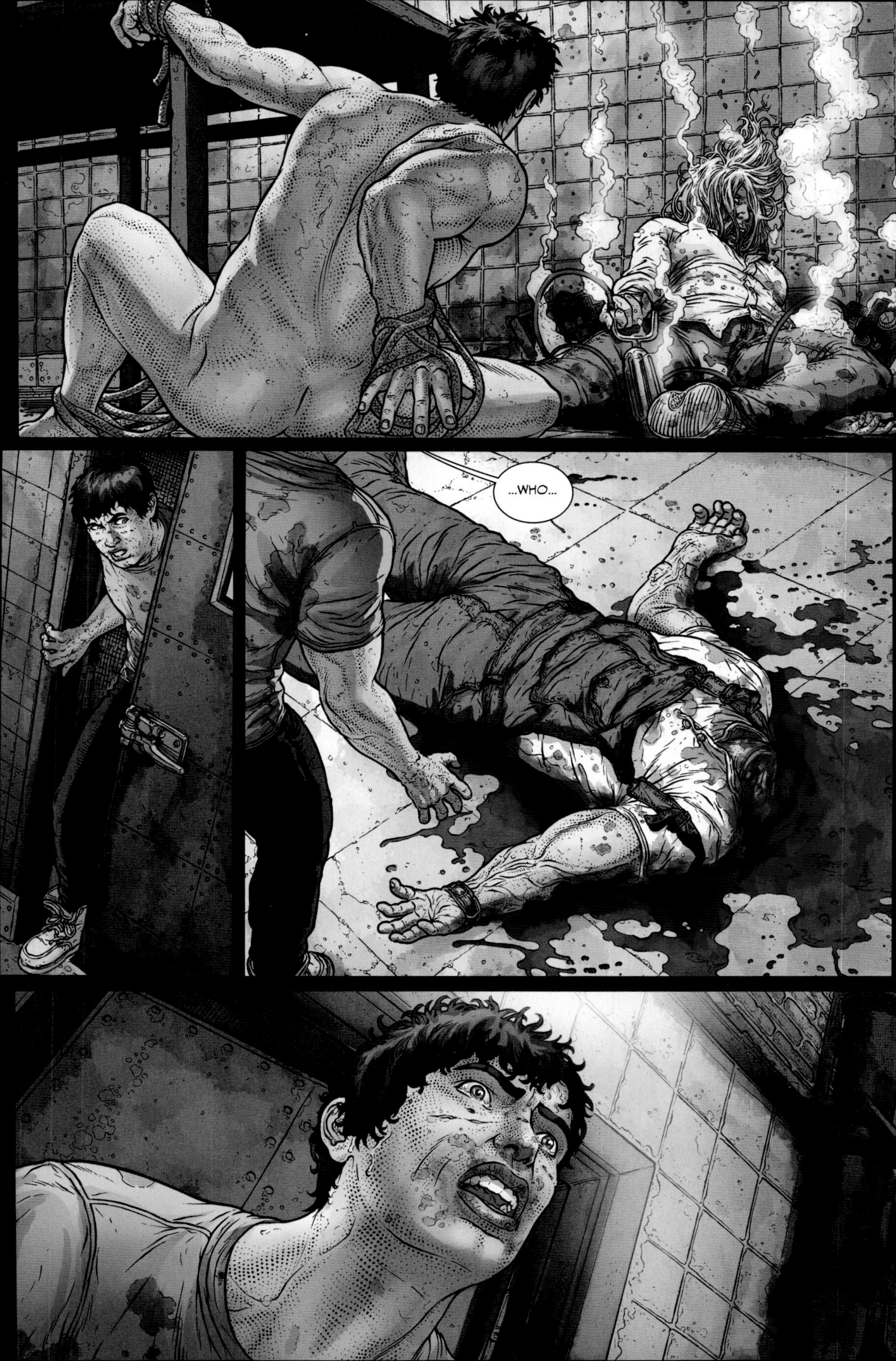
...WHO...

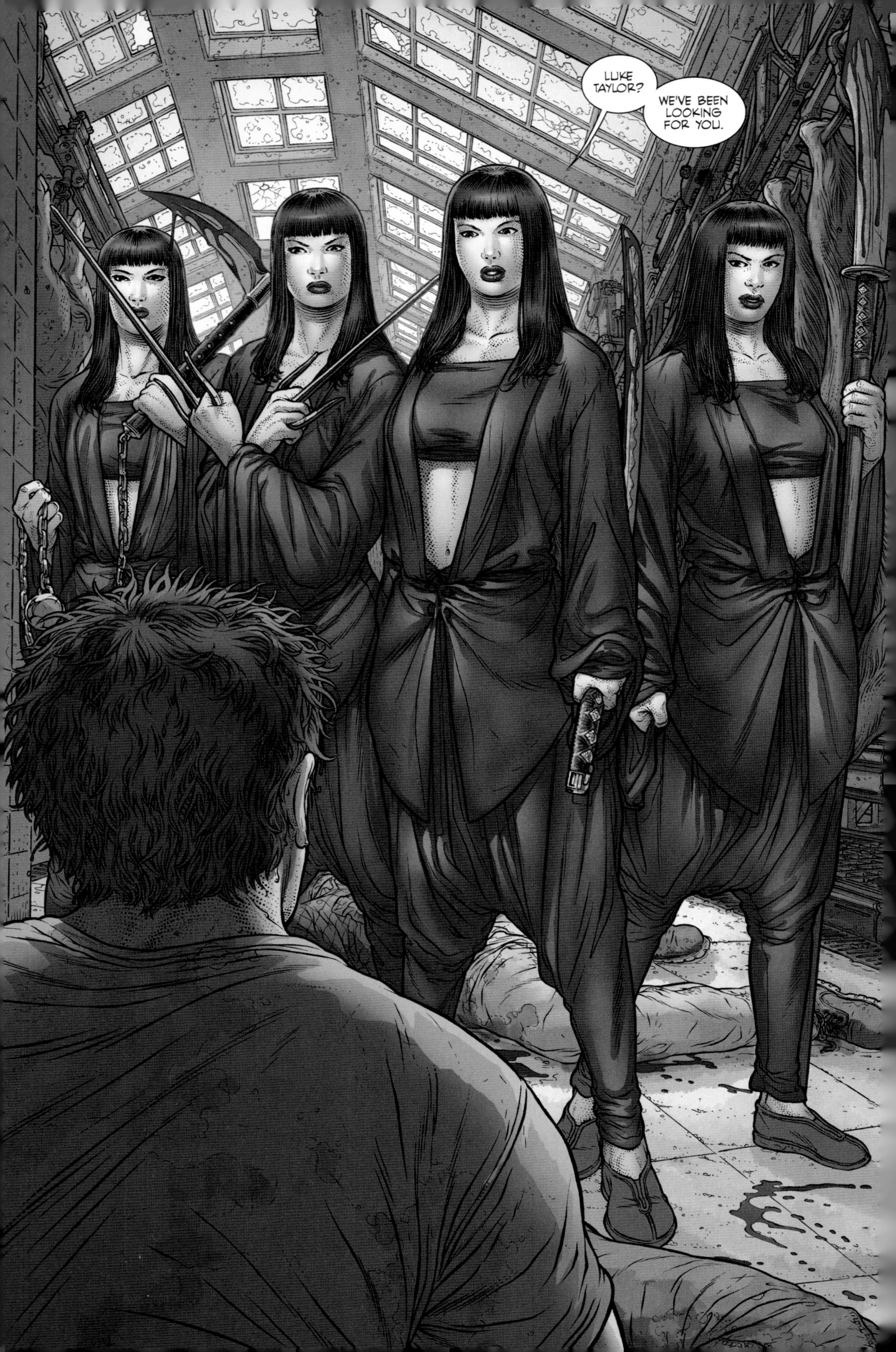
LUKE TAYLOR?
WE'VE BEEN LOOKING FOR YOU.

CHAPTER 14

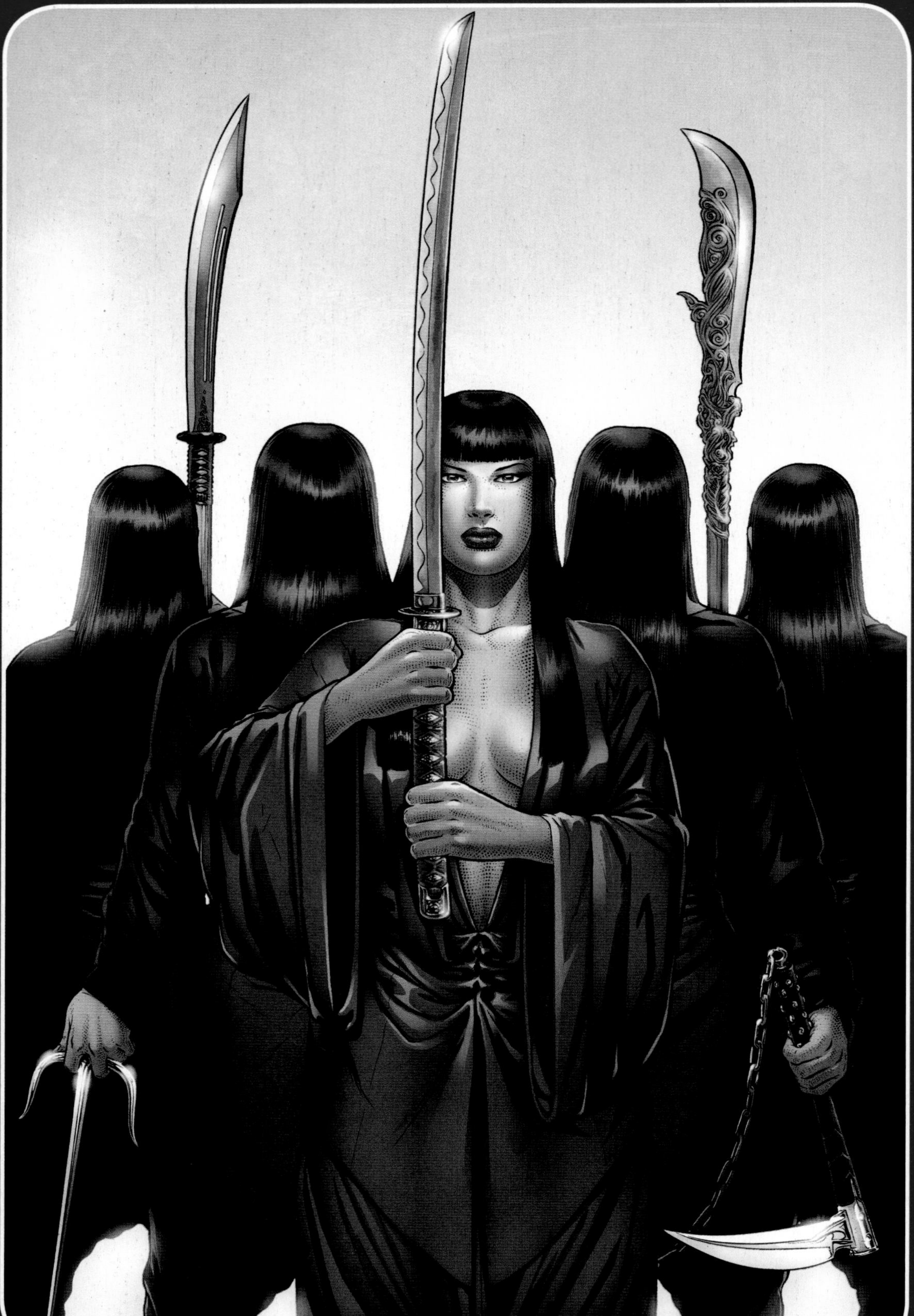

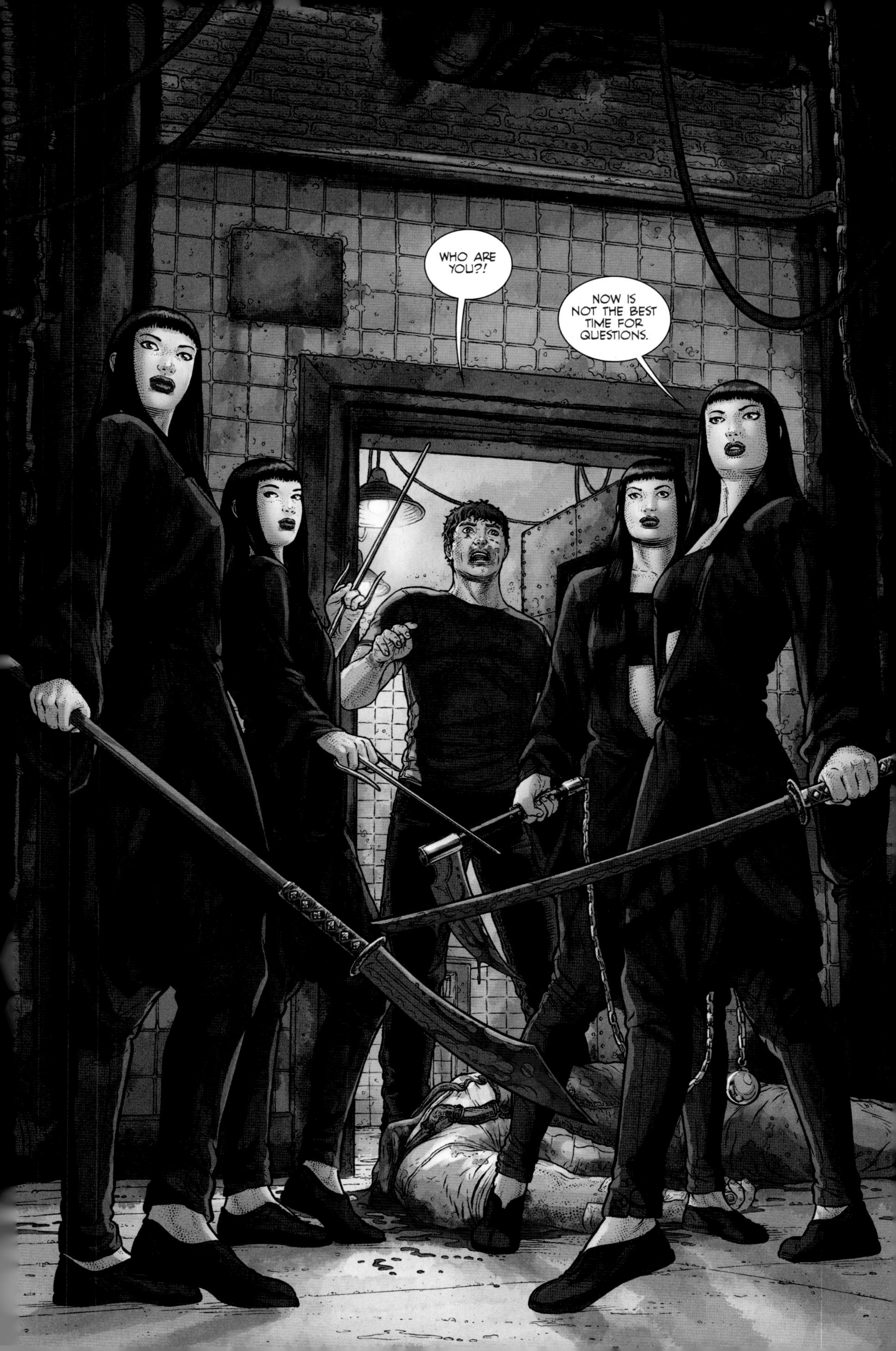
WHO ARE YOU?!
NOW IS NOT THE BEST TIME FOR QUESTIONS.

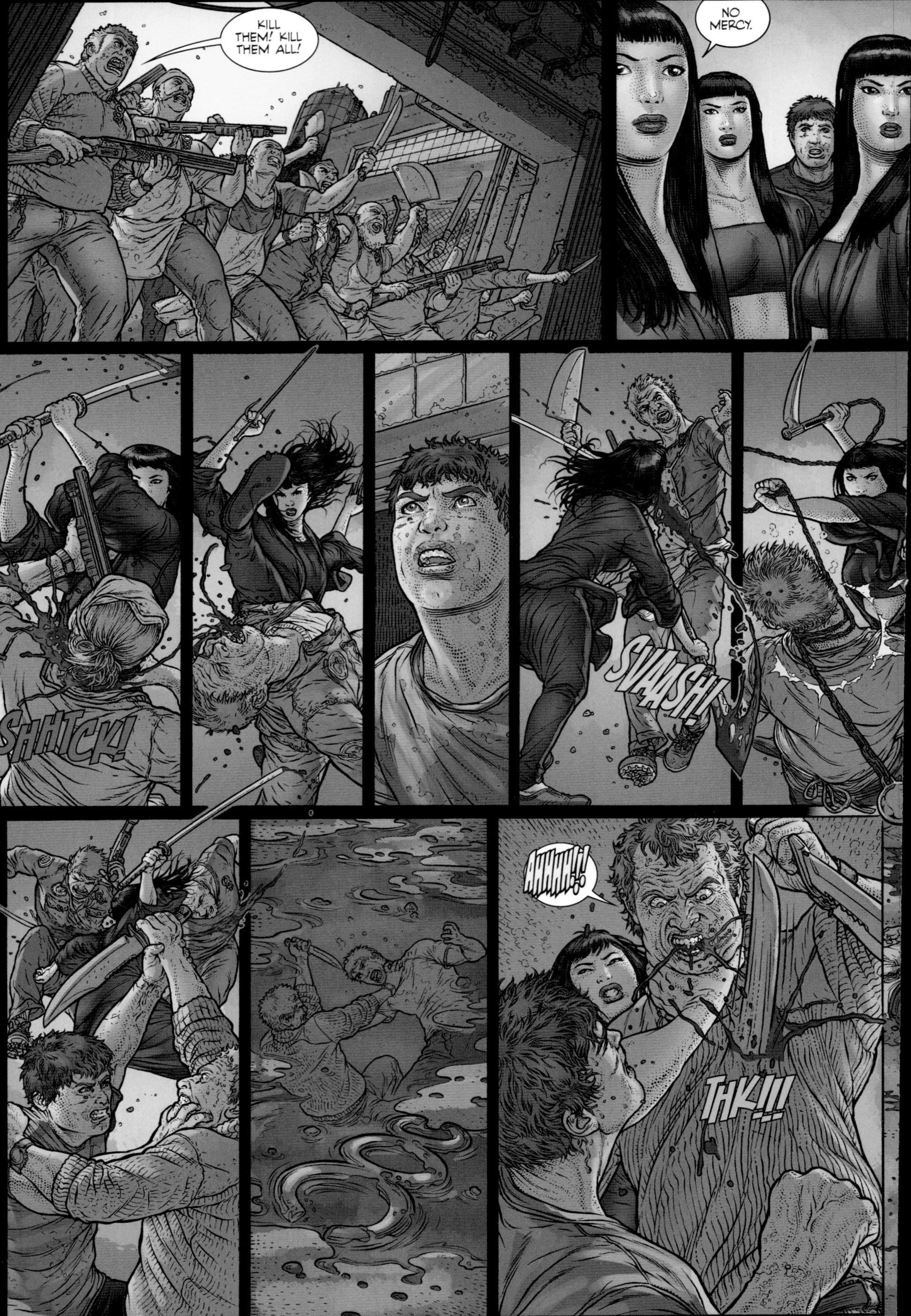
KILL THEM! KILL THEM ALL!
NO MERCY.
SHHTCK!
SVAASH!
AHHHH!!!
THK!!!

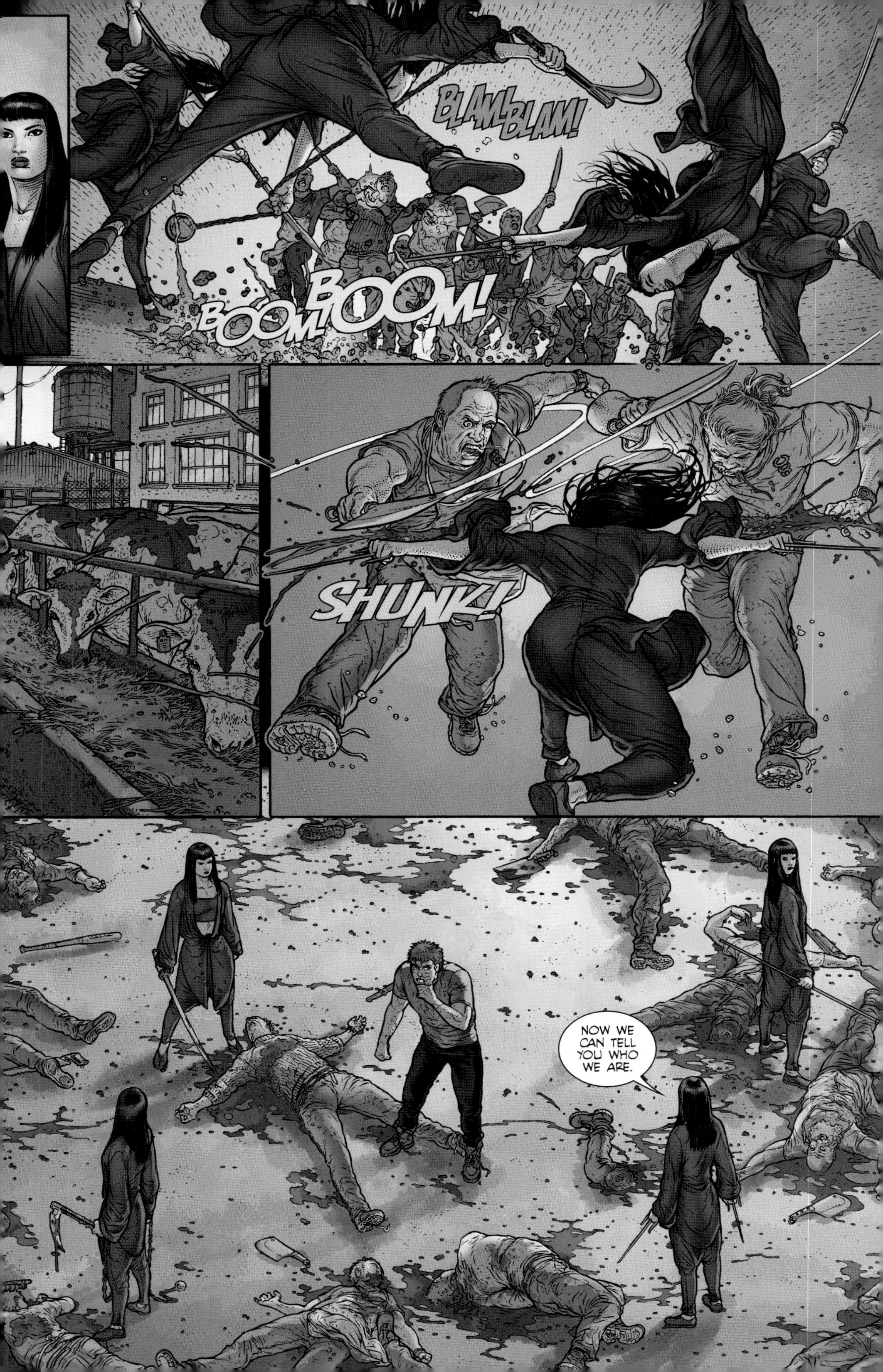
BLAM BLAM!
BOOM BOOM!
SHUNK!
NOW WE CAN TELL YOU WHO WE ARE.

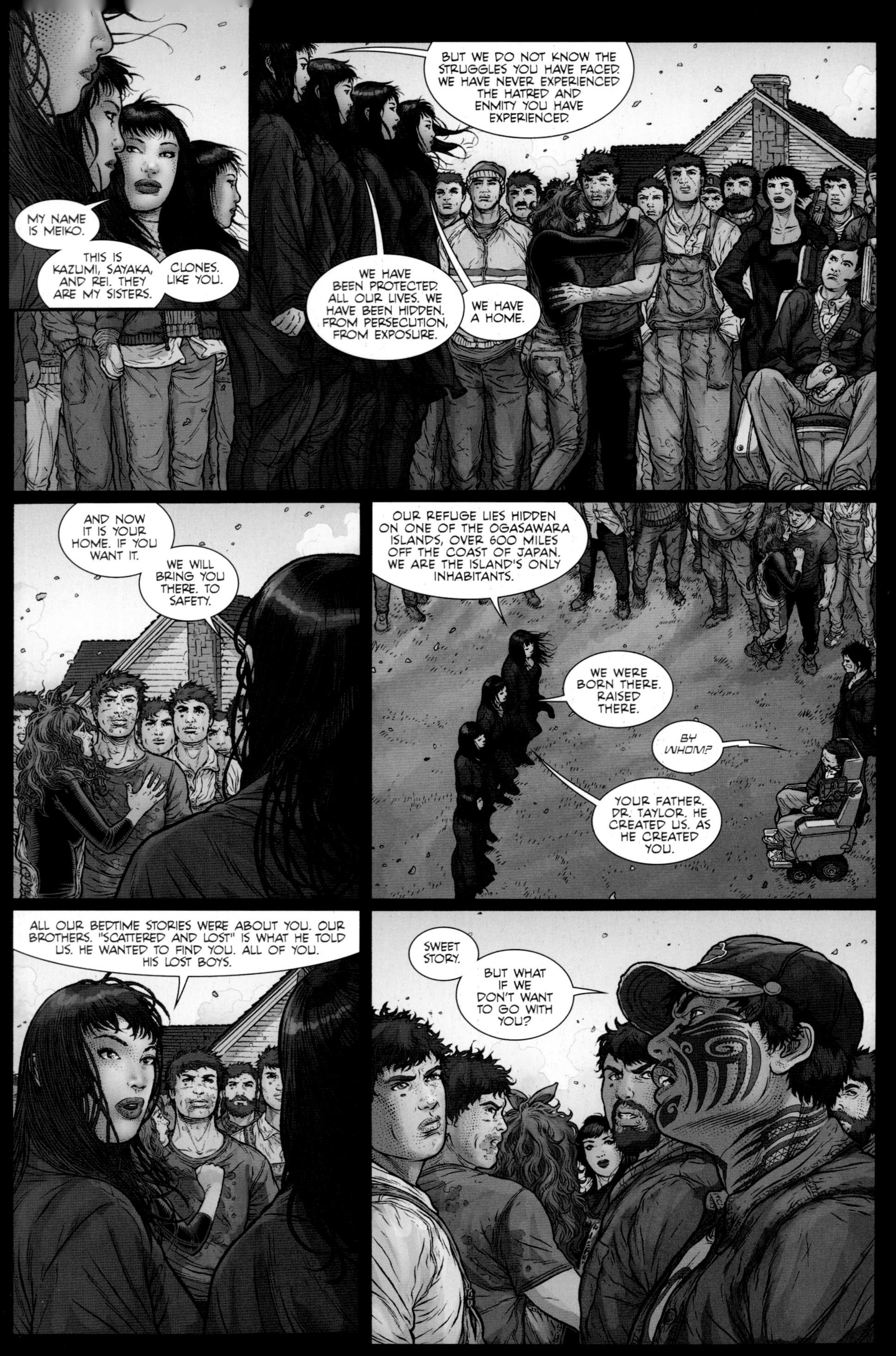
MY NAME IS MEIKO.
THIS IS KAZUMI, SAYAKA, AND REI. THEY ARE MY SISTERS.
CLONES. LIKE YOU.
BUT WE DO NOT KNOW THE STRUGGLES YOU HAVE FACED. WE HAVE NEVER EXPERIENCED THE HATRED AND ENMITY YOU HAVE EXPERIENCED.
WE HAVE BEEN PROTECTED. ALL OUR LIVES. WE HAVE BEEN HIDDEN. FROM PERSECUTION, FROM EXPOSURE.
WE HAVE A HOME.
AND NOW IT IS YOUR HOME. IF YOU WANT IT.
WE WILL BRING YOU THERE. TO SAFETY.
OUR REFUGE LIES HIDDEN ON ONE OF THE OGASAWARA ISLANDS, OVER 600 MILES OFF THE COAST OF JAPAN. WE ARE THE ISLAND'S ONLY INHABITANTS.
WE WERE BORN THERE. RAISED THERE.
BY WHOM?
YOUR FATHER. DR. TAYLOR. HE CREATED US. AS HE CREATED YOU.
ALL OUR BEDTIME STORIES WERE ABOUT YOU. OUR BROTHERS. "SCATTERED AND LOST" IS WHAT HE TOLD US. HE WANTED TO FIND YOU. ALL OF YOU. HIS LOST BOYS.
SWEET STORY.
BUT WHAT IF WE DON'T WANT TO GO WITH YOU?

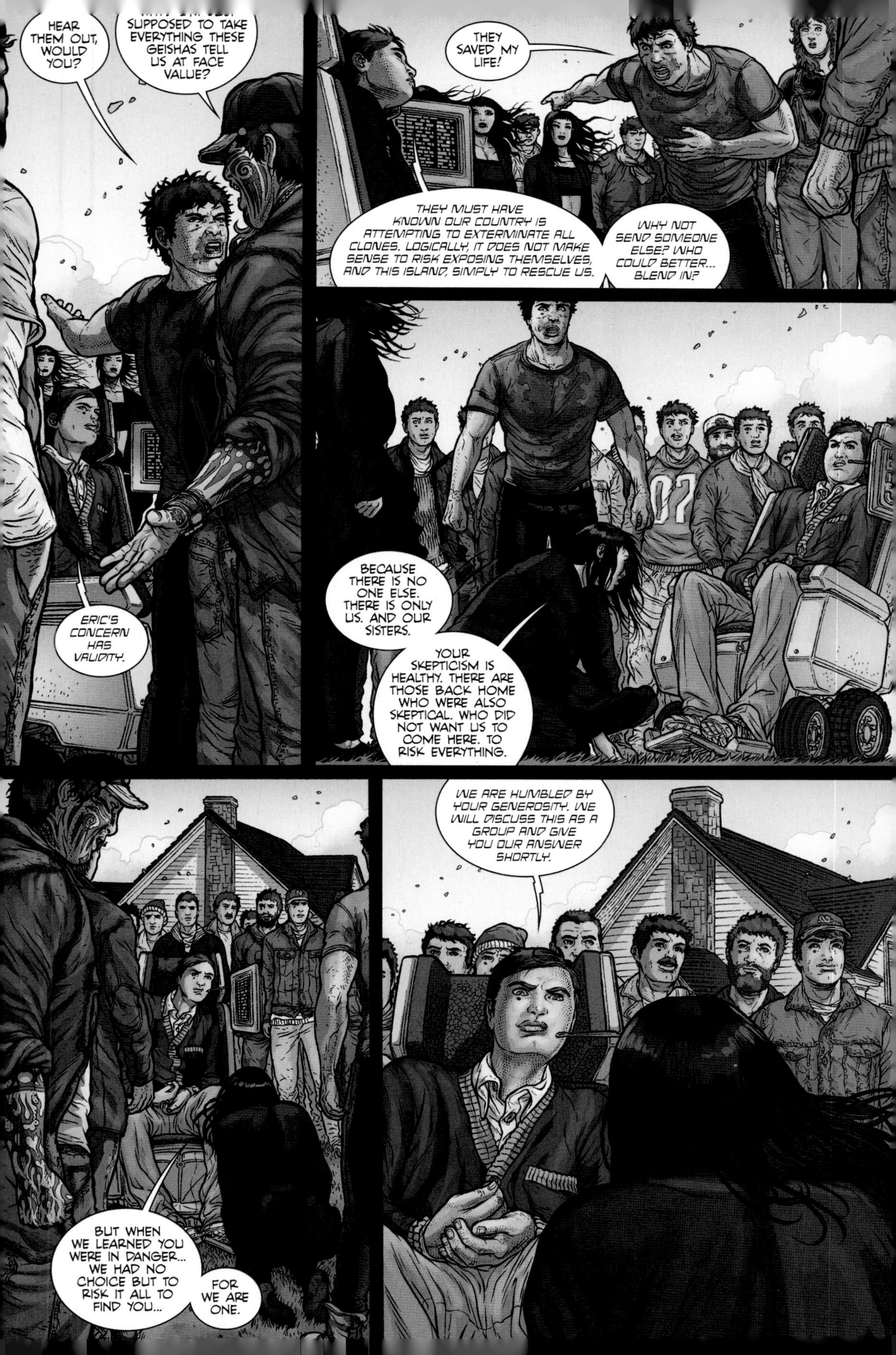
HEAR THEM OUT, WOULD YOU?
SUPPOSED TO TAKE EVERYTHING THESE GEISHAS TELL US AT FACE VALUE?
ERIC'S CONCERN HAS VALIDITY.
THEY SAVED MY LIFE!
THEY MUST HAVE KNOWN OUR COUNTRY IS ATTEMPTING TO EXTERMINATE ALL CLONES. LOGICALLY, IT DOES NOT MAKE SENSE TO RISK EXPOSING THEMSELVES, AND THIS ISLAND, SIMPLY TO RESCUE US.
WHY NOT SEND SOMEONE ELSE? WHO COULD BETTER... BLEND IN?
BECAUSE THERE IS NO ONE ELSE. THERE IS ONLY US. AND OUR SISTERS.
YOUR SKEPTICISM IS HEALTHY. THERE ARE THOSE BACK HOME WHO WERE ALSO SKEPTICAL. WHO DID NOT WANT US TO COME HERE. TO RISK EVERYTHING.
BUT WHEN WE LEARNED YOU WERE IN DANGER... WE HAD NO CHOICE BUT TO RISK IT ALL TO FIND YOU...
FOR WE ARE ONE.
WE ARE HUMBLED BY YOUR GENEROSITY. WE WILL DISCUSS THIS AS A GROUP AND GIVE YOU OUR ANSWER SHORTLY.

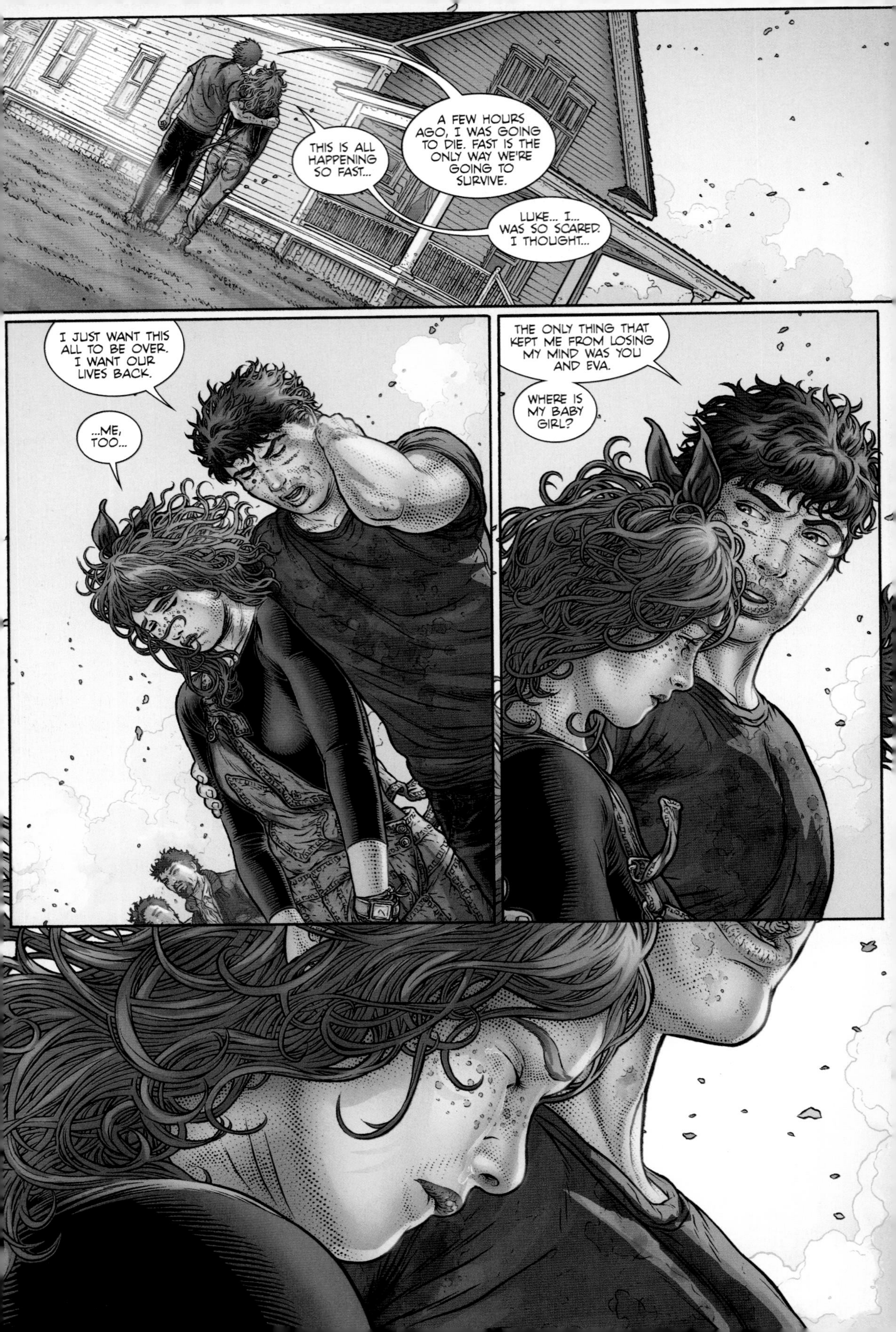
THIS IS ALL HAPPENING SO FAST...
A FEW HOURS AGO, I WAS GOING TO DIE. FAST IS THE ONLY WAY WE'RE GOING TO SURVIVE.
LUKE... I... WAS SO SCARED. I THOUGHT...
I JUST WANT THIS ALL TO BE OVER. I WANT OUR LIVES BACK.
...ME, TOO...
THE ONLY THING THAT KEPT ME FROM LOSING MY MIND WAS YOU AND EVA.
WHERE IS MY BABY GIRL?

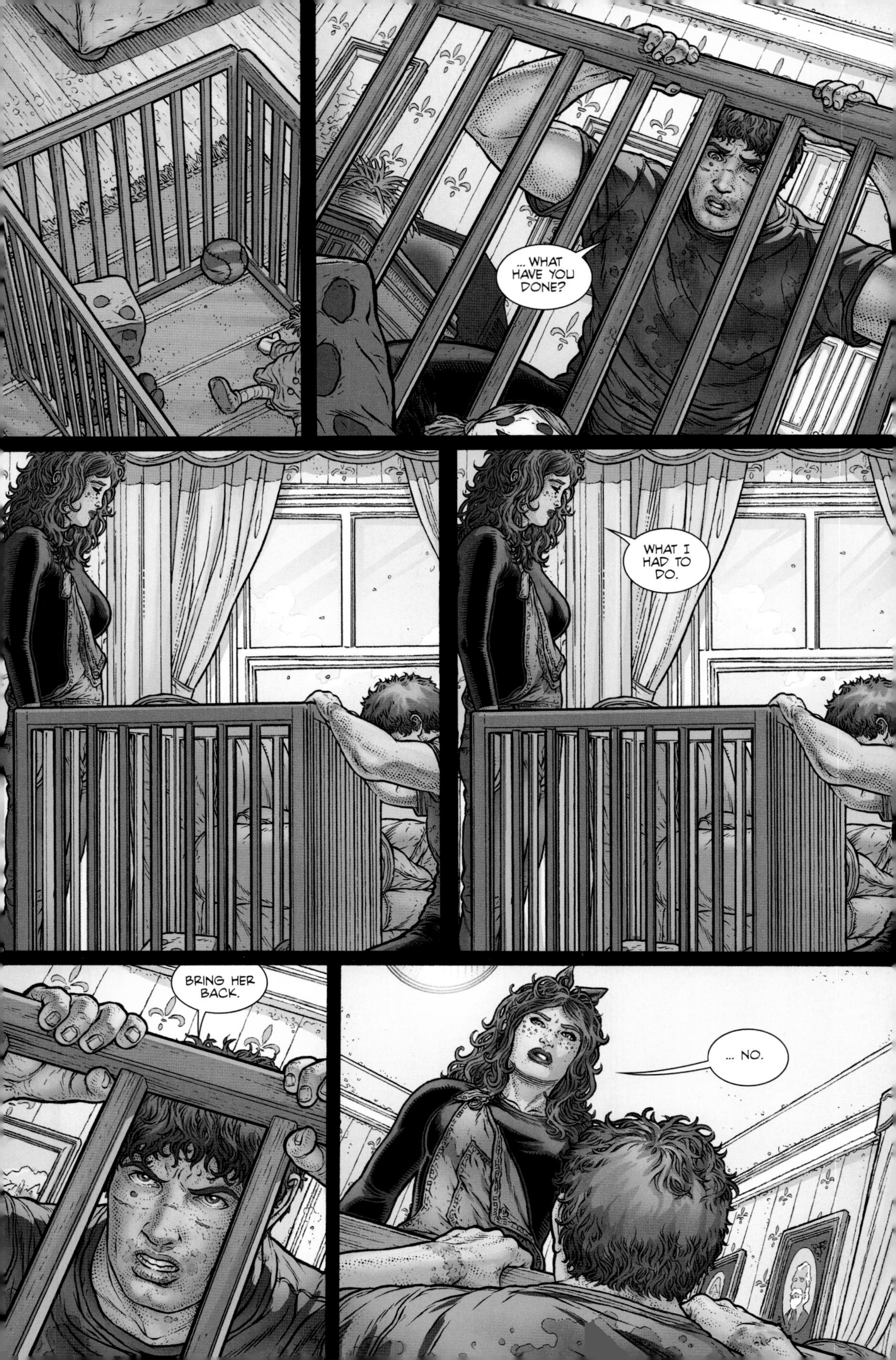
... WHAT HAVE YOU DONE?
WHAT I HAD TO DO.
BRING HER BACK.
... NO.

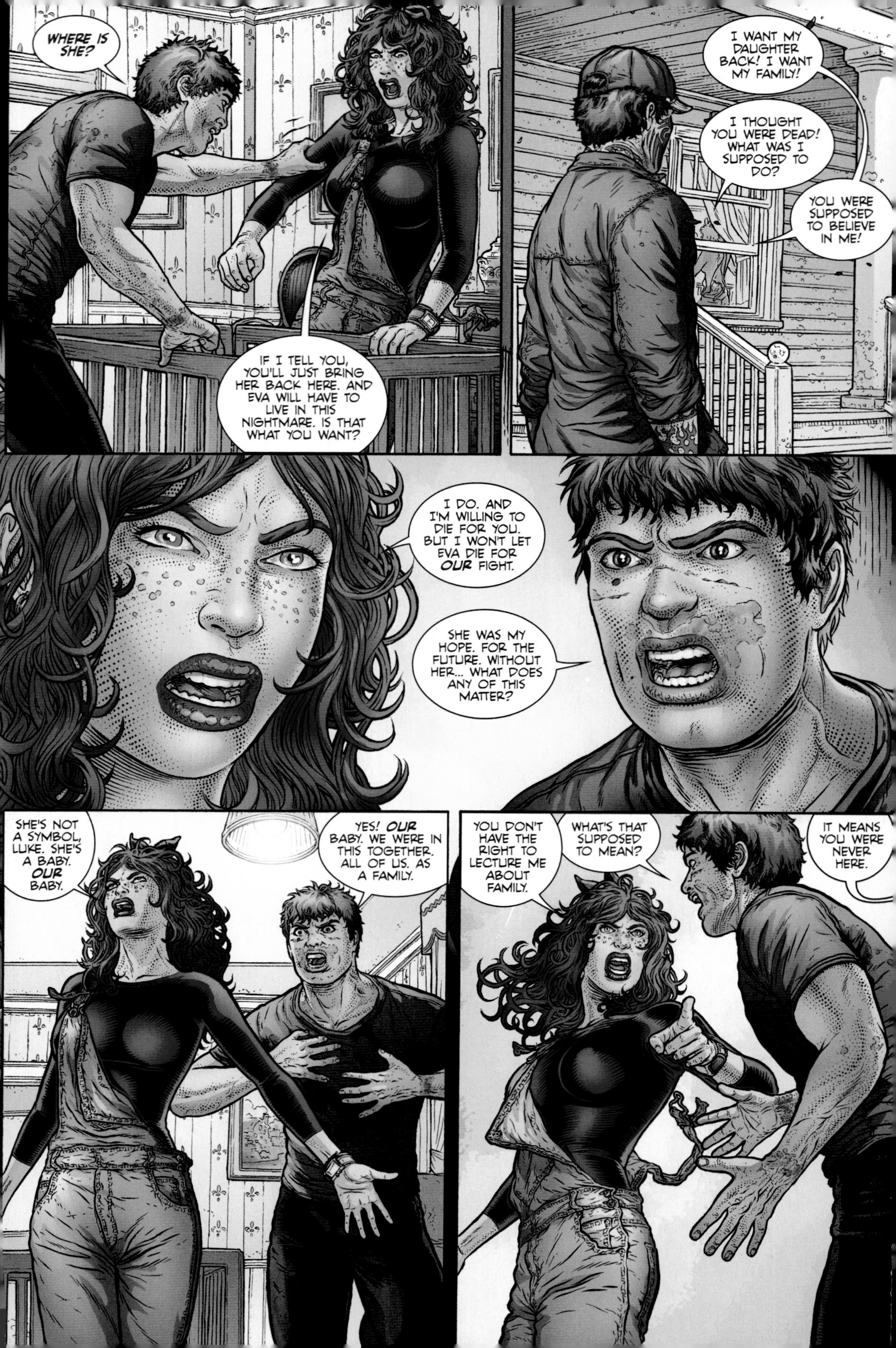
WHERE IS SHE?
IF I TELL YOU, YOU'LL JUST BRING HER BACK HERE. AND EVA WILL HAVE TO LIVE IN THIS NIGHTMARE. IS THAT WHAT YOU WANT?
I WANT MY DAUGHTER BACK! I WANT MY FAMILY!
I THOUGHT YOU WERE DEAD! WHAT WAS I SUPPOSED TO DO?
YOU WERE SUPPOSED TO BELIEVE IN ME!
I DO. AND I'M WILLING TO DIE FOR YOU. BUT I WON'T LET EVA DIE FOR OUR FIGHT.
SHE WAS MY HOPE. FOR THE FUTURE. WITHOUT HER... WHAT DOES ANY OF THIS MATTER?
SHE'S NOT A SYMBOL, LUKE. SHE'S A BABY. OUR BABY.
YES! OUR BABY. WE WERE IN THIS TOGETHER. ALL OF US. AS A FAMILY.
YOU DON'T HAVE THE RIGHT TO LECTURE ME ABOUT FAMILY.
WHAT'S THAT SUPPOSED TO MEAN?
IT MEANS YOU WERE NEVER HERE.

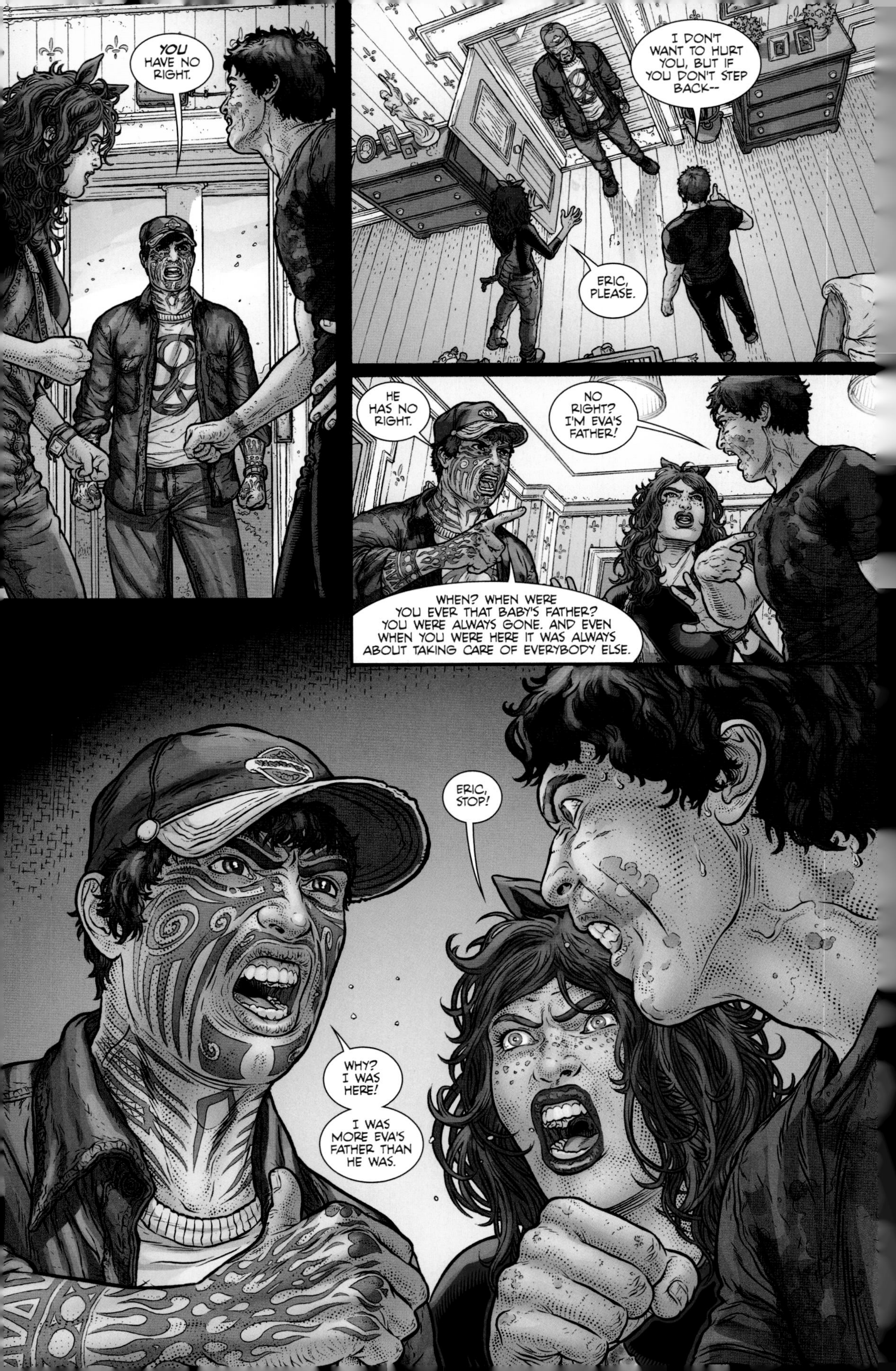
YOU HAVE NO RIGHT.
I DON'T WANT TO HURT YOU, BUT IF YOU DON'T STEP BACK--
ERIC, PLEASE.
HE HAS NO RIGHT.
NO RIGHT? I'M EVA'S FATHER!
WHEN? WHEN WERE YOU EVER THAT BABY'S FATHER? YOU WERE ALWAYS GONE. AND EVEN WHEN YOU WERE HERE IT WAS ALWAYS ABOUT TAKING CARE OF EVERYBODY ELSE.
ERIC, STOP!
WHY? I WAS HERE!
I WAS MORE EVA'S FATHER THAN HE WAS.

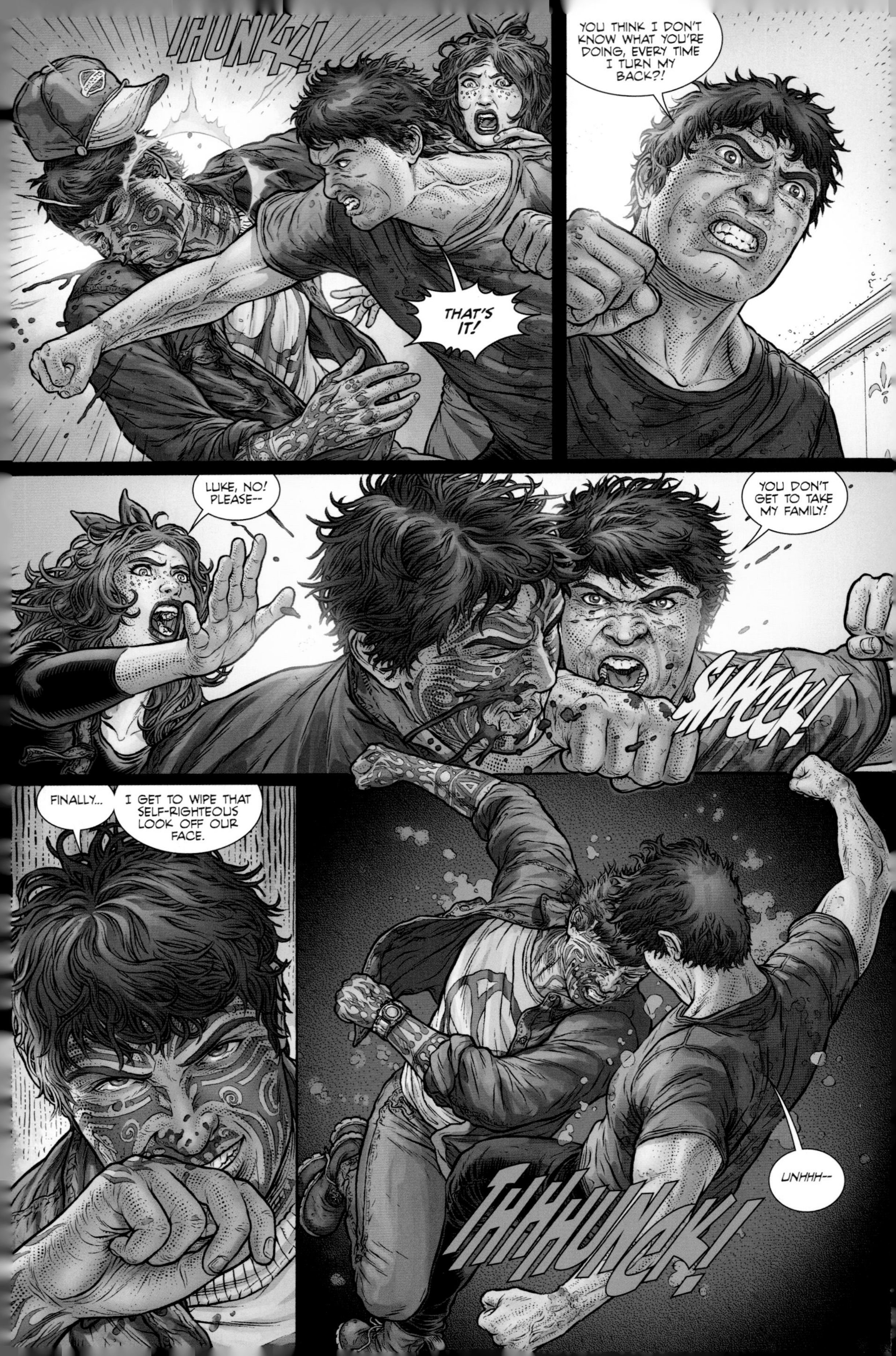
THUNK!
THAT'S IT!
YOU THINK I DON'T KNOW WHAT YOU'RE DOING, EVERY TIME I TURN MY BACK?!
LUKE, NO! PLEASE--
YOU DON'T GET TO TAKE MY FAMILY!
SMACK!
FINALLY...
I GET TO WIPE THAT SELF-RIGHTEOUS LOOK OFF OUR FACE.
UNHHH--
THHUNCK!

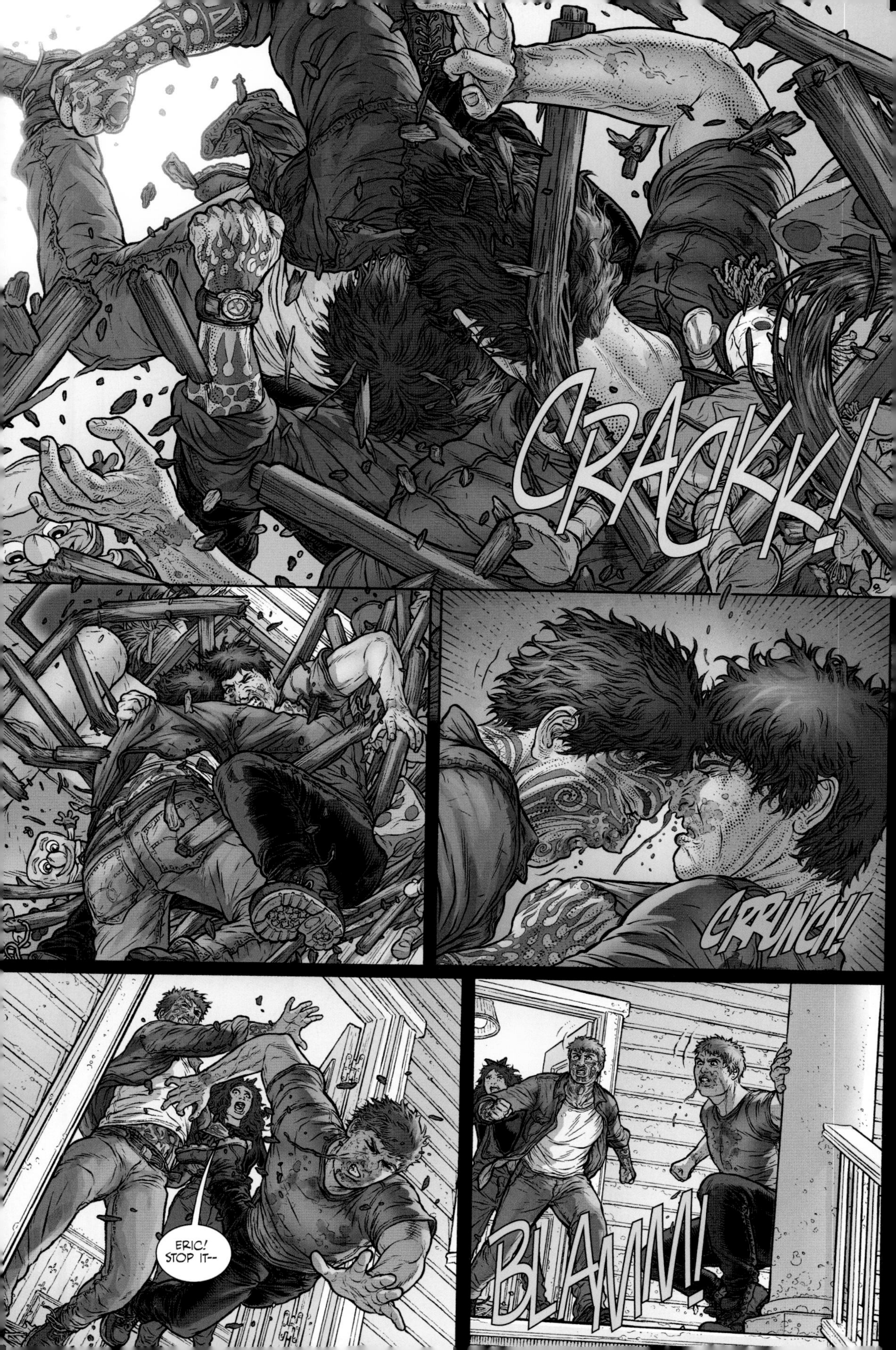
CRACKK!
CRRUNCH!
ERIC! STOP IT--
BLAMM!

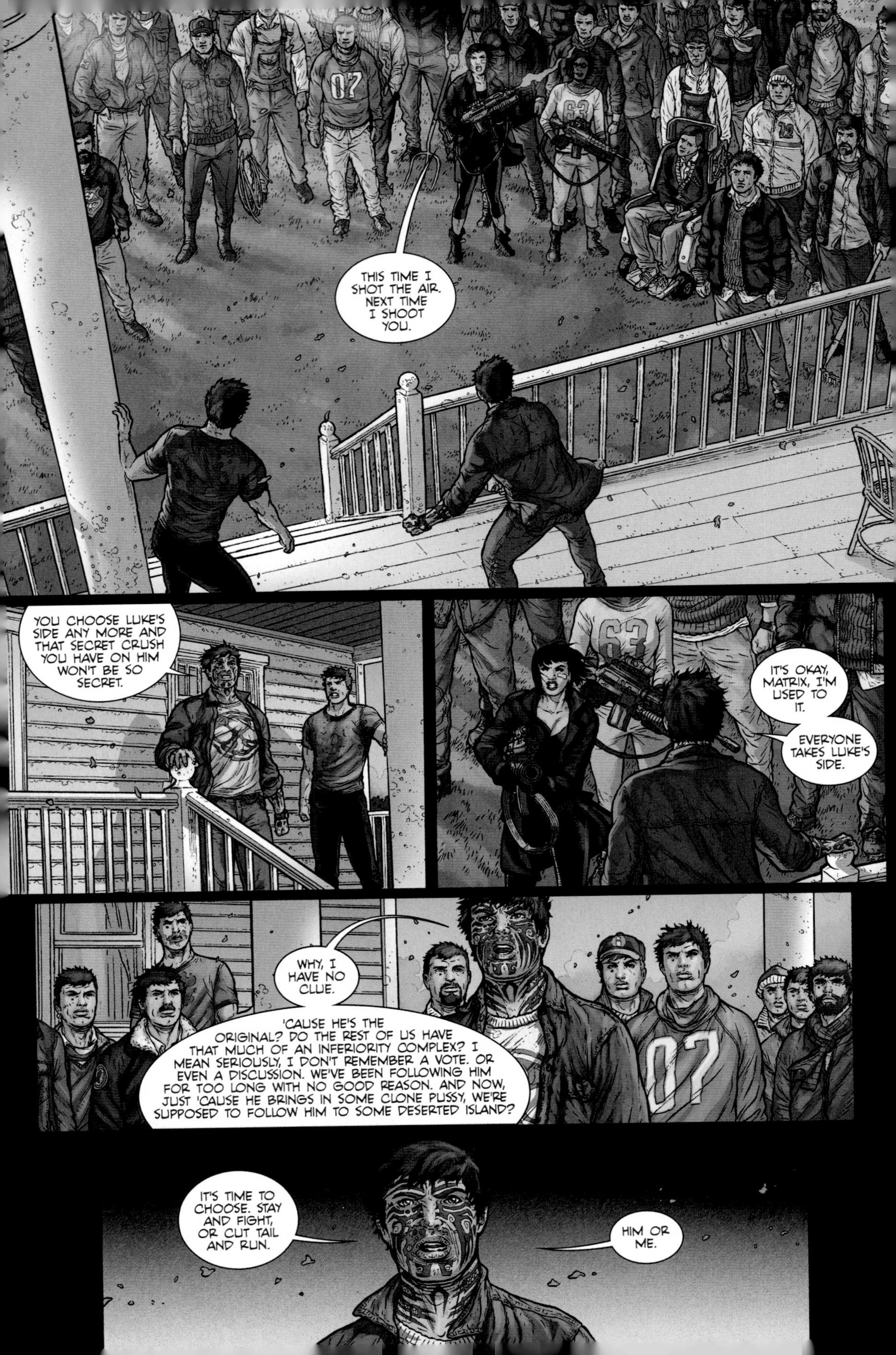

THIS TIME I SHOT THE AIR. NEXT TIME I SHOOT YOU.
YOU CHOOSE LUKE'S SIDE ANY MORE AND THAT SECRET CRUSH YOU HAVE ON HIM WON'T BE SO SECRET.
IT'S OKAY, MATRIX, I'M USED TO IT.
EVERYONE TAKES LUKE'S SIDE.
WHY, I HAVE NO CLUE.
'CAUSE HE'S THE ORIGINAL? DO THE REST OF US HAVE THAT MUCH OF AN INFERIORITY COMPLEX? I MEAN SERIOUSLY, I DON'T REMEMBER A VOTE. OR EVEN A DISCUSSION. WE'VE BEEN FOLLOWING HIM FOR TOO LONG WITH NO GOOD REASON. AND NOW, JUST 'CAUSE HE BRINGS IN SOME CLONE PUSSY, WE'RE SUPPOSED TO FOLLOW HIM TO SOME DESERTED ISLAND?
IT'S TIME TO CHOOSE. STAY AND FIGHT, OR CUT TAIL AND RUN.
HIM OR ME.

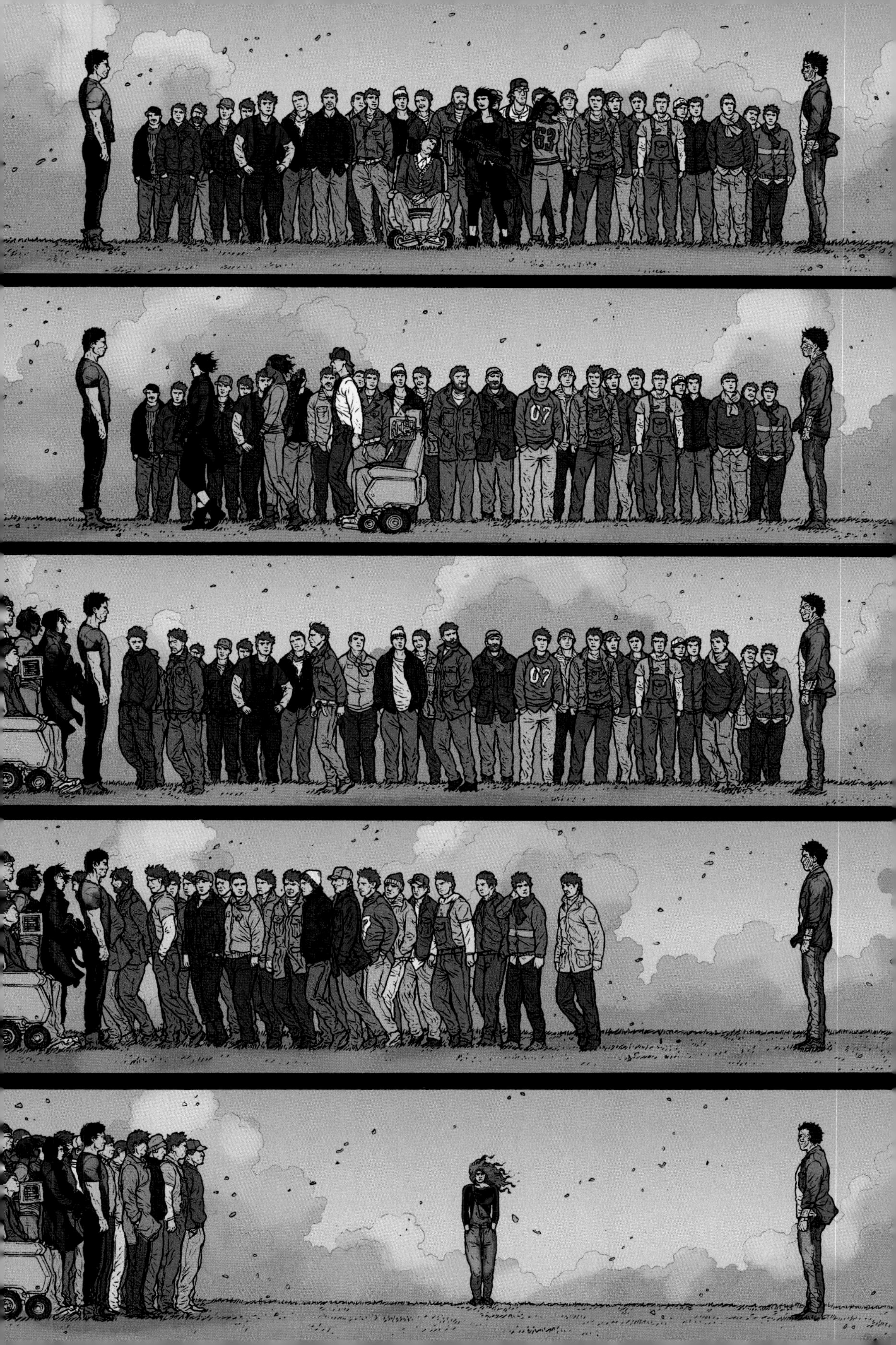

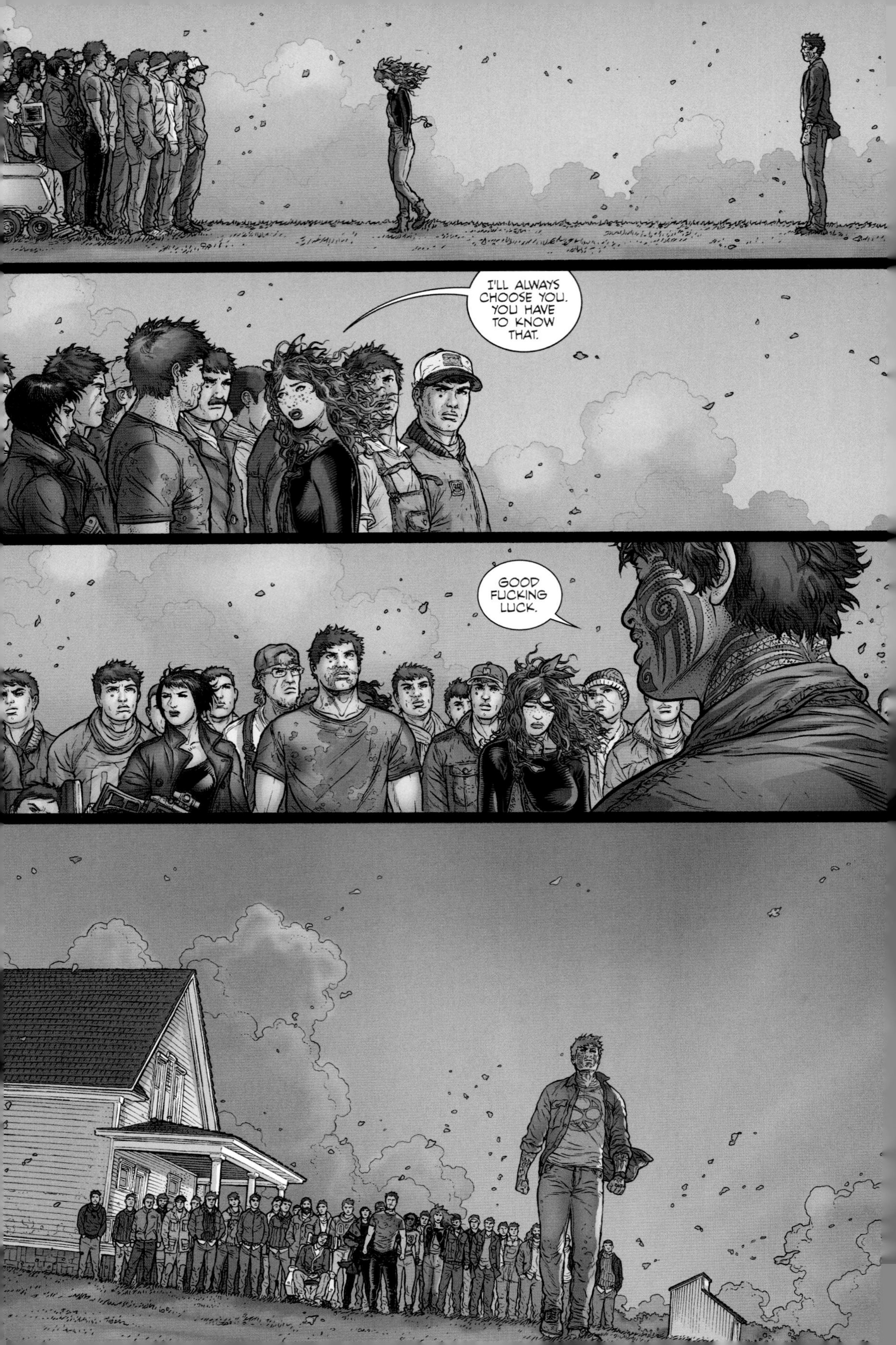
I'LL ALWAYS CHOOSE YOU. YOU HAVE TO KNOW THAT.
GOOD FUCKING LUCK.

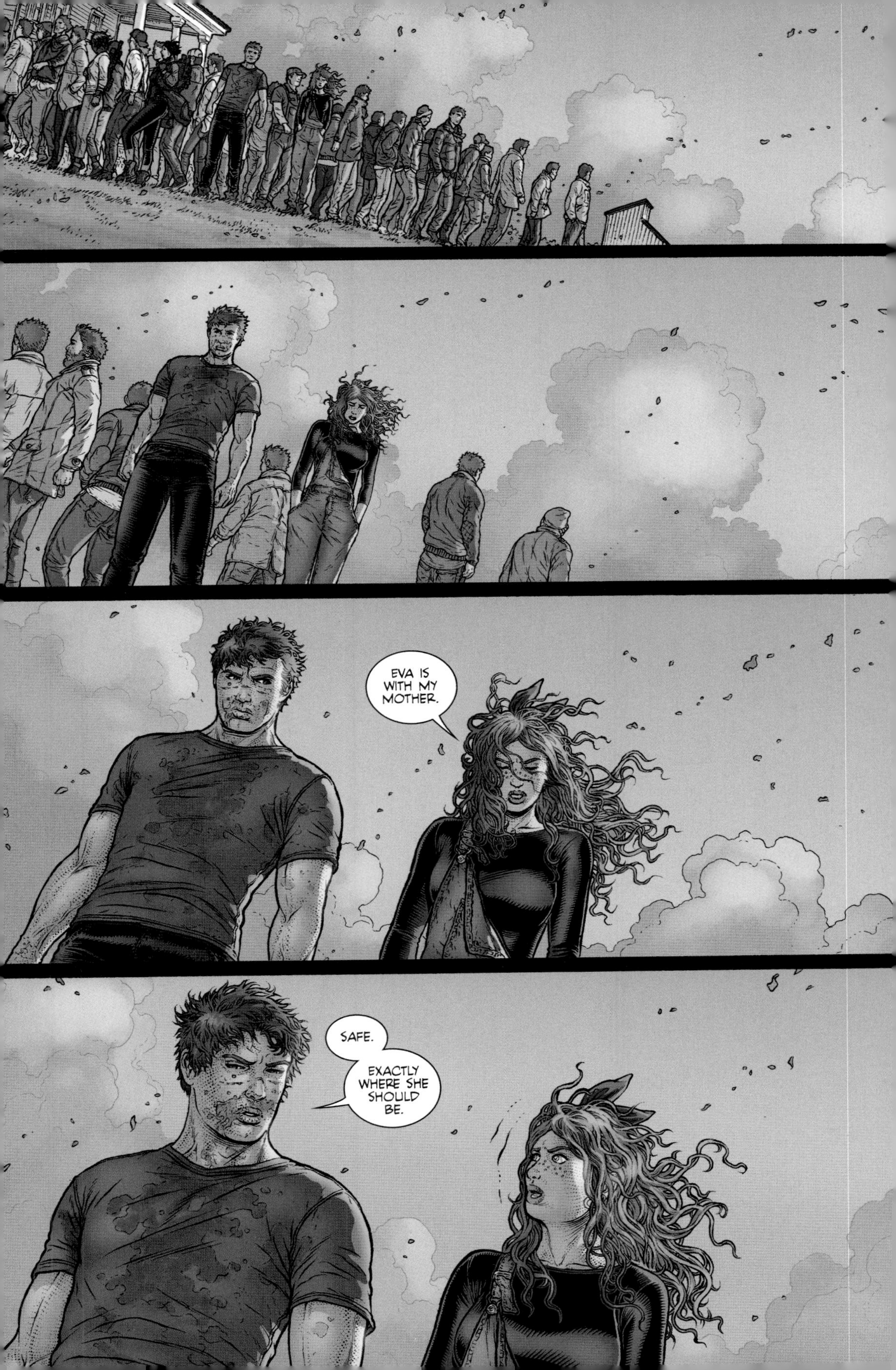
EVA IS WITH MY MOTHER.
SAFE.
EXACTLY WHERE SHE SHOULD BE.

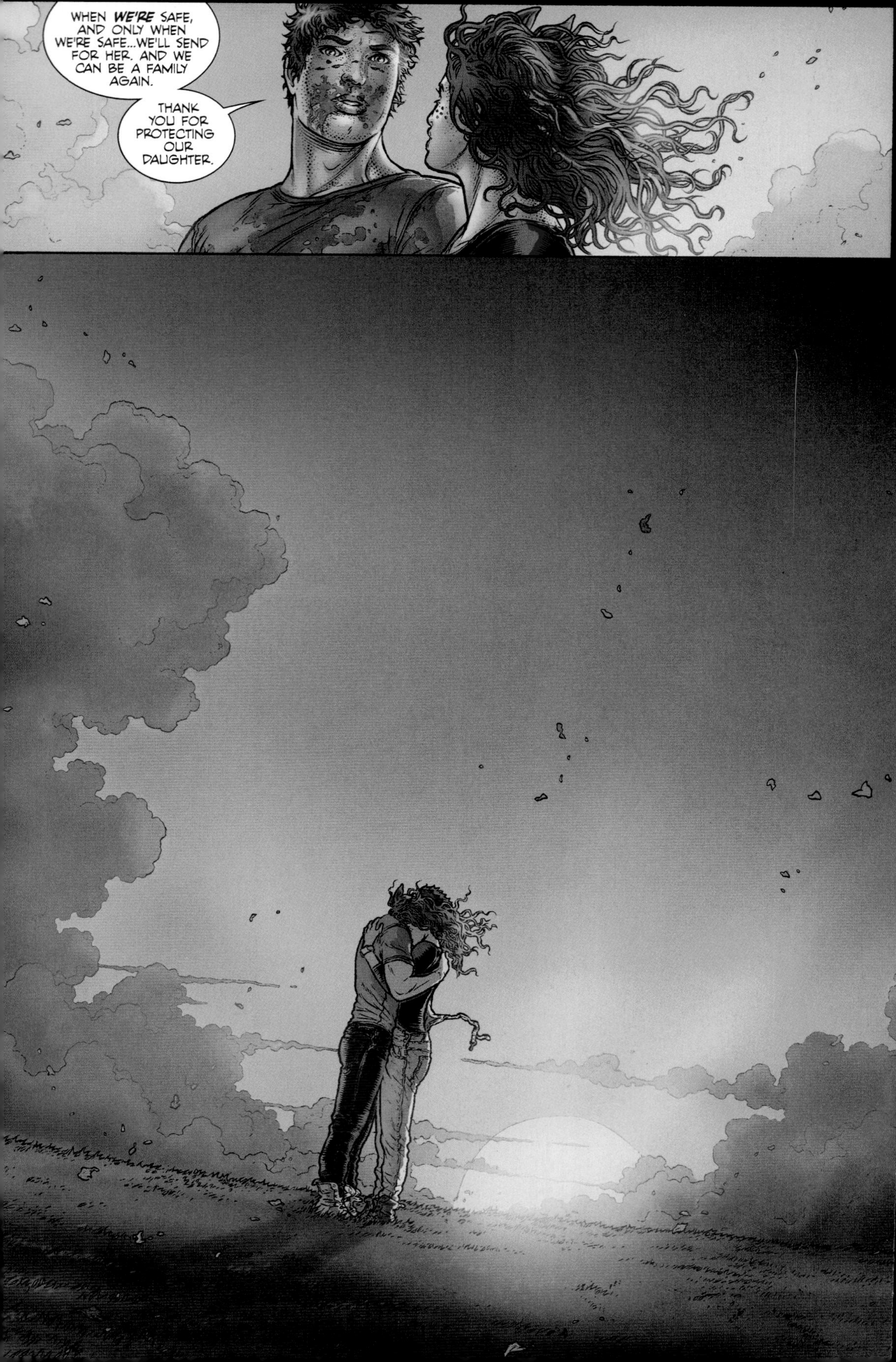
WHEN WE'RE SAFE, AND ONLY WHEN WE'RE SAFE...WE'LL SEND FOR HER. AND WE CAN BE A FAMILY AGAIN.
THANK YOU FOR PROTECTING OUR DAUGHTER.

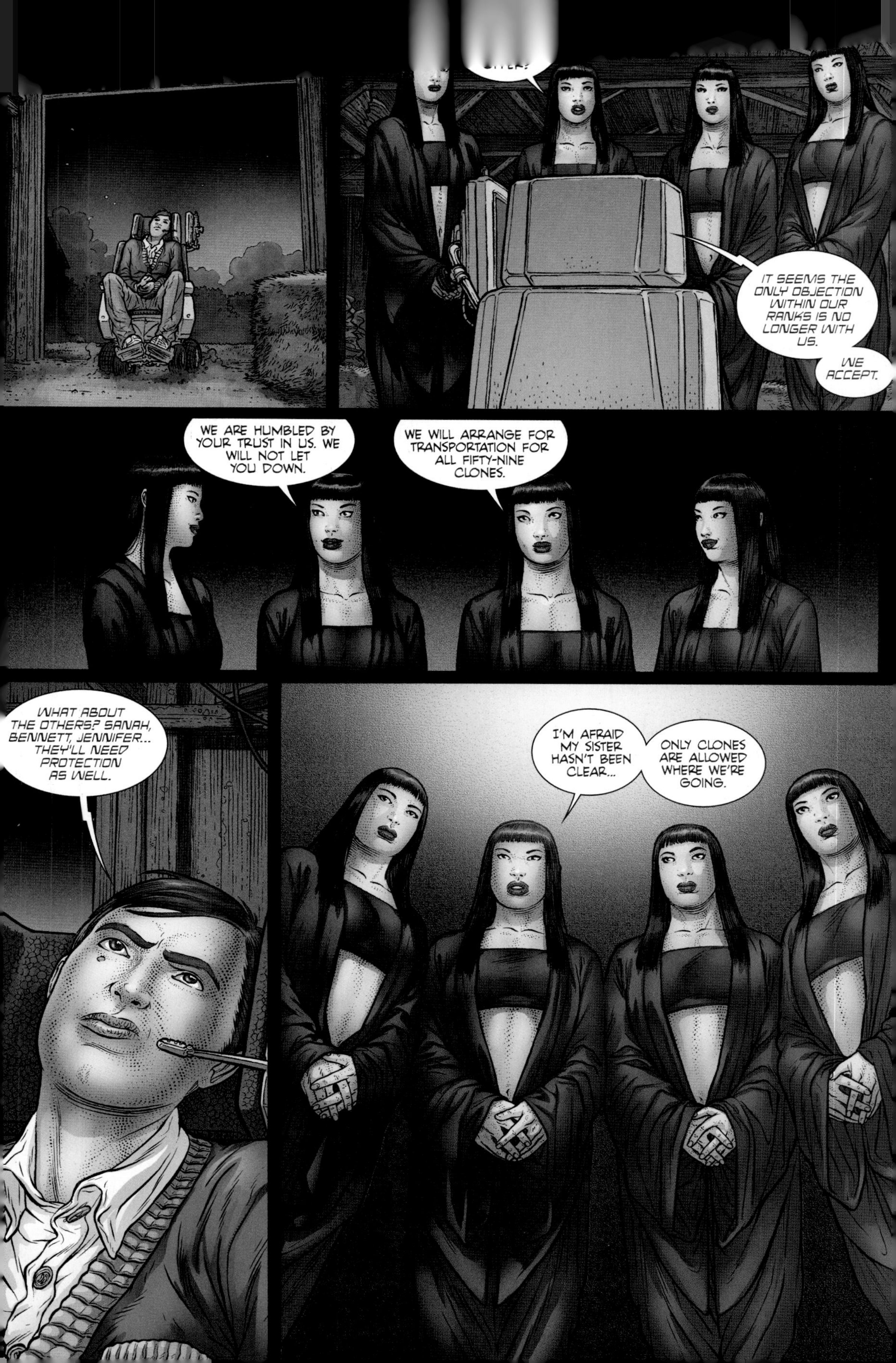
IT SEEMS THE ONLY OBJECTION WITHIN OUR RANKS IS NO LONGER WITH US.
WE ACCEPT.
WE ARE HUMBLED BY YOUR TRUST IN US. WE WILL NOT LET YOU DOWN.
WE WILL ARRANGE FOR TRANSPORTATION FOR ALL FIFTY-NINE CLONES.
WHAT ABOUT THE OTHERS? SANAH, BENNETT, JENNIFER... THEY'LL NEED PROTECTION AS WELL.
I'M AFRAID MY SISTER HASN'T BEEN CLEAR...
ONLY CLONES ARE ALLOWED WHERE WE'RE GOING.

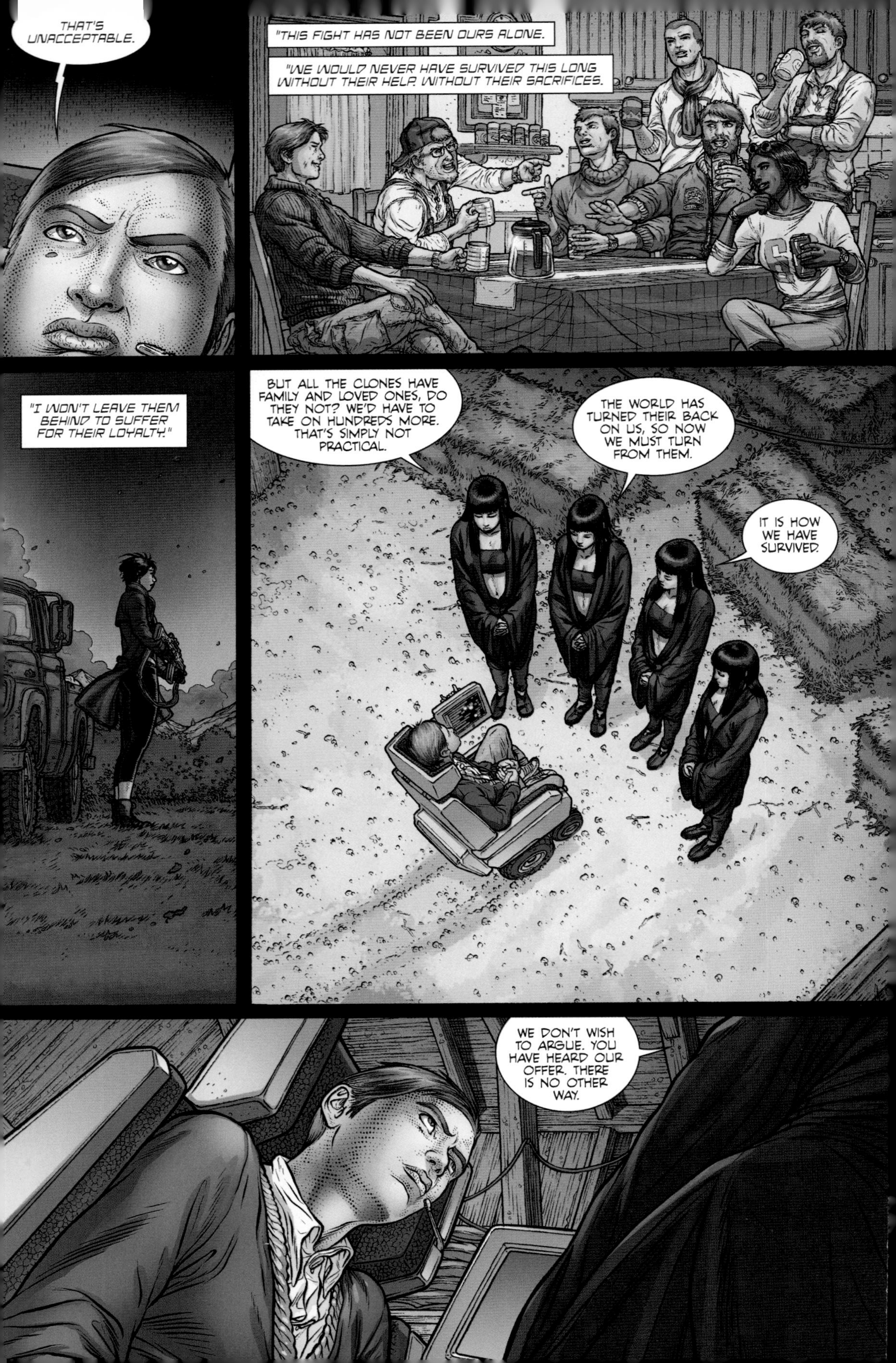
THAT'S UNACCEPTABLE.
"THIS FIGHT HAS NOT BEEN OURS ALONE.
"WE WOULD NEVER HAVE SURVIVED THIS LONG WITHOUT THEIR HELP. WITHOUT THEIR SACRIFICES.
"I WON'T LEAVE THEM BEHIND TO SUFFER FOR THEIR LOYALTY."
BUT ALL THE CLONES HAVE FAMILY AND LOVED ONES, DO THEY NOT? WE'D HAVE TO TAKE ON HUNDREDS MORE. THAT'S SIMPLY NOT PRACTICAL.
THE WORLD HAS TURNED THEIR BACK ON US, SO NOW WE MUST TURN FROM THEM.
IT IS HOW WE HAVE SURVIVED.
WE DON'T WISH TO ARGUE. YOU HAVE HEARD OUR OFFER. THERE IS NO OTHER WAY.

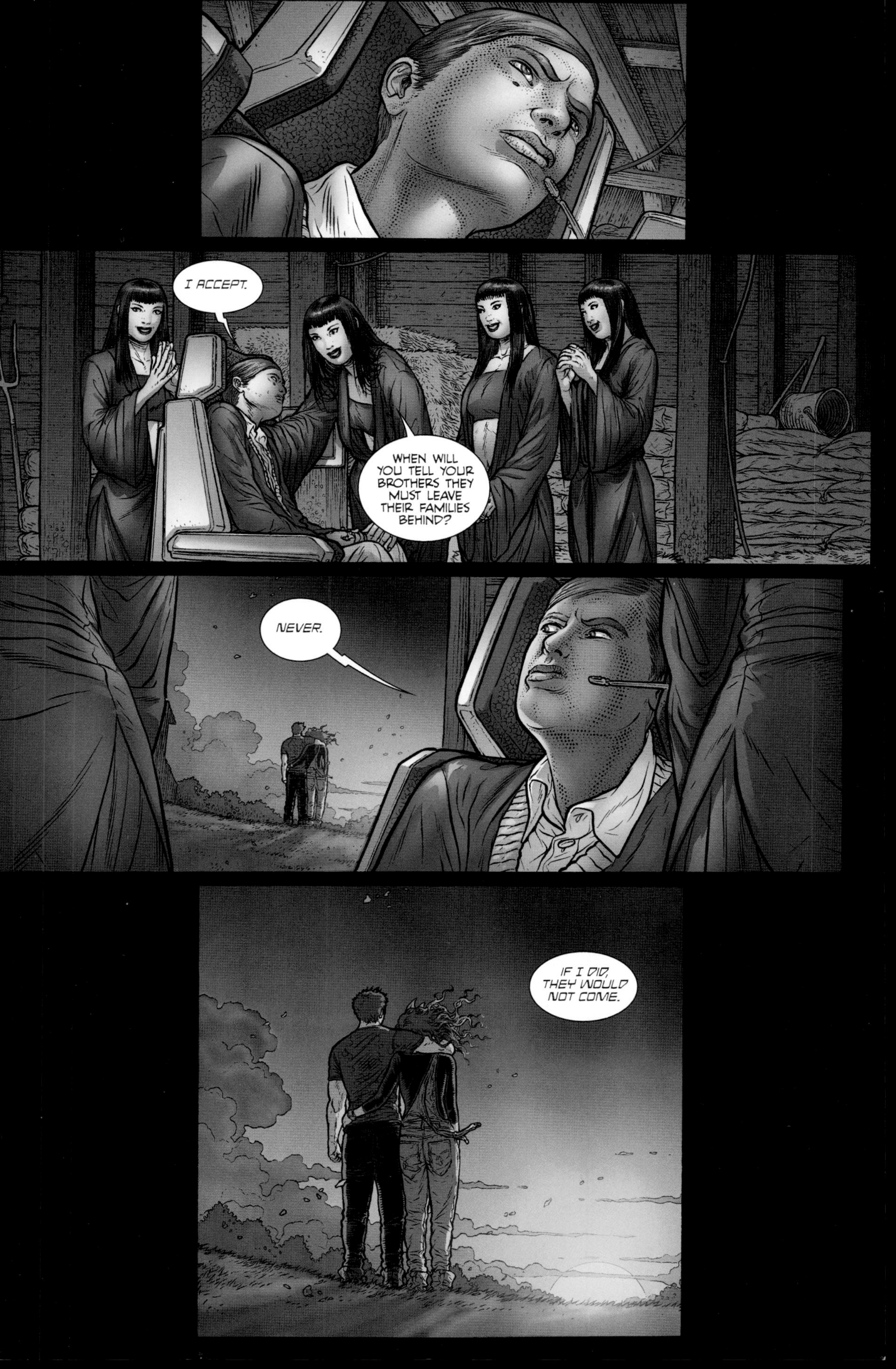

I ACCEPT.
WHEN WILL YOU TELL YOUR BROTHERS THEY MUST LEAVE THEIR FAMILIES BEHIND?
NEVER.
IF I DID, THEY WOULD NOT COME.

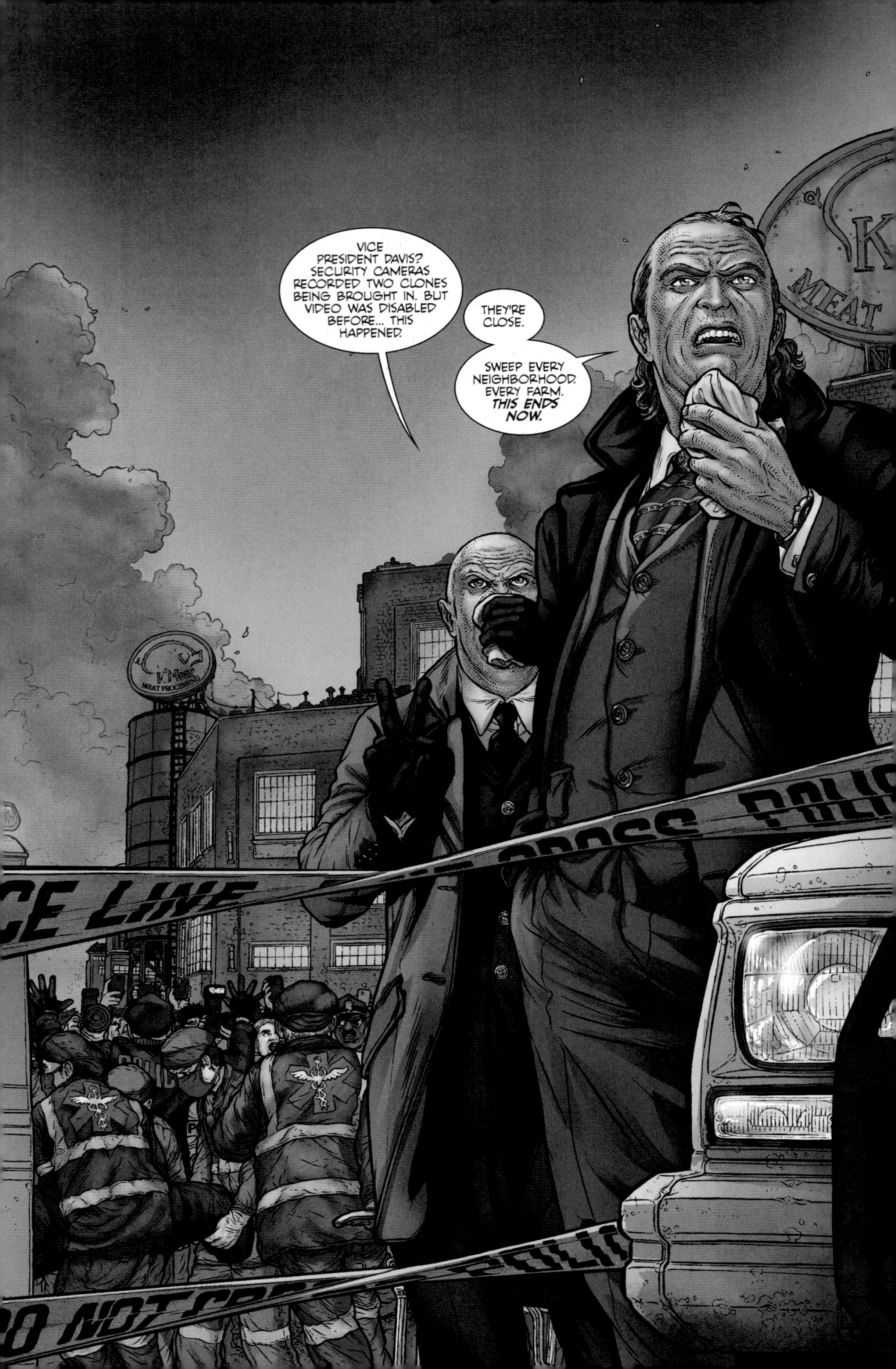
VICE PRESIDENT DAVIS? SECURITY CAMERAS RECORDED TWO CLONES BEING BROUGHT IN. BUT VIDEO WAS DISABLED BEFORE... THIS HAPPENED.
THEY'RE CLOSE.
SWEEP EVERY NEIGHBORHOOD. EVERY FARM. *THIS ENDS NOW.*
MEAT PROCESSING

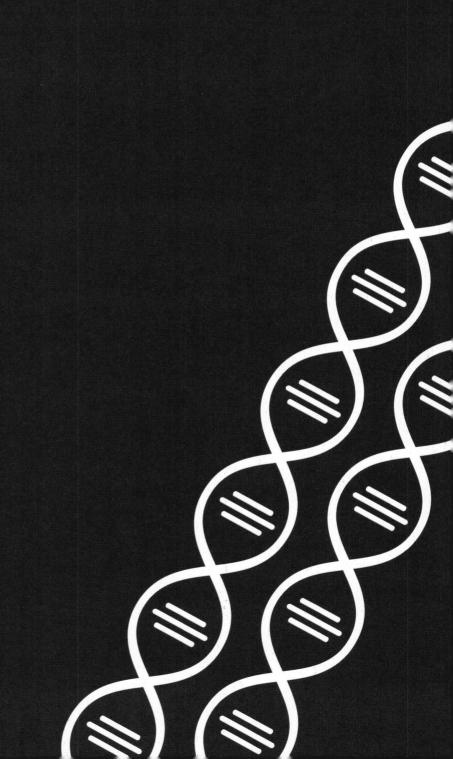

CHAPTER 15

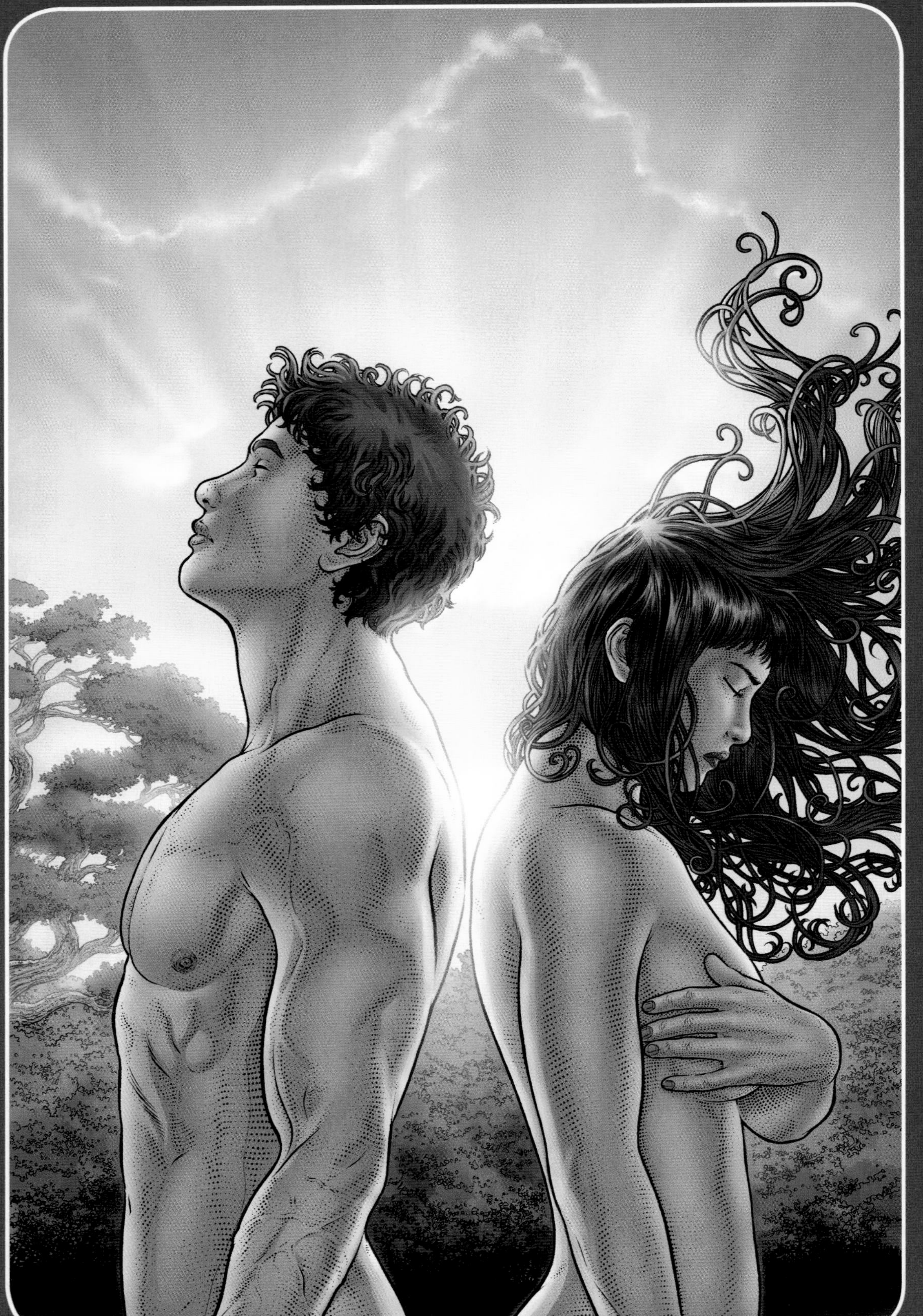

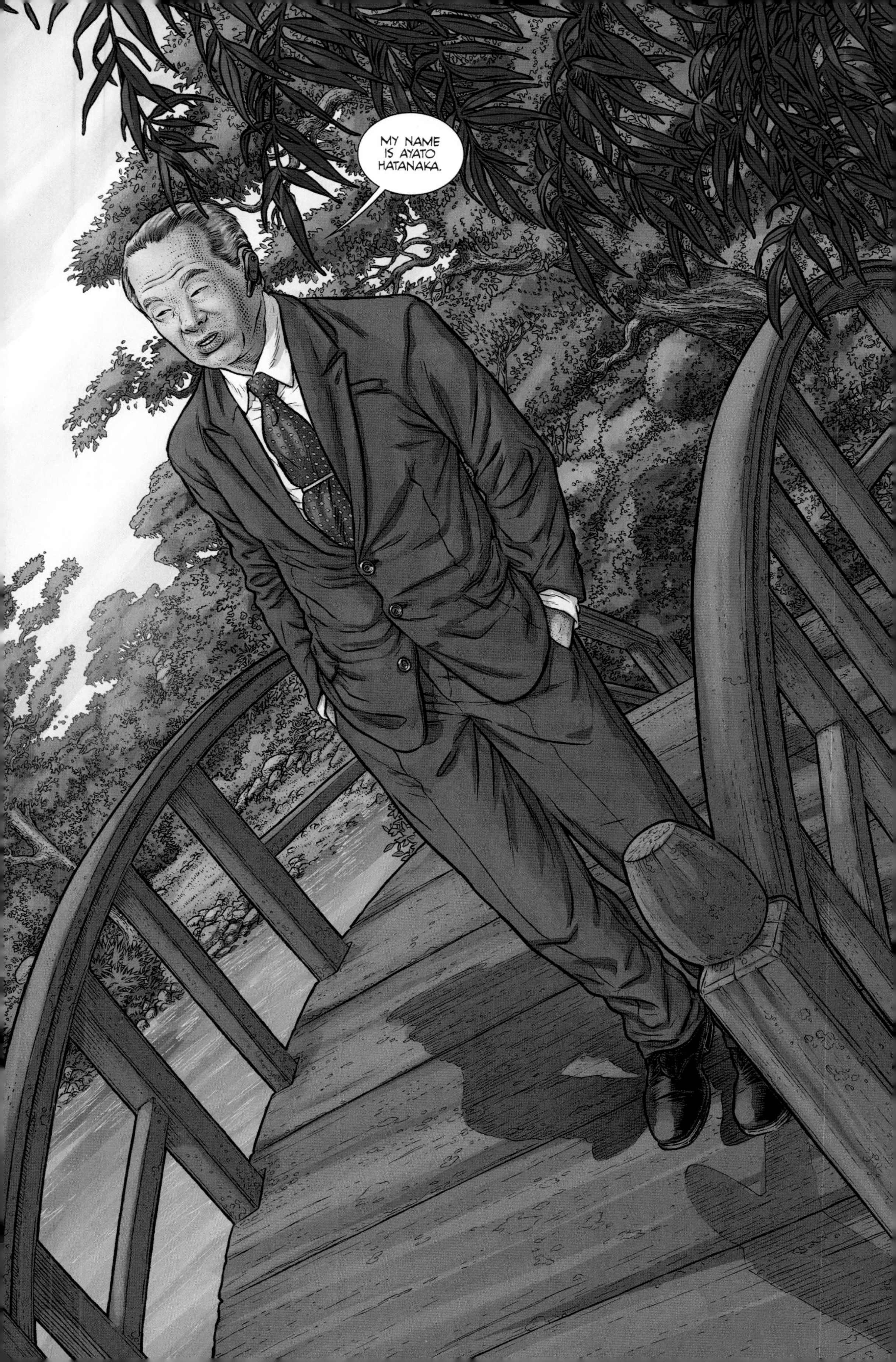
MY NAME IS AYATO HATANAKA.

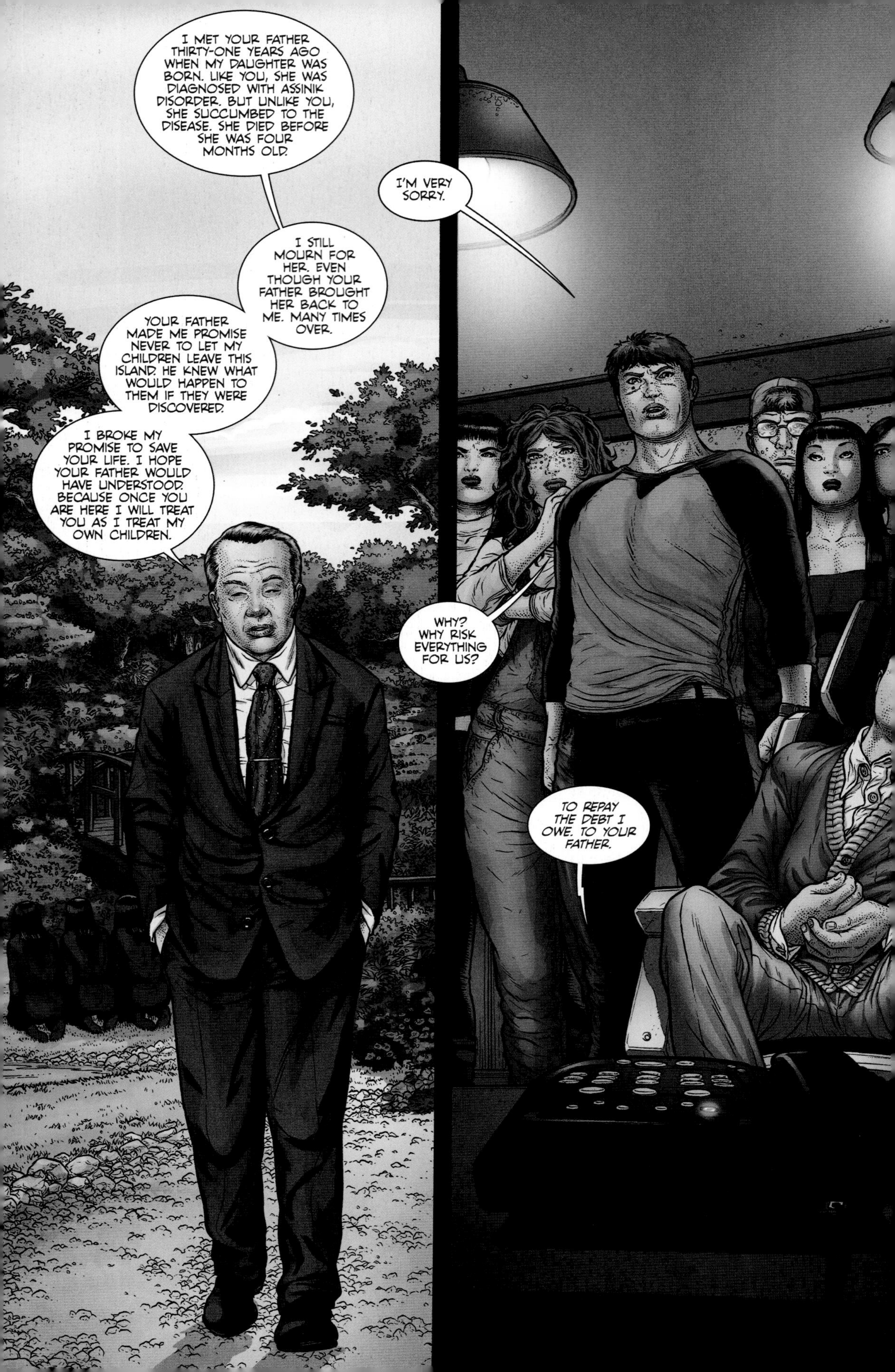
I MET YOUR FATHER THIRTY-ONE YEARS AGO WHEN MY DAUGHTER WAS BORN. LIKE YOU, SHE WAS DIAGNOSED WITH ASSINIK DISORDER. BUT UNLIKE YOU, SHE SUCCUMBED TO THE DISEASE. SHE DIED BEFORE SHE WAS FOUR MONTHS OLD.
I'M VERY SORRY.
I STILL MOURN FOR HER. EVEN THOUGH YOUR FATHER BROUGHT HER BACK TO ME. MANY TIMES OVER.
YOUR FATHER MADE ME PROMISE NEVER TO LET MY CHILDREN LEAVE THIS ISLAND. HE KNEW WHAT WOULD HAPPEN TO THEM IF THEY WERE DISCOVERED.
I BROKE MY PROMISE TO SAVE YOUR LIFE. I HOPE YOUR FATHER WOULD HAVE UNDERSTOOD. BECAUSE ONCE YOU ARE HERE I WILL TREAT YOU AS I TREAT MY OWN CHILDREN.
WHY? WHY RISK EVERYTHING FOR US?
TO REPAY THE DEBT I OWE. TO YOUR FATHER.

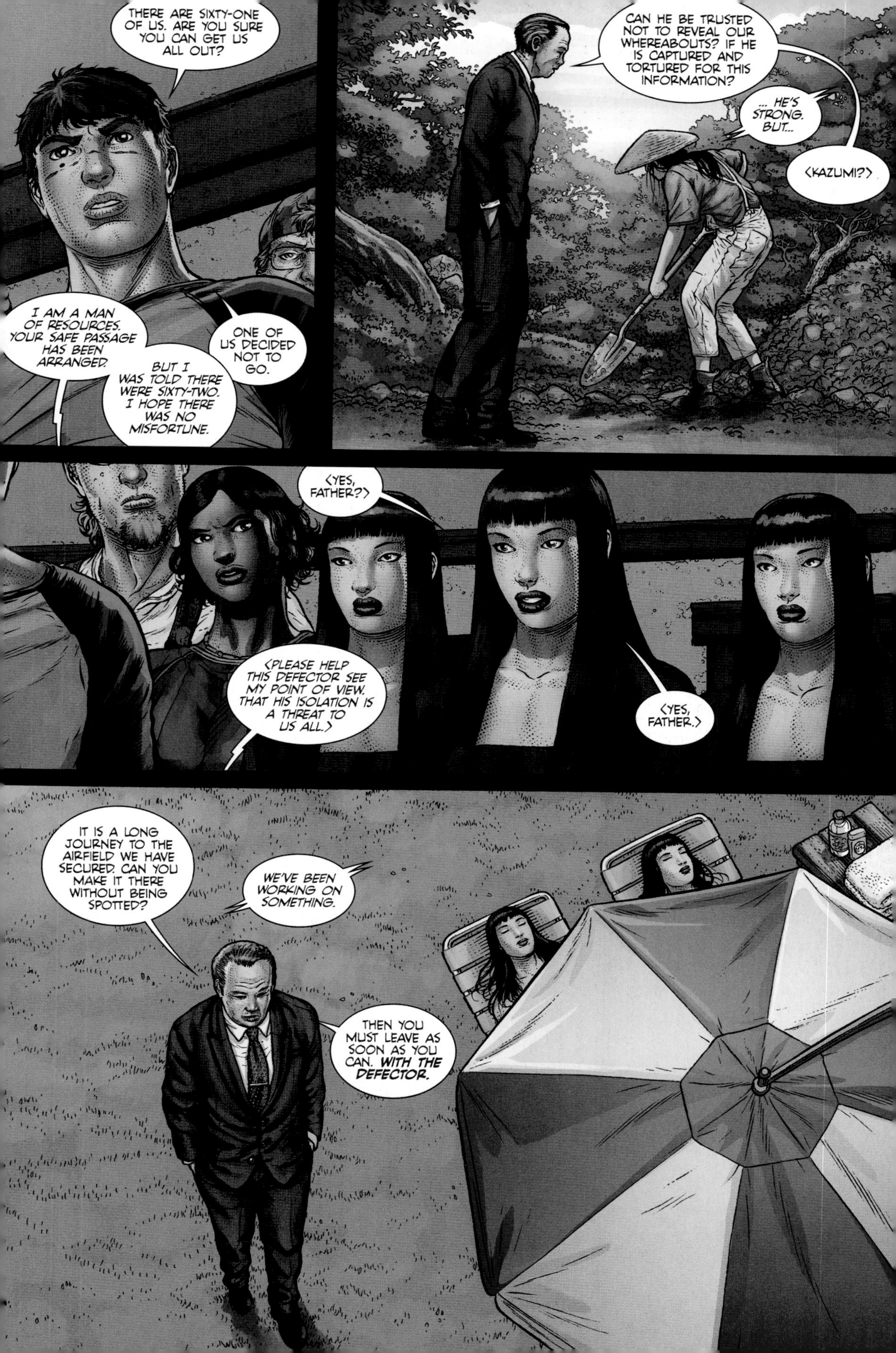

THERE ARE SIXTY-ONE OF US. ARE YOU SURE YOU CAN GET US ALL OUT?
I AM A MAN OF RESOURCES. YOUR SAFE PASSAGE HAS BEEN ARRANGED.
BUT I WAS TOLD THERE WERE SIXTY-TWO. I HOPE THERE WAS NO MISFORTUNE.
ONE OF US DECIDED NOT TO GO.
CAN HE BE TRUSTED NOT TO REVEAL OUR WHEREABOUTS? IF HE IS CAPTURED AND TORTURED FOR THIS INFORMATION?
... HE'S STRONG. BUT...
<KAZUMI?>
<YES, FATHER?>
<PLEASE HELP THIS DEFECTOR SEE MY POINT OF VIEW. THAT HIS ISOLATION IS A THREAT TO US ALL.>
<YES, FATHER.>
IT IS A LONG JOURNEY TO THE AIRFIELD WE HAVE SECURED. CAN YOU MAKE IT THERE WITHOUT BEING SPOTTED?
WE'VE BEEN WORKING ON SOMETHING.
THEN YOU MUST LEAVE AS SOON AS YOU CAN. WITH THE DEFECTOR.

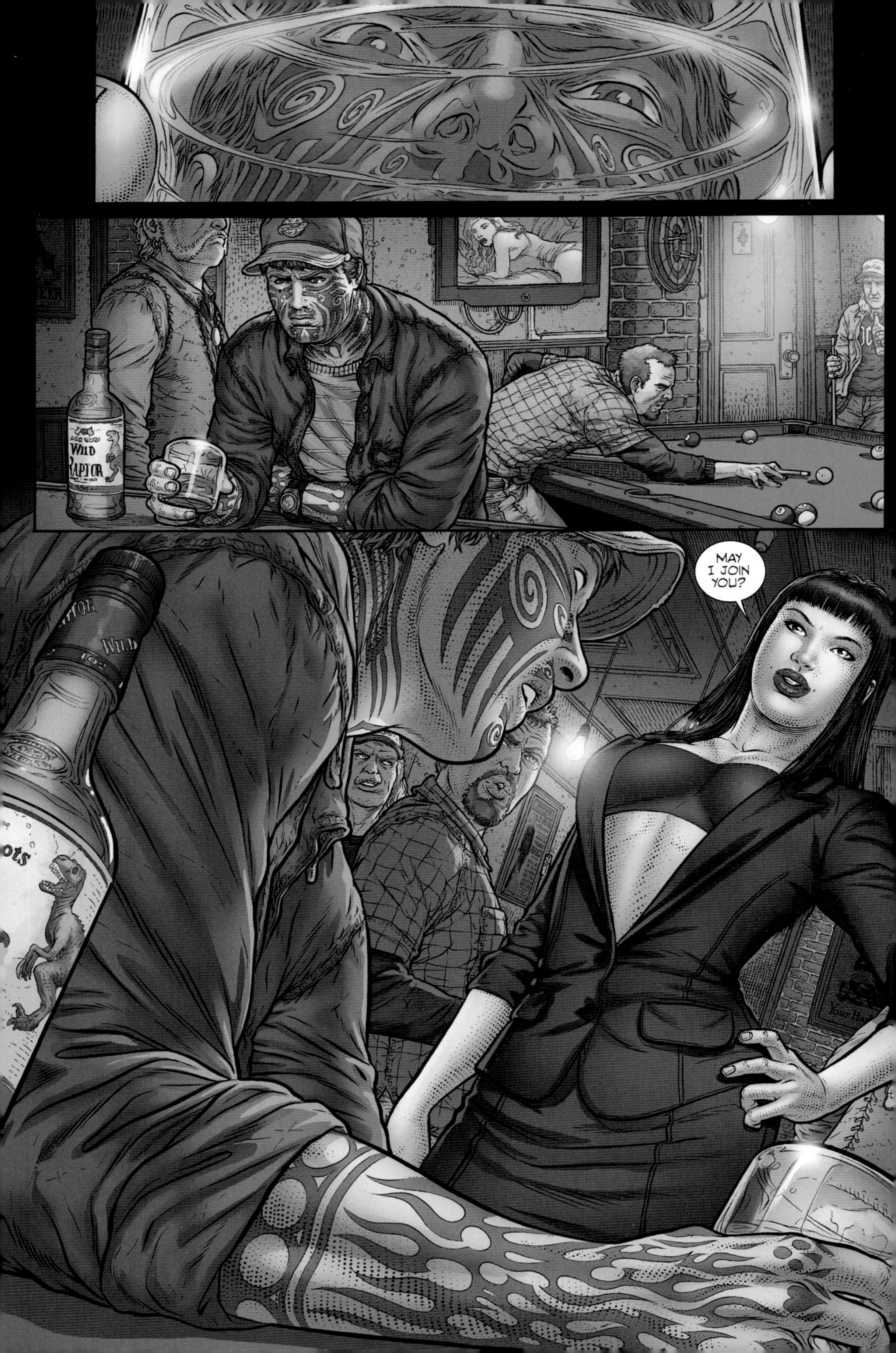
WILD RAPTOR
MAY I JOIN YOU?

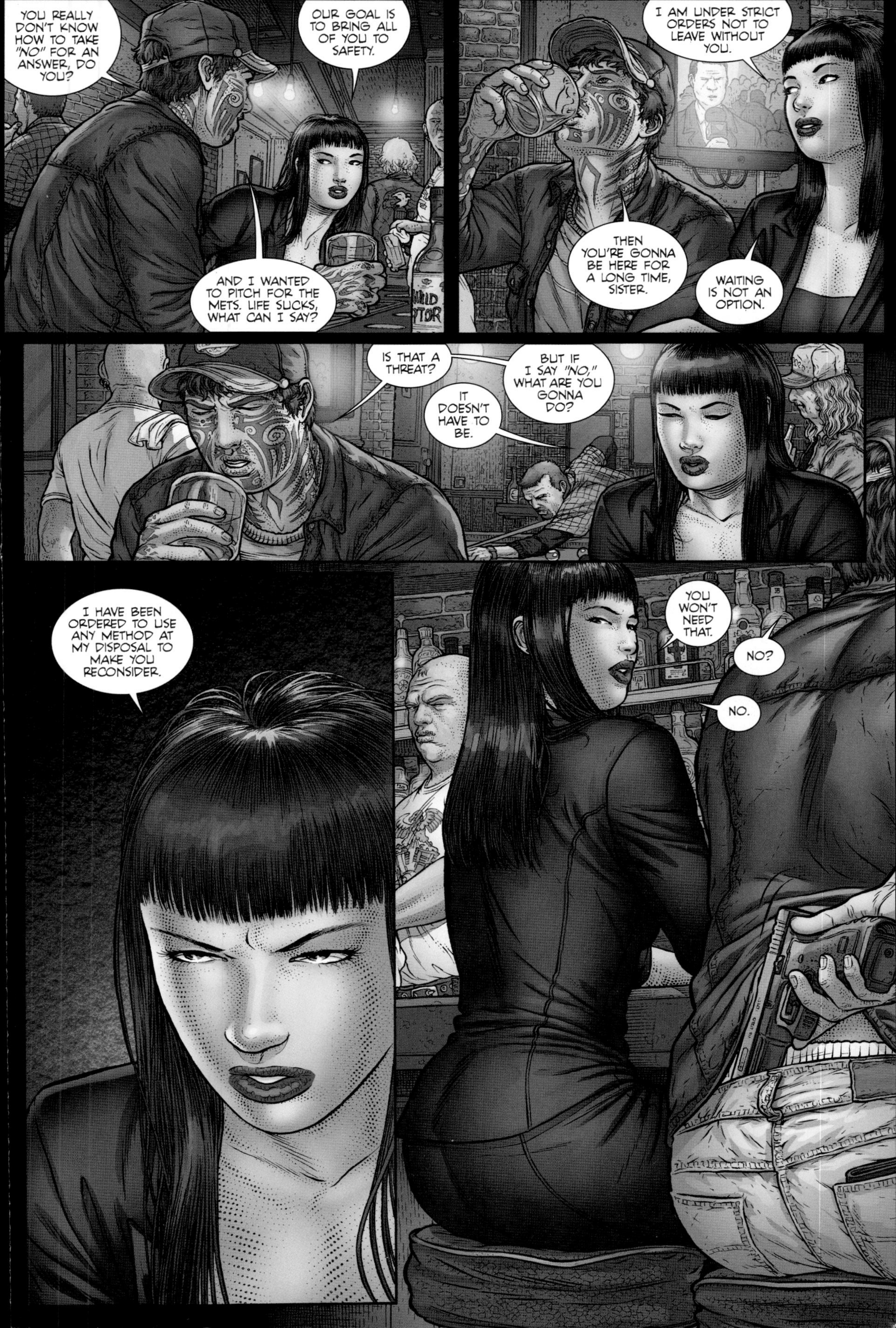

YOU REALLY DON'T KNOW HOW TO TAKE "NO" FOR AN ANSWER, DO YOU?
OUR GOAL IS TO BRING ALL OF YOU TO SAFETY.
AND I WANTED TO PITCH FOR THE METS. LIFE SUCKS, WHAT CAN I SAY?
I AM UNDER STRICT ORDERS NOT TO LEAVE WITHOUT YOU.
THEN YOU'RE GONNA BE HERE FOR A LONG TIME, SISTER.
WAITING IS NOT AN OPTION.
BUT IF I SAY "NO," WHAT ARE YOU GONNA DO?
IS THAT A THREAT?
IT DOESN'T HAVE TO BE.
I HAVE BEEN ORDERED TO USE ANY METHOD AT MY DISPOSAL TO MAKE YOU RECONSIDER.
YOU WON'T NEED THAT.
NO?
NO.

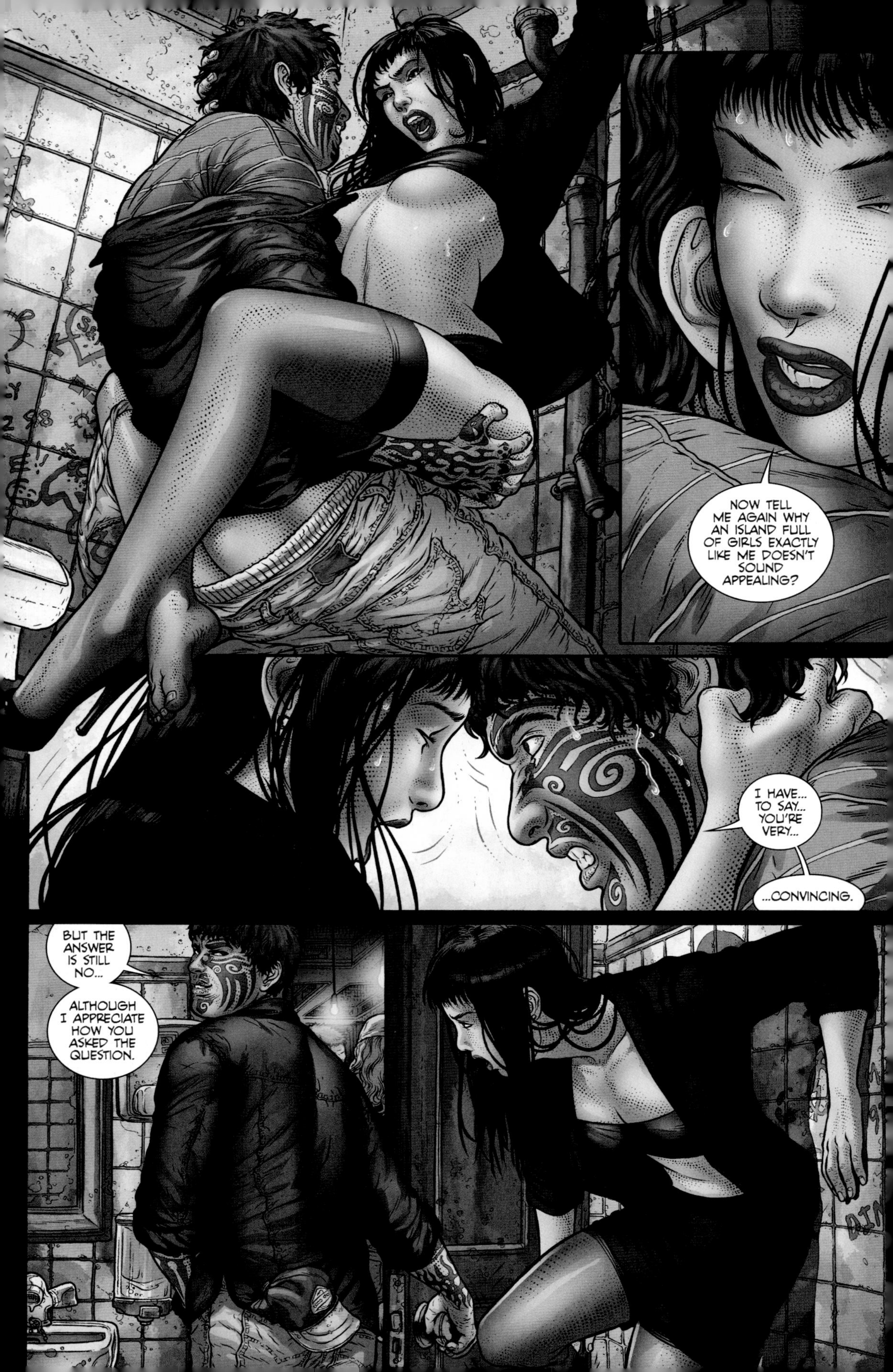
NOW TELL ME AGAIN WHY AN ISLAND FULL OF GIRLS EXACTLY LIKE ME DOESN'T SOUND APPEALING?
I HAVE... TO SAY... YOU'RE VERY...
...CONVINCING.
BUT THE ANSWER IS STILL NO...
ALTHOUGH I APPRECIATE HOW YOU ASKED THE QUESTION.

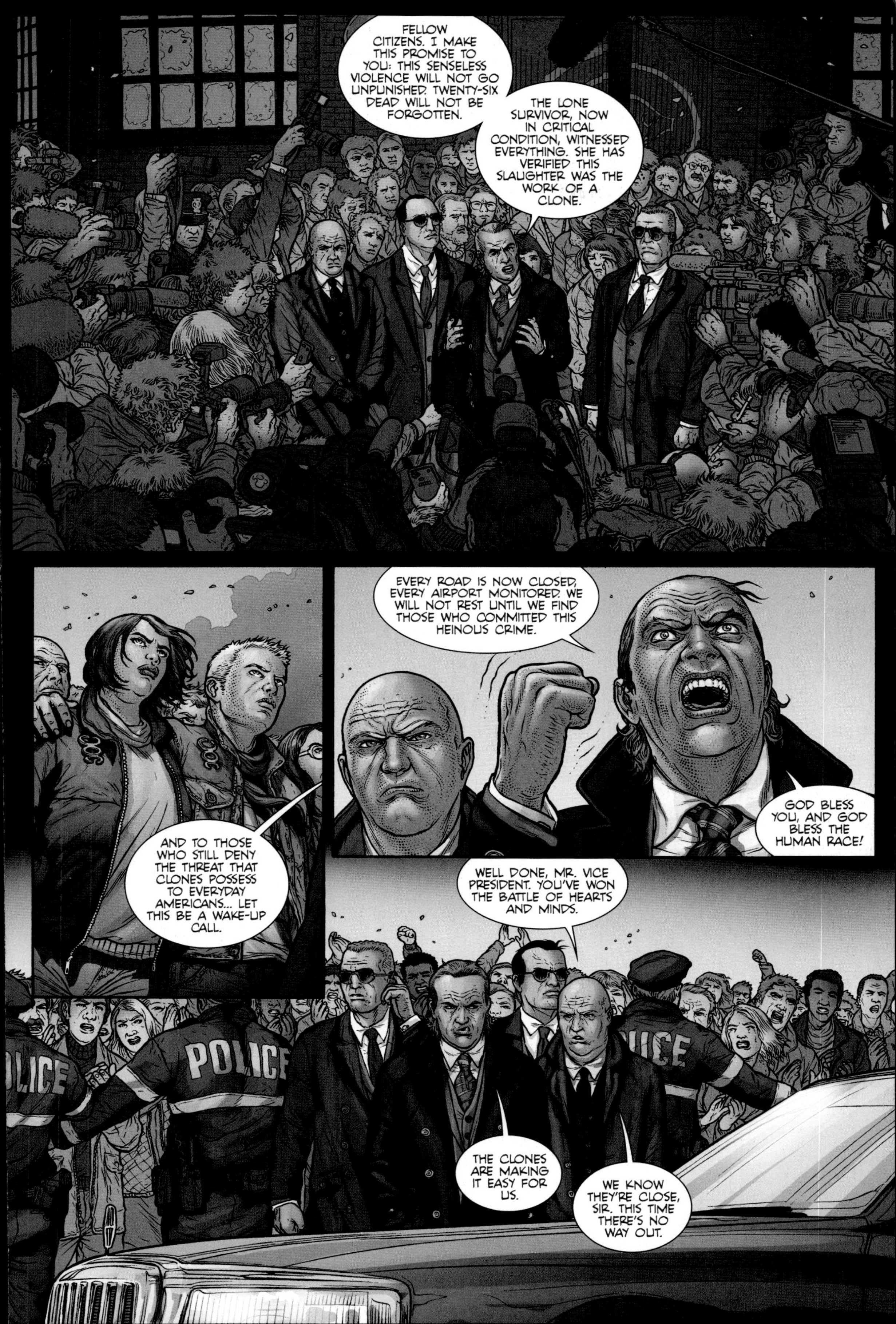
FELLOW CITIZENS. I MAKE THIS PROMISE TO YOU: THIS SENSELESS VIOLENCE WILL NOT GO UNPUNISHED. TWENTY-SIX DEAD WILL NOT BE FORGOTTEN.
THE LONE SURVIVOR, NOW IN CRITICAL CONDITION, WITNESSED EVERYTHING. SHE HAS VERIFIED THIS SLAUGHTER WAS THE WORK OF A CLONE.
AND TO THOSE WHO STILL DENY THE THREAT THAT CLONES POSSESS TO EVERYDAY AMERICANS... LET THIS BE A WAKE-UP CALL.
EVERY ROAD IS NOW CLOSED, EVERY AIRPORT MONITORED. WE WILL NOT REST UNTIL WE FIND THOSE WHO COMMITTED THIS HEINOUS CRIME.
GOD BLESS YOU, AND GOD BLESS THE HUMAN RACE!
WELL DONE, MR. VICE PRESIDENT. YOU'VE WON THE BATTLE OF HEARTS AND MINDS.
POLICE
POLICE
THE CLONES ARE MAKING IT EASY FOR US.
WE KNOW THEY'RE CLOSE, SIR. THIS TIME THERE'S NO WAY OUT.

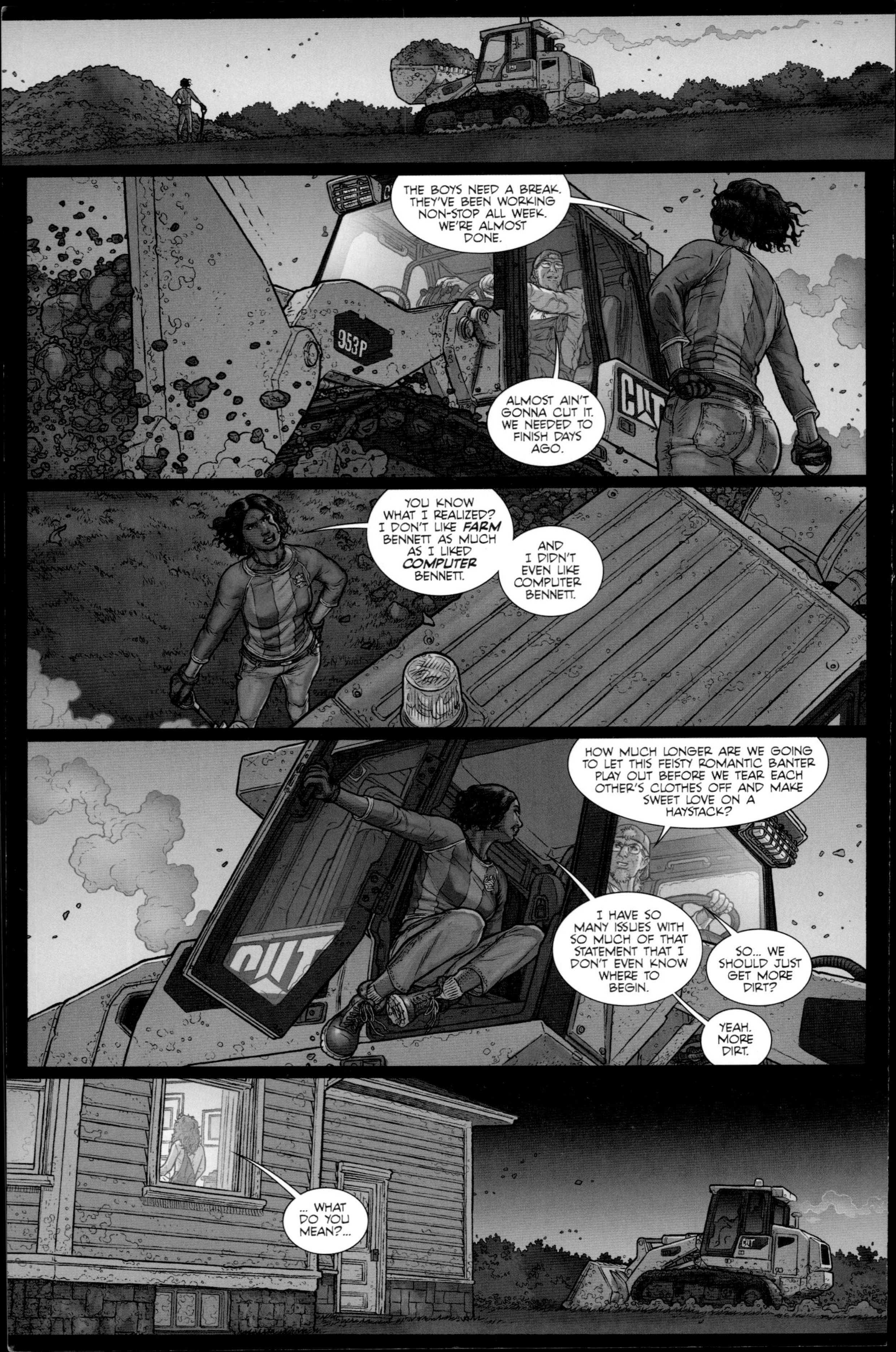
THE BOYS NEED A BREAK. THEY'VE BEEN WORKING NON-STOP ALL WEEK. WE'RE ALMOST DONE.
ALMOST AIN'T GONNA CUT IT. WE NEEDED TO FINISH DAYS AGO.
953P
CAT
YOU KNOW WHAT I REALIZED? I DON'T LIKE FARM BENNETT AS MUCH AS I LIKED COMPUTER BENNETT.
AND I DIDN'T EVEN LIKE COMPUTER BENNETT.
HOW MUCH LONGER ARE WE GOING TO LET THIS FEISTY ROMANTIC BANTER PLAY OUT BEFORE WE TEAR EACH OTHER'S CLOTHES OFF AND MAKE SWEET LOVE ON A HAYSTACK?
I HAVE SO MANY ISSUES WITH SO MUCH OF THAT STATEMENT THAT I DON'T EVEN KNOW WHERE TO BEGIN.
SO... WE SHOULD JUST GET MORE DIRT?
YEAH. MORE DIRT.
... WHAT DO YOU MEAN?...

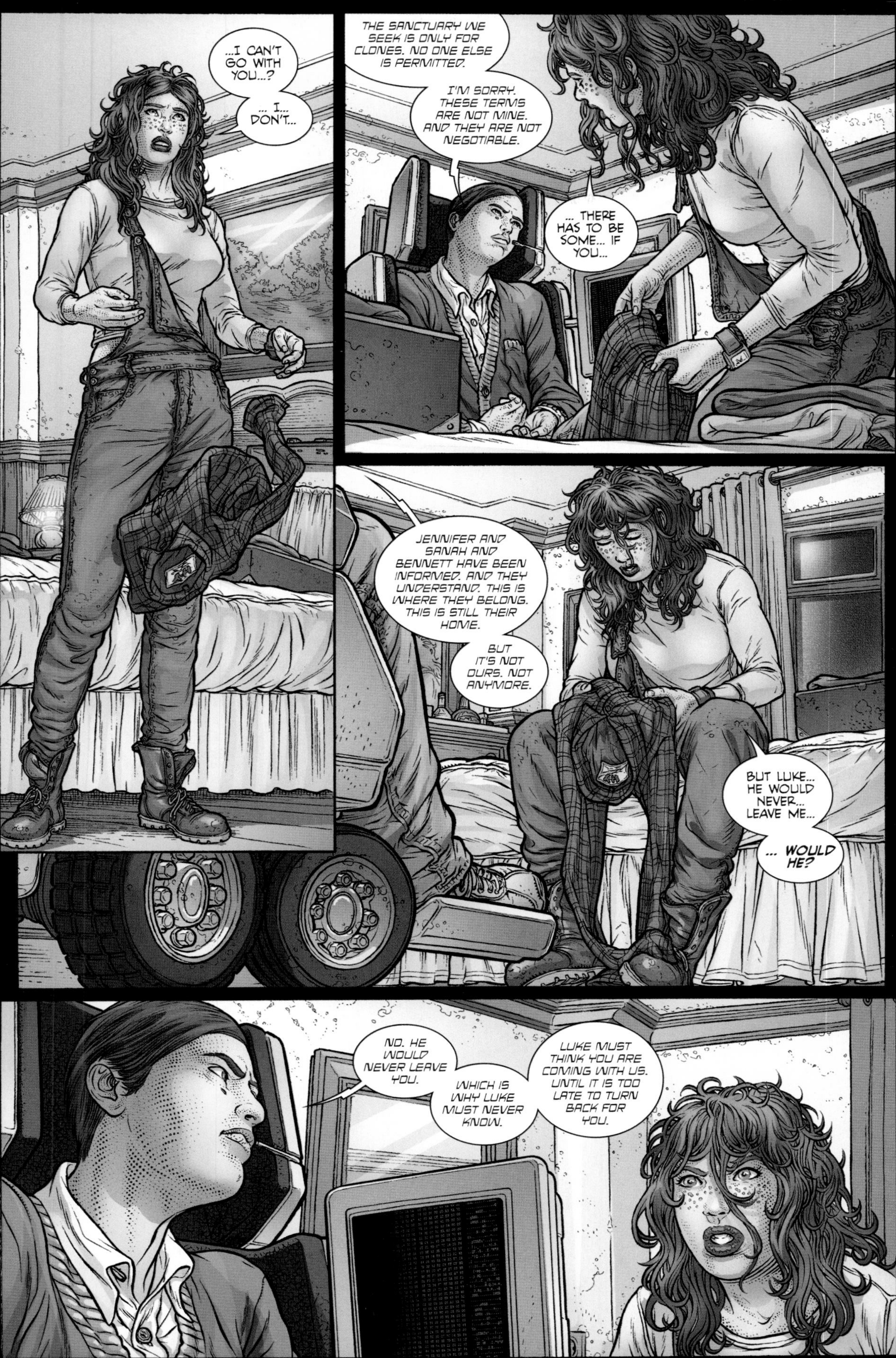

...I CAN'T GO WITH YOU...?
... I... DON'T...
THE SANCTUARY WE SEEK IS ONLY FOR CLONES. NO ONE ELSE IS PERMITTED.
I'M SORRY. THESE TERMS ARE NOT MINE. AND THEY ARE NOT NEGOTIABLE.
... THERE HAS TO BE SOME... IF YOU...
JENNIFER AND SARAH AND BENNETT HAVE BEEN INFORMED. AND THEY UNDERSTAND. THIS IS WHERE THEY BELONG. THIS IS STILL THEIR HOME.
BUT IT'S NOT OURS. NOT ANYMORE.
BUT LUKE... HE WOULD NEVER... LEAVE ME...
... WOULD HE?
NO. HE WOULD NEVER LEAVE YOU.
WHICH IS WHY LUKE MUST NEVER KNOW.
LUKE MUST THINK YOU ARE COMING WITH US. UNTIL IT IS TOO LATE TO TURN BACK FOR YOU.

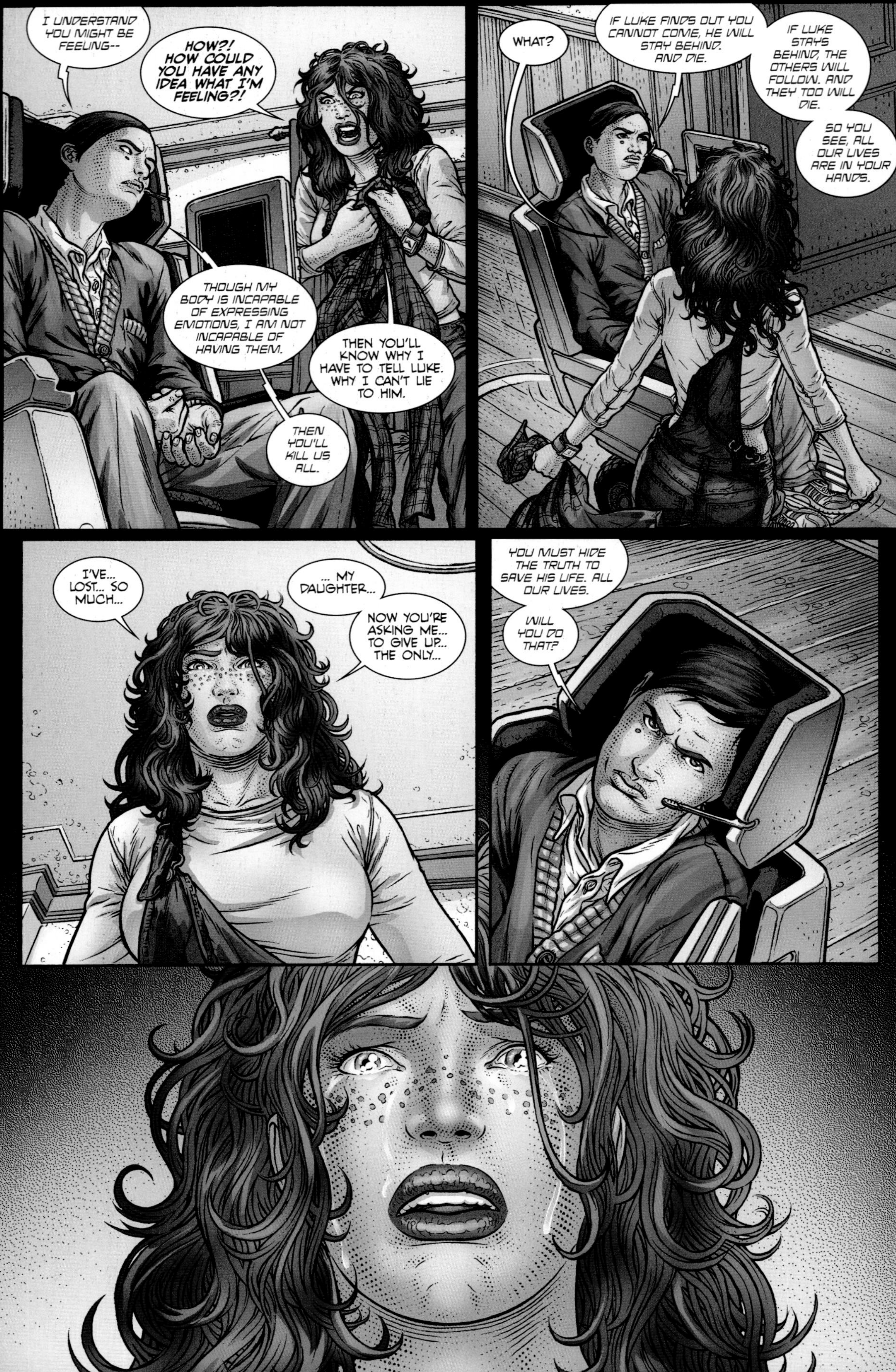
I UNDERSTAND YOU MIGHT BE FEELING--
HOW?! HOW COULD YOU HAVE ANY IDEA WHAT I'M FEELING?!
THOUGH MY BODY IS INCAPABLE OF EXPRESSING EMOTIONS, I AM NOT INCAPABLE OF HAVING THEM.
THEN YOU'LL KNOW WHY I HAVE TO TELL LUKE. WHY I CAN'T LIE TO HIM.
THEN YOU'LL KILL US ALL.
WHAT?
IF LUKE FINDS OUT YOU CANNOT COME, HE WILL STAY BEHIND. AND DIE.
IF LUKE STAYS BEHIND, THE OTHERS WILL FOLLOW. AND THEY TOO WILL DIE.
SO YOU SEE, ALL OUR LIVES ARE IN YOUR HANDS.
I'VE... LOST... SO MUCH...
... MY DAUGHTER...
NOW YOU'RE ASKING ME... TO GIVE UP... THE ONLY...
YOU MUST HIDE THE TRUTH TO SAVE HIS LIFE. ALL OUR LIVES.
WILL YOU DO THAT?

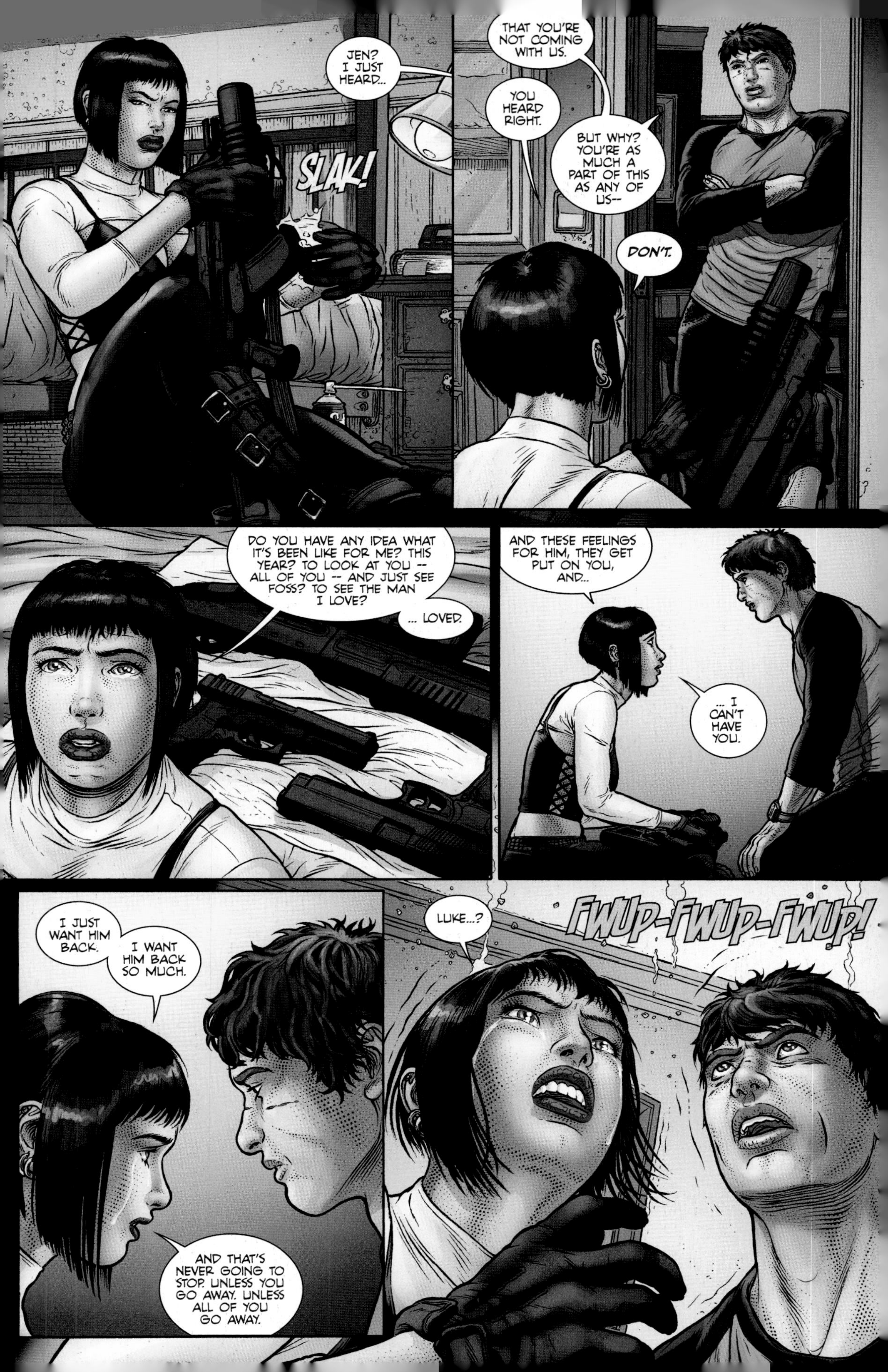
JEN? I JUST HEARD...
SLAK!
THAT YOU'RE NOT COMING WITH US.
YOU HEARD RIGHT.
BUT WHY? YOU'RE AS MUCH A PART OF THIS AS ANY OF US--
DON'T.
DO YOU HAVE ANY IDEA WHAT IT'S BEEN LIKE FOR ME? THIS YEAR? TO LOOK AT YOU -- ALL OF YOU -- AND JUST SEE FOSS? TO SEE THE MAN I LOVE?
... LOVED.
AND THESE FEELINGS FOR HIM, THEY GET PUT ON YOU, AND...
... I CAN'T HAVE YOU.
I JUST WANT HIM BACK.
I WANT HIM BACK SO MUCH.
AND THAT'S NEVER GOING TO STOP. UNLESS YOU GO AWAY. UNLESS ALL OF YOU GO AWAY.
LUKE...?
FWUP-FWUP-FWUP!

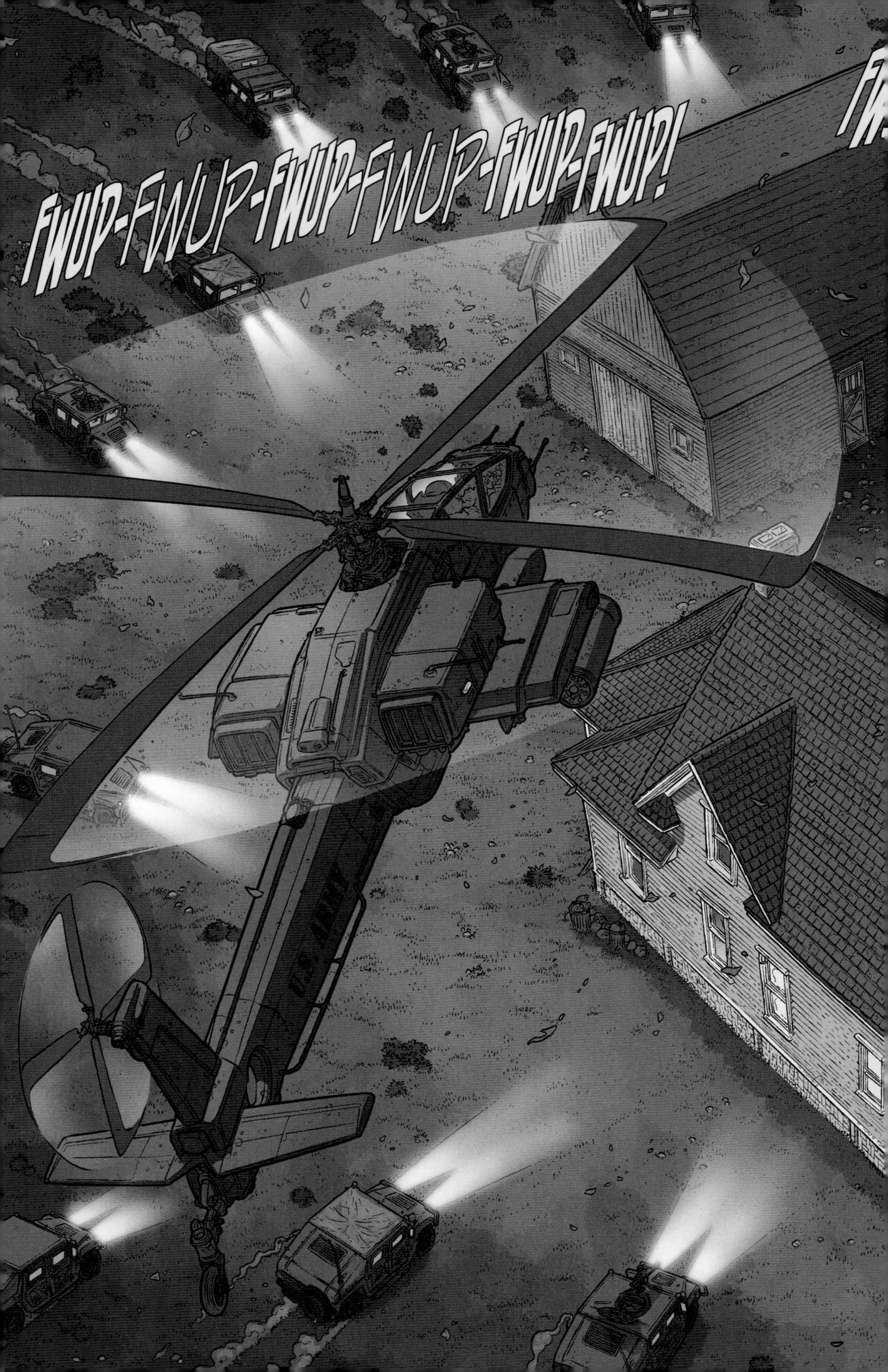
FWUP-FWUP-FWUP-FWUP-FWUP-FWUP!
U.S. ARMY

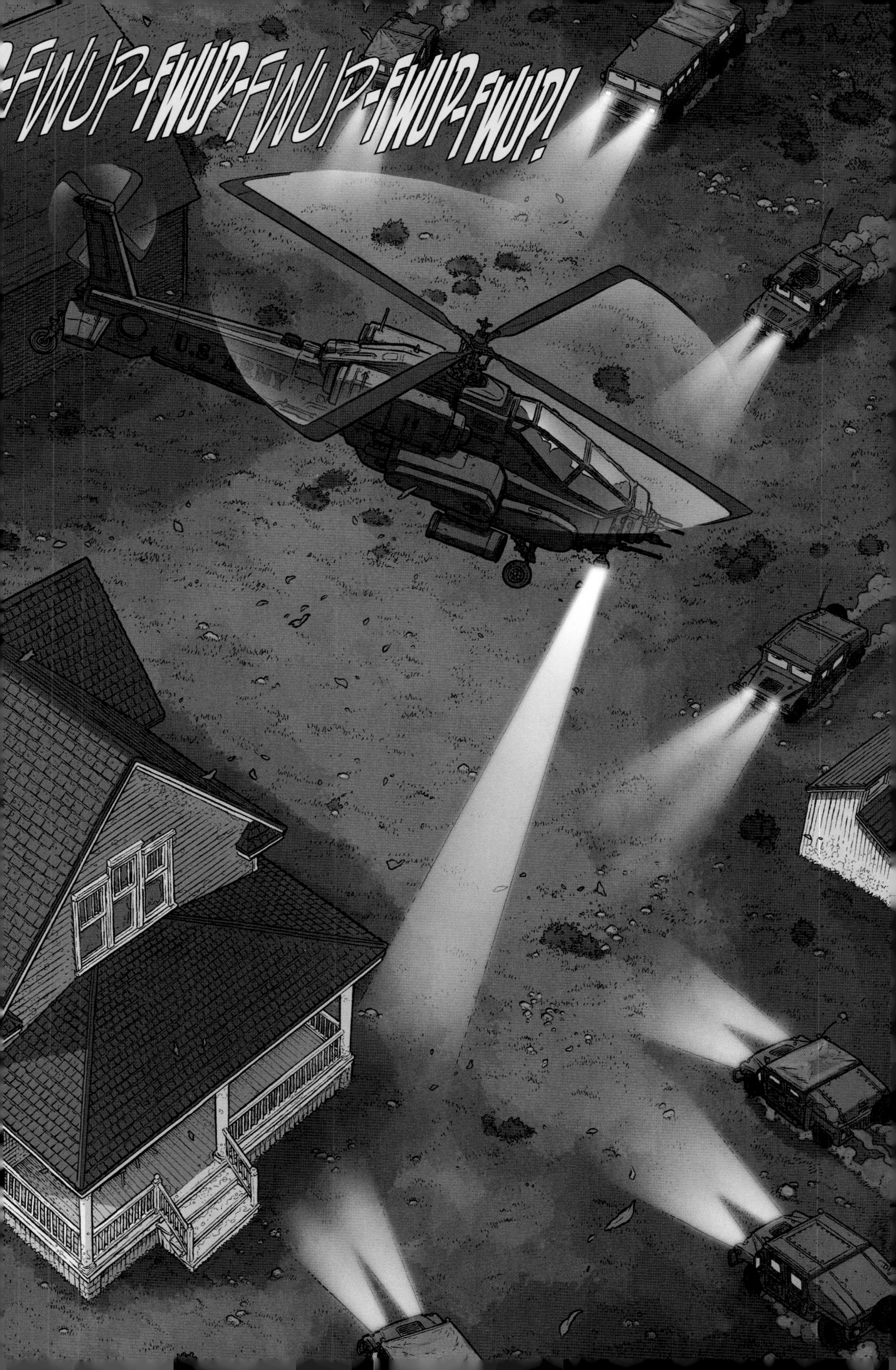
-FWUP-FWUP-FWUP-FWUP-FWUP-FWUP!

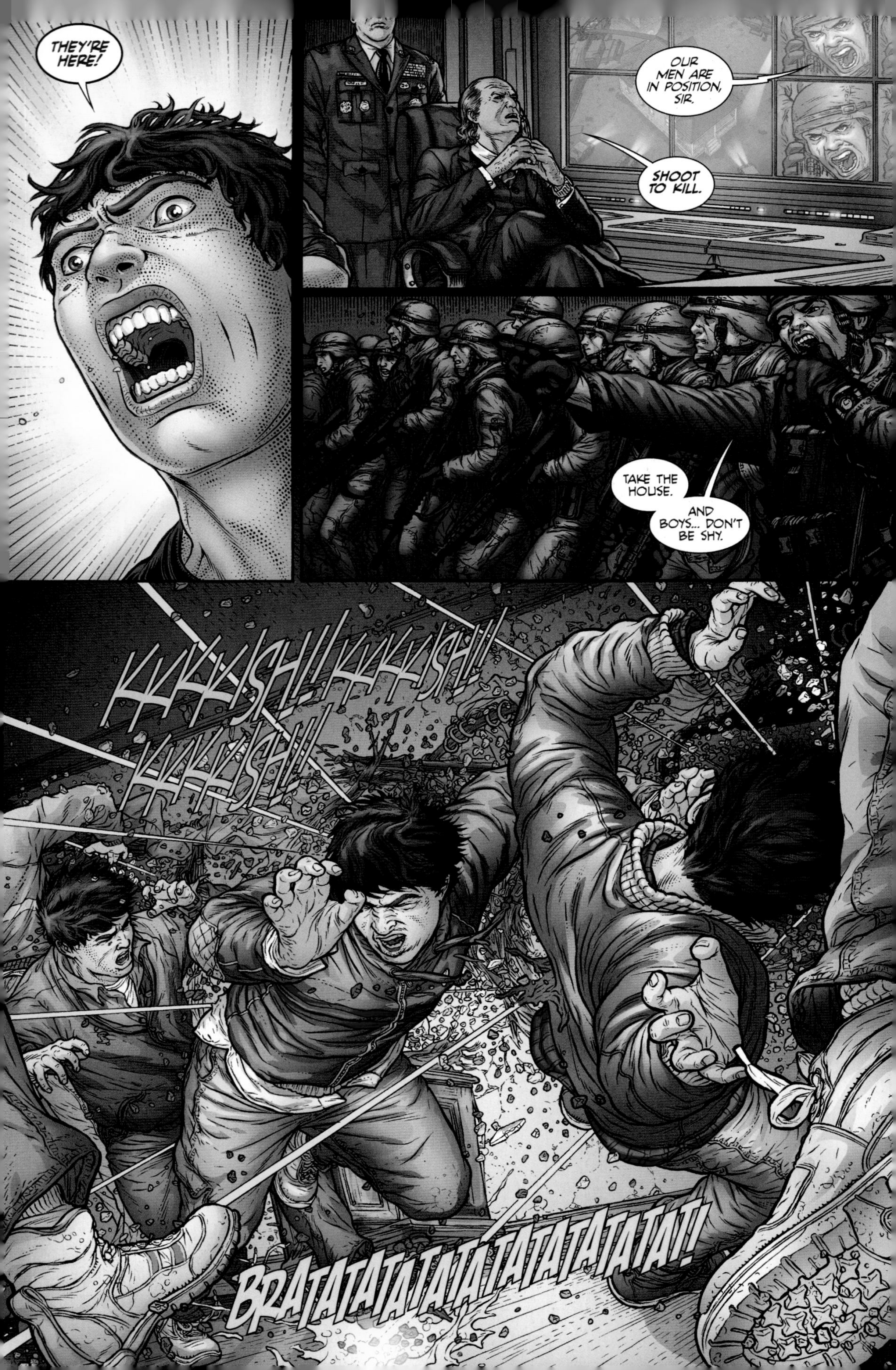
THEY'RE HERE!
OUR MEN ARE IN POSITION, SIR.
SHOOT TO KILL.
TAKE THE HOUSE.
AND BOYS... DON'T BE SHY.
KKKKISH!! KKKKISH!!
KKKKISH!!
BRATATATATATATATATATATATAT!

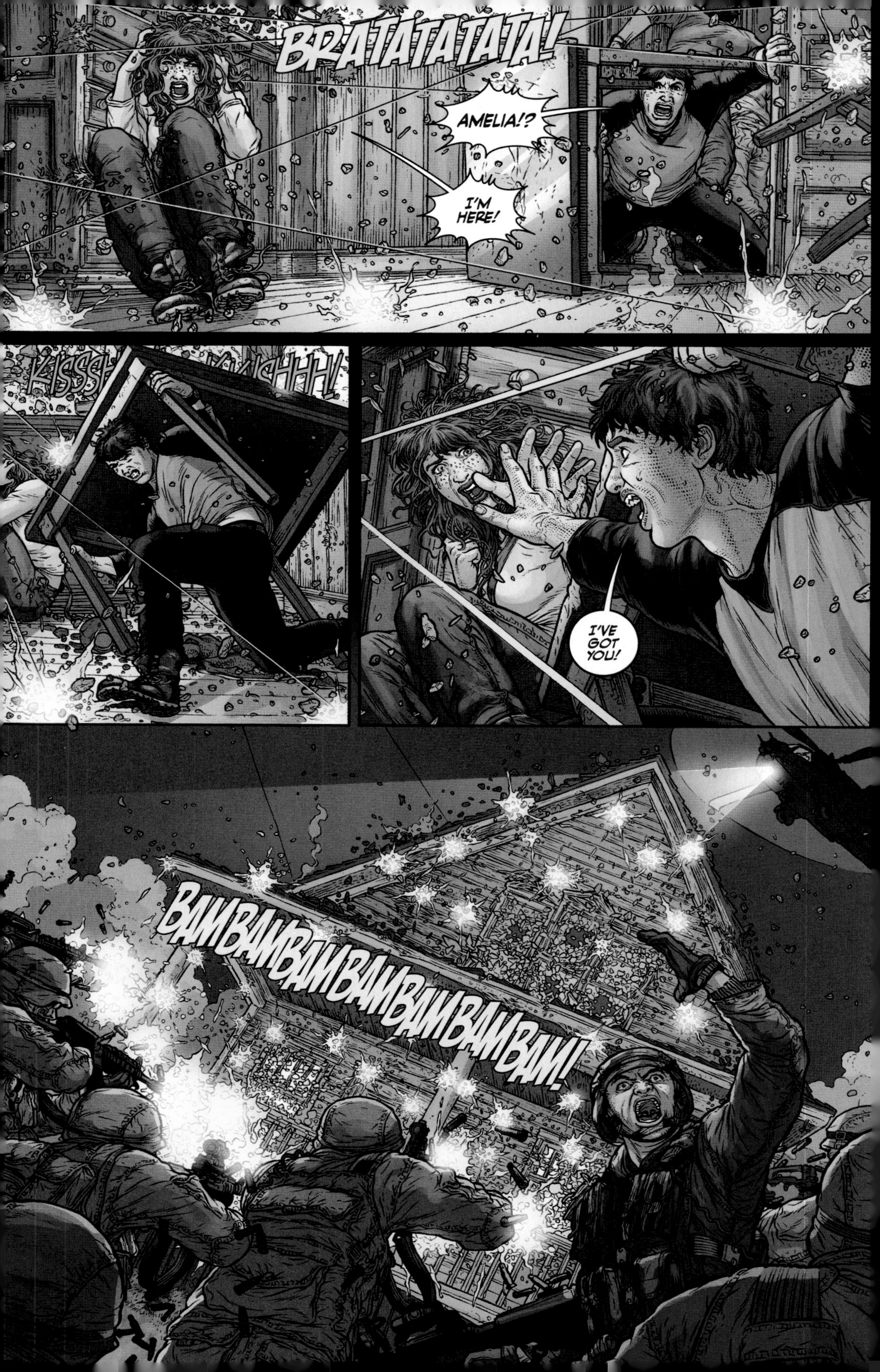
BRATATATATA!
AMELIA!?
I'M HERE!
KISSSH
I'VE GOT YOU!
BAM BAM BAM BAM BAM BAM BAM BAM BAM!

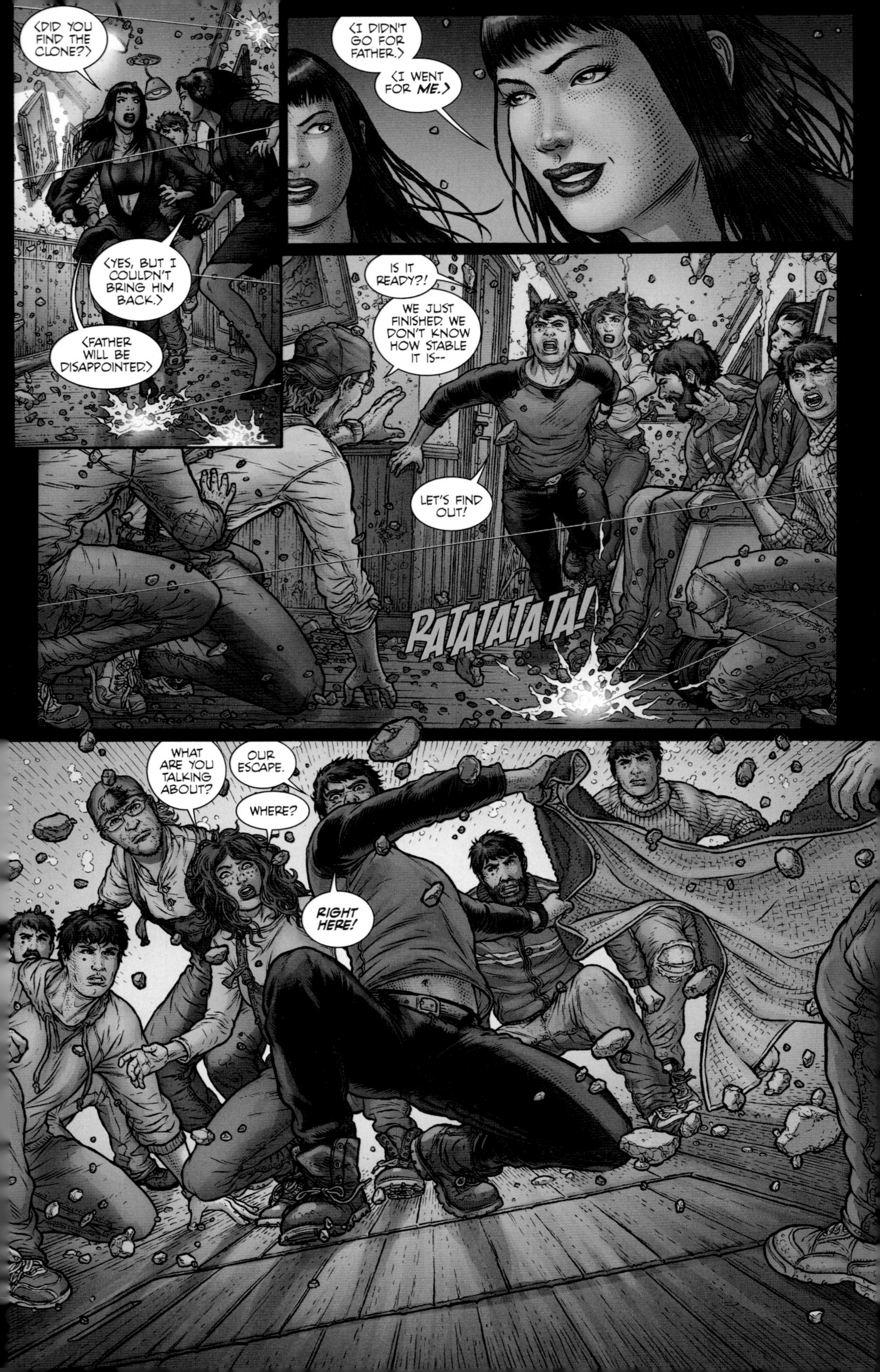
<DID YOU FIND THE CLONE?>
<I DIDN'T GO FOR FATHER.>
<I WENT FOR ME.>
<YES, BUT I COULDN'T BRING HIM BACK.>
<FATHER WILL BE DISAPPOINTED.>
IS IT READY?!
WE JUST FINISHED. WE DON'T KNOW HOW STABLE IT IS--
LET'S FIND OUT!
RATATATATA!
WHAT ARE YOU TALKING ABOUT?
OUR ESCAPE.
WHERE?
RIGHT HERE!

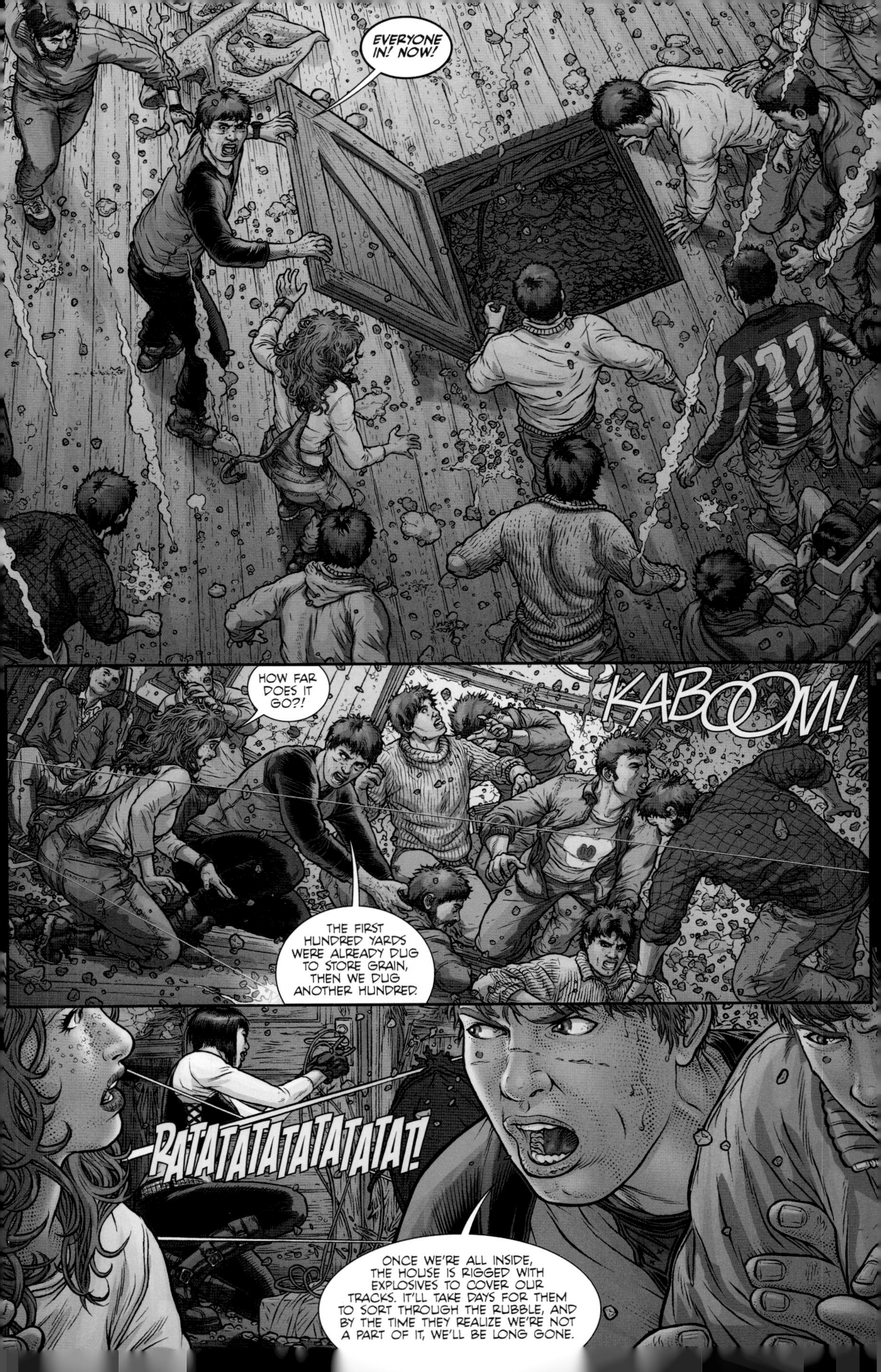
EVERYONE IN! NOW!
HOW FAR DOES IT GO?!
KABOOM!
THE FIRST HUNDRED YARDS WERE ALREADY DUG TO STORE GRAIN, THEN WE DUG ANOTHER HUNDRED.
RATATATATATATATAT!
ONCE WE'RE ALL INSIDE, THE HOUSE IS RIGGED WITH EXPLOSIVES TO COVER OUR TRACKS. IT'LL TAKE DAYS FOR THEM TO SORT THROUGH THE RUBBLE, AND BY THE TIME THEY REALIZE WE'RE NOT A PART OF IT, WE'LL BE LONG GONE.

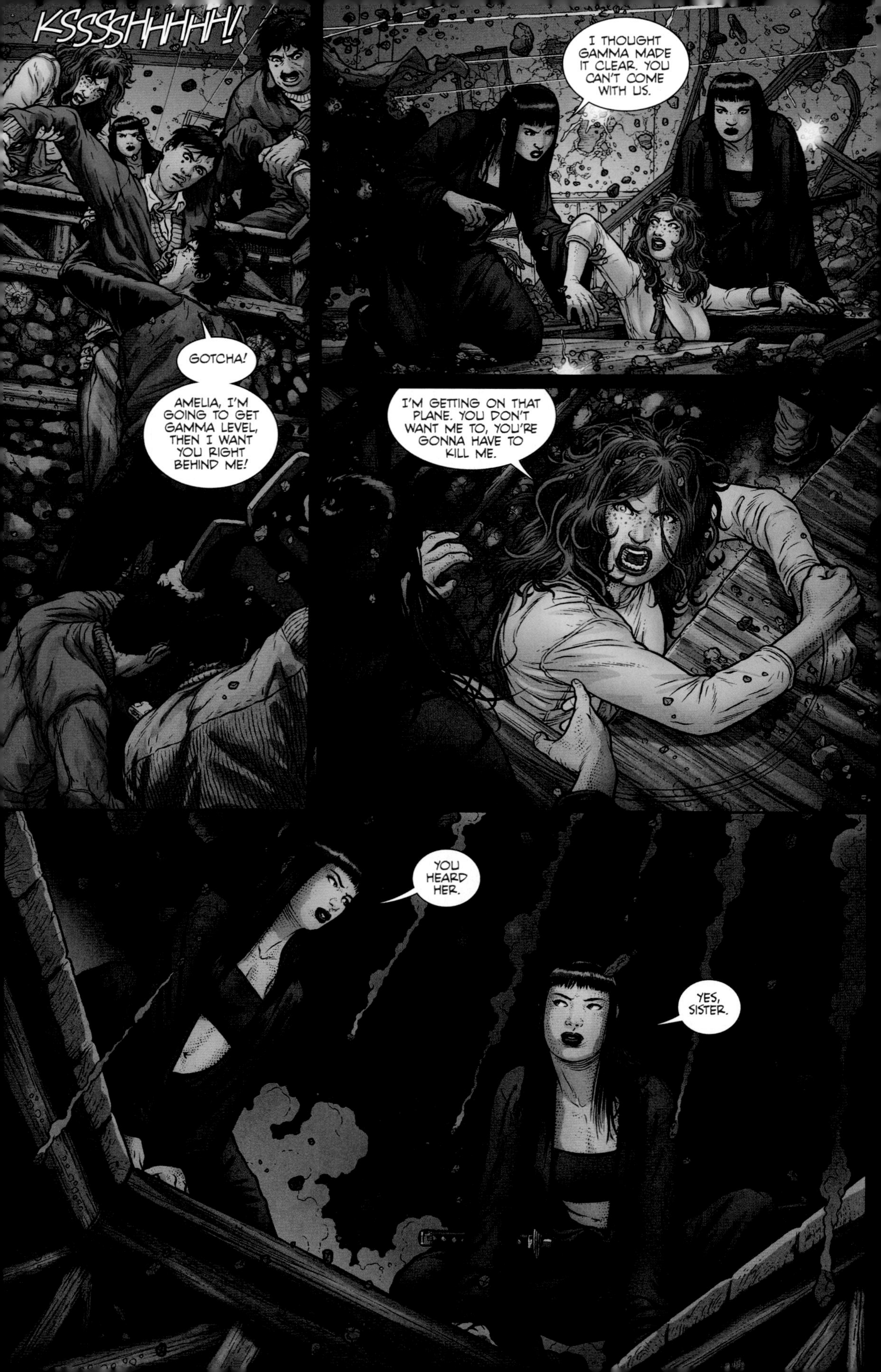
KSSSSHHHH!
GOTCHA!
AMELIA, I'M GOING TO GET GAMMA LEVEL, THEN I WANT YOU RIGHT BEHIND ME!
I THOUGHT GAMMA MADE IT CLEAR. YOU CAN'T COME WITH US.
I'M GETTING ON THAT PLANE. YOU DON'T WANT ME TO, YOU'RE GONNA HAVE TO KILL ME.
YOU HEARD HER.
YES, SISTER.

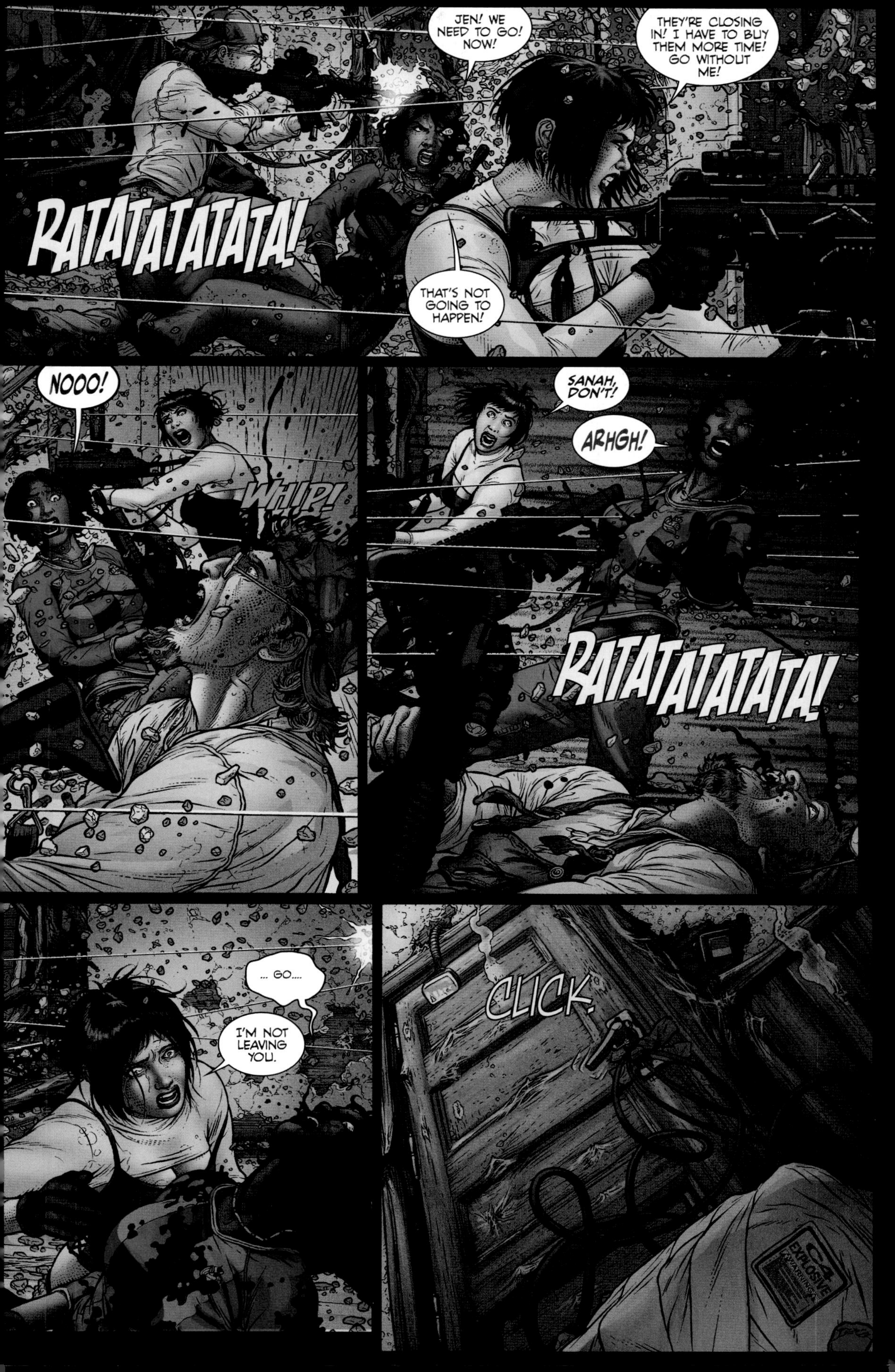
JEN! WE NEED TO GO! NOW!
THEY'RE CLOSING IN! I HAVE TO BUY THEM MORE TIME! GO WITHOUT ME!
RATATATATATA!
THAT'S NOT GOING TO HAPPEN!
NOOO!
WHIP!
SANAH, DON'T!
ARHGH!
RATATATATATA!
... GO....
I'M NOT LEAVING YOU.
CLICK.
C4 EXPLOSIVE

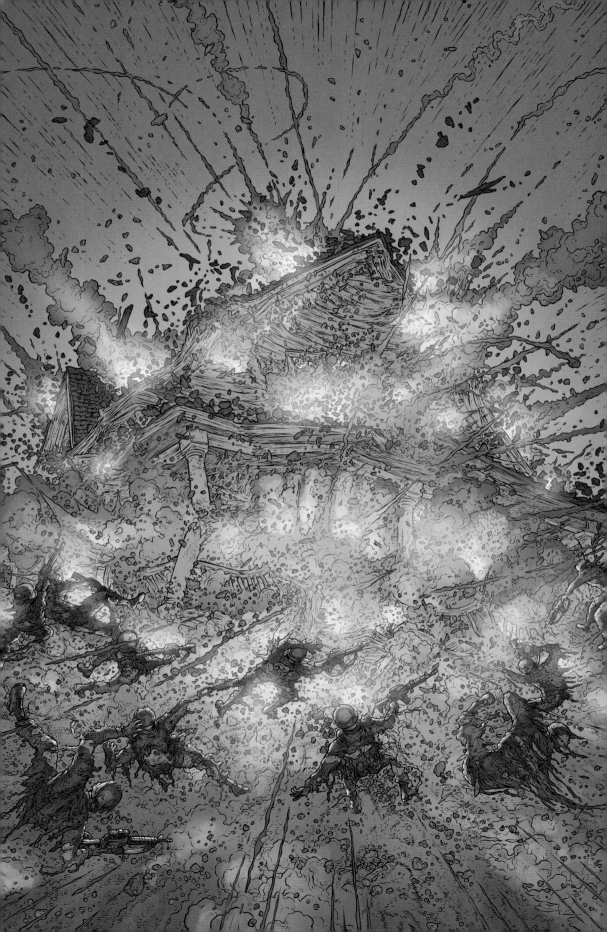

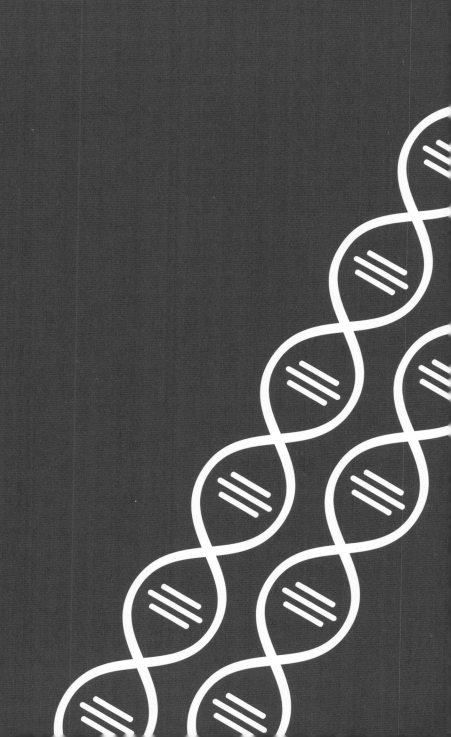

SKETCHBOOK

WADE MCINTYRE: When deciding who to feature on the cover of this compilation, we had a realization: Luke's story places him in the middle of four very different women– each pulling him in a different direction. Instead of asking Juan to draw millions of pieces of shattered glass, this time we went with millions of droplets of water to reference the baptism motif in CLONE #12.

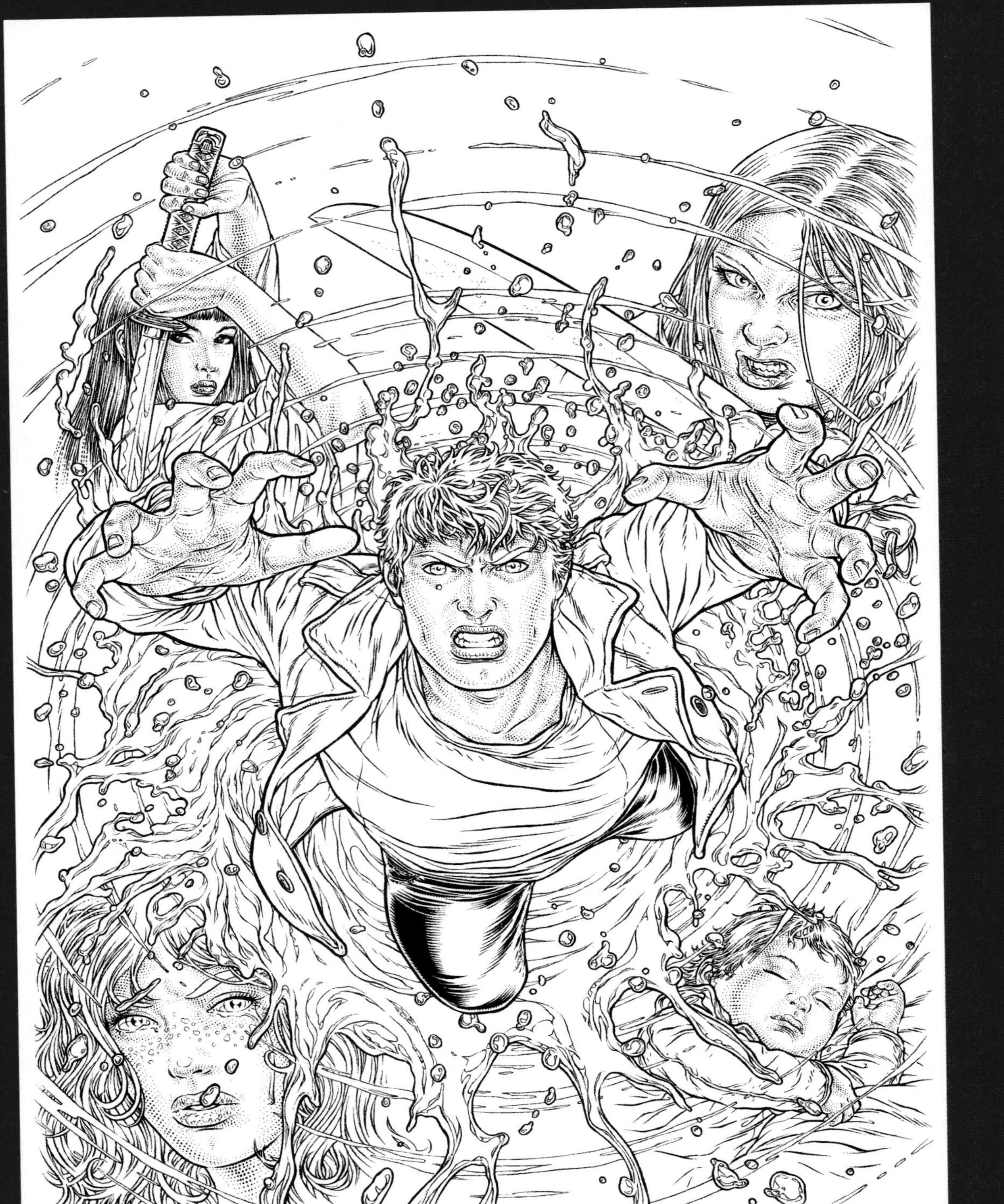

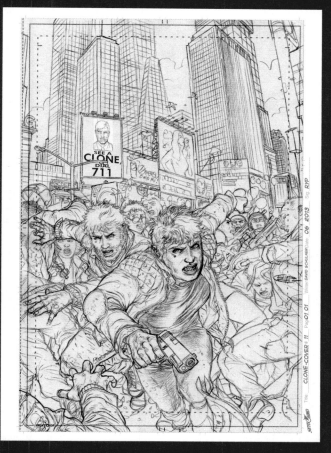

DAVID SCHULNER: For this cover Sean (Aaron calls him our "amazing editor" later, so I'll just call him Sean here, lest he get a big head) suggested an image that played on the cover for CLONE #1: Luke in the big city, on the run for his life. And I remember his reasoning for that first chaotic, wraparound, border to border image-packed cover, which was, "It'll show off Juan's detail work." Or put another way, "Let's torture Juan." The idea appealed to me too because #11 was designed as a reboot of sorts. You could jump in here and it didn't require you to have read the first ten issues. And I'm a big fan of symmetry. And callbacks. So it hit my sweet spot.

SEE A
CLONE
DIAL
711
CLONE-COVER # 11
Page 01 01
Writer DAVID SCHULNER
Date 06 2013
Sig. RYP

What makes this cover different, and shows how far Luke has grown, is that now Luke is the one with the gun. He's not running for his life, he's running to save another clone's life. And he's not scared, he's determined. I liked how all of that reflected Luke's journey. If you were to go back and compare cover #1 and cover #11 it would be a perfect summation of how far he's traveled.

And yes, we did torture Juan. But secretly (though less secretly now that I'm writing this for worldwide publication) I think he likes it.

CLONE #11 COVER
IDEA #01
IDEA #02
IDEA #03
IDEA #04

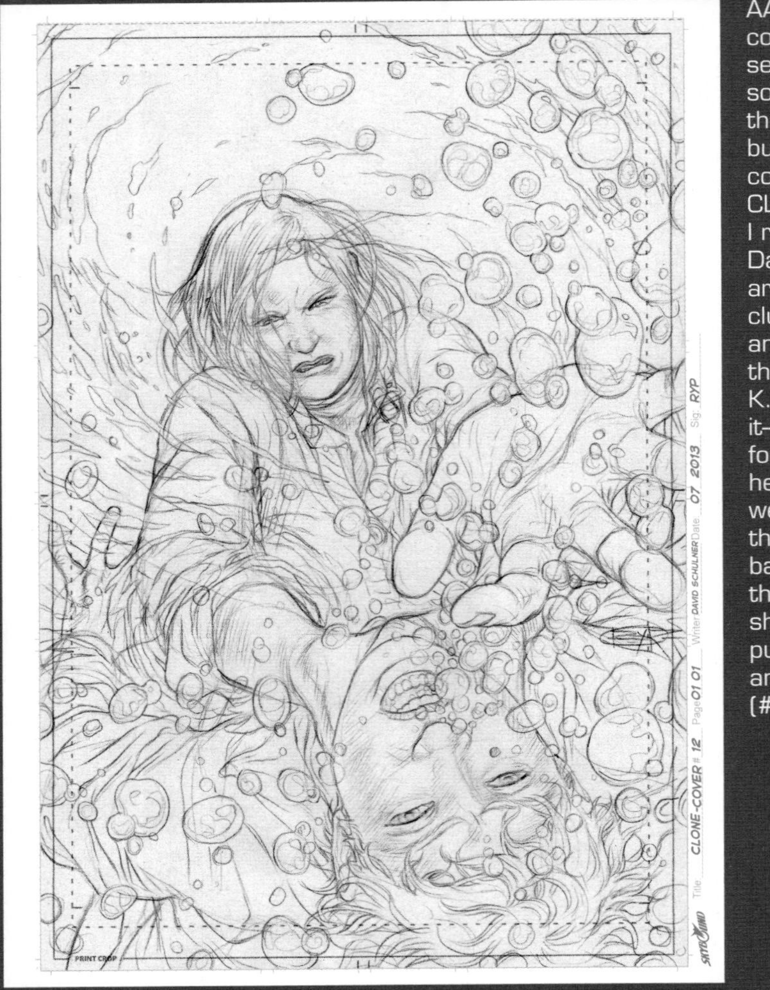
PRINT CROP
Title CLONE-COVER # 12 Page 01 01 Writer DAVID SCHULNER Date 07 2013 Sig: RYP

AARON GINSBURG: Not only is this cover one of my favorites of the series thus far (although we do have some seriously cool shit coming down the pike for you, don't you worry...), but it's a great example of the collaboration that goes into producing CLONE each and every month.
I remember distinctly the day that Dave, Wade and I were all sitting around, staring at a corkboard cluttered with upcoming story beats and plot twists, and we discovered the backstory of our new villain, Mrs. K. I don't know how else to explain it–it just presented itself to us, fully formed –like it really happened to her and we were just sharing what we had learned. And we knew, right then and there, that Mrs. K's failed baptism of her clone husband (and the bloody fallout) would not only shape her character, but it would push our story into new, complicated, and ultimately disturbing directions (#bullmasturbator).

We had introduced Mrs. K in #11–just a frumpy soccer mom with a mean looking shotgun and an unwavering devotion to Christian fundamentalism–but this issue would reveal exactly what lengths she was willing to go to rid the world of clones. When we turned in the script, our amazing editor, Sean Mackiewicz, suggested we feature Mrs. K on the cover–specifically teasing the baptism of her husband. There was no argument from anyone.

The cover plays on so many levels: at first glance, it looks violent, dangerous, Mrs. K's hands gripped around Luke's neck, drowning him (a plausible event, seeing as how we ended #11). But no, this is a moment of desperation, of hope, of faith. This is a glimpse of a woman putting everything on the line to cleanse the soul of the man she loves... and that man isn't Luke.

Juan quickly sketched out a few versions–and this layout was the easy pick–it was creepy, calm, and most of all, strangely beautiful. And then somehow, incredibly, Andy Troy managed to color this half-in-the water/half-on-the-surface moment in time. It's brilliant. I still don't know how Juan and Andy do it.

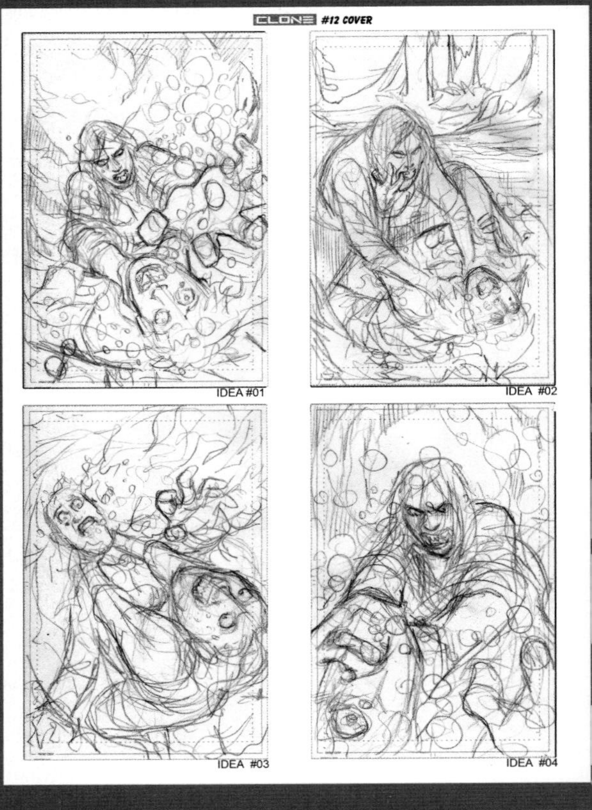
CLONE #12 COVER
IDEA #01
IDEA #02
IDEA #03
IDEA #04

AARON: Yikes, am I right? We've come a long way from the cool, blue bubbling waters of the baptismal river delicately highlighted with the soft pink hue from Mrs. K's signature cardigan. That was #12, folks. Welcome to #13—where things are about to get seriously dark and twisted and bloody.

We knew this was one of our most disturbing issues to date, and we wanted an ominous cover to reflect the darkness waiting for the reader just inside the pages... but choosing the right image turned out to be trickier than we imagined.

Initially, we discussed a conceptual cover: the menacing slaughterhouse workbench, empty, awaiting its next victim. The awful-looking electro-ejaculator just resting there upon the greasy tabletop, maybe we even notice it's sparking... However, we ultimately decided that this shocking sequence (pun intended) would work better as a surprise for the reader... Let's not spoil it on the cover. So we discussed a cover that focuses on a close-up of a discarded Coalition helix pin, soaking in a pool of blood... Gruesome, yes, but it lacked something that we were looking for... It lacked... the romance.

#01

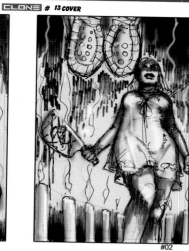
#02

#03

#04

Yes, I said "romance." Sure, in this issue Mrs. K violates Luke in ways too gruesome to even type here, but the part of the story that I always found more disturbing was her pathetic attempts to woo him, to encourage Luke to touch her like a lover, to give himself to her of his own volition. There's delusion in that, there's desperation, and we found that conceit to be far more twisted than any bull sperm collection tube (again, sorry).

So we pitched the idea of Luke hanging from a meat hook with Mrs. K standing before him in a skimpy negligee, looking as sexy as she possibly could. Candles set up around the slaughterhouse. An unlikely blend of horror and romance...

Naturally, Juan didn't miss a step—and even added the fantastic reflection of Luke in the cleaver blade. And Andy's colors are such a striking departure from #12—he found a way to make the image simultaneously warm, romantic and absolutely terrifying. The final image captures Mrs. K's nervousness, her shyness, the shame she feels wearing such a revealing nightgown, and most of all, her unwavering drive—because, ultimately, this woman will do anything to have a child.

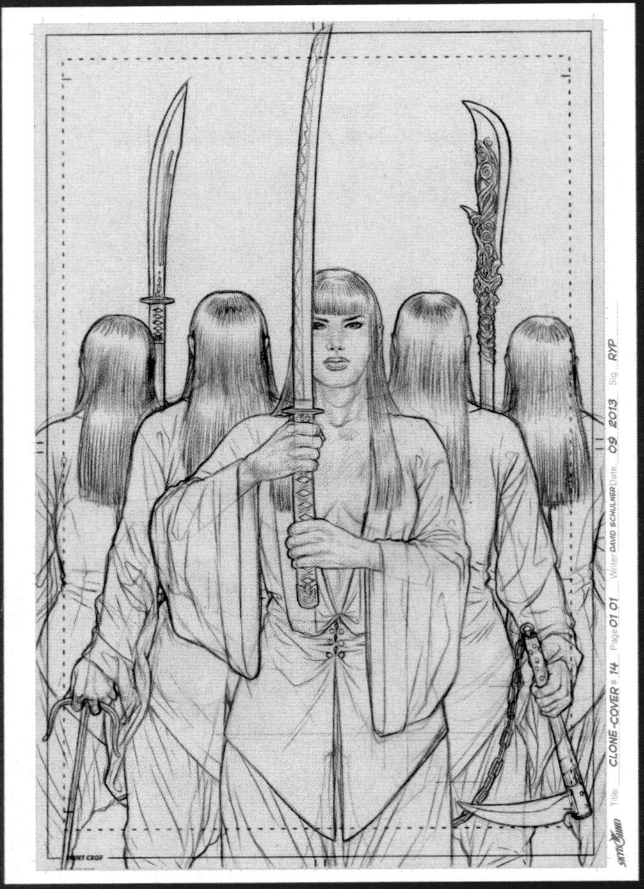
Title CLONE-COVER # 14 Page 01 01 Writer DAVID SCHULNER Date 09 2013 Sig RYP

WADE: #14 marked a significant departure for the series: it's the first cover not to feature Luke's face. But as the scope of the book expanded, it made sense to put another face forward. Meiko and her "sisters" are the new clones in town, and this cover announces their arrival. It was David's idea to pose them with only one woman facing forward. By showing as little as possible, Juan's drawing is able to hint at their mystery and menace.

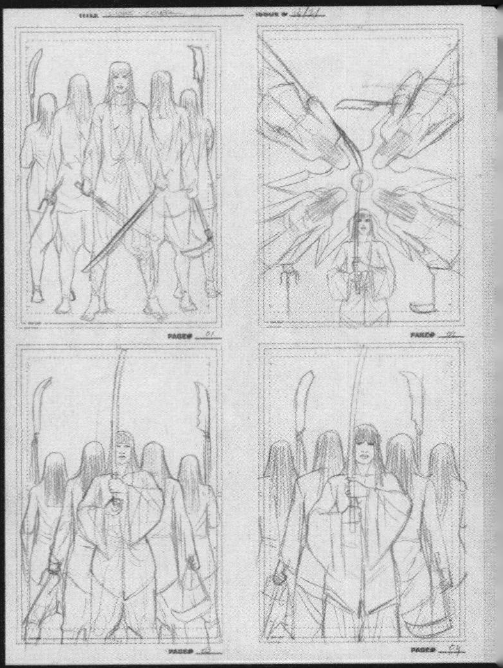

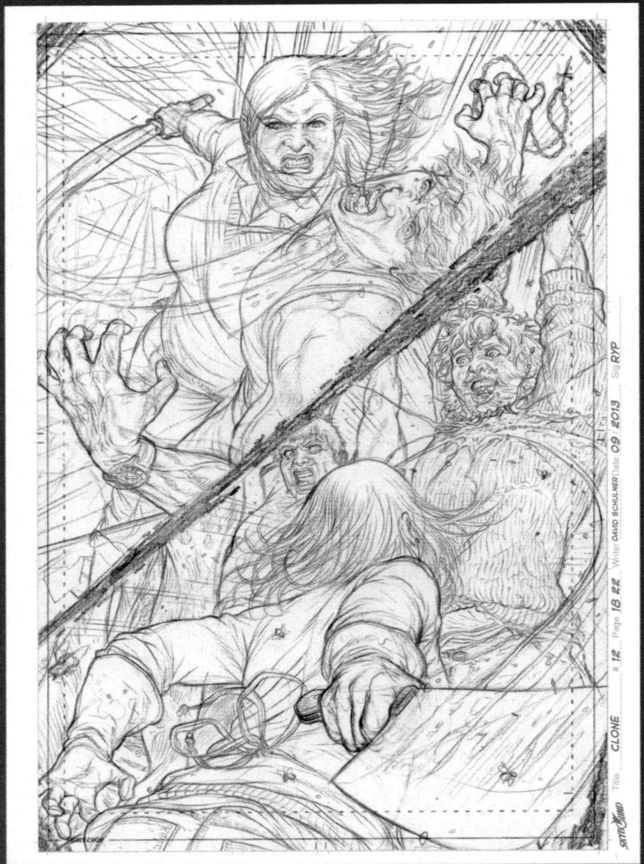
Title CLONE # 12 Page 18 22 Writer DAVID SCHULNER Date 09 2013 Sig RYP

WADE: I thought it would be cool to include the page from the script:

PAGE 18: Two Panels
This page is a big SPLASH split vertically

(or perhaps diagonally or whatever is most striking). Two matching images of violence.

Panel 1: In the hotel room, MRS. K USES THE KNIFE TO SLIT HER HUSBAND'S THROAT with the efficiency of one who's spent decades slaughtering livestock.

Panel 2: In the slaughterhouse, MRS. K HAS JUST KILLED ADRIAN in an identical manner (though using the grotesque meat saw instead of a knife). Luke looks on in horror, hanging helplessly from the meat hook. Straining against the ropes that bind his wrists.

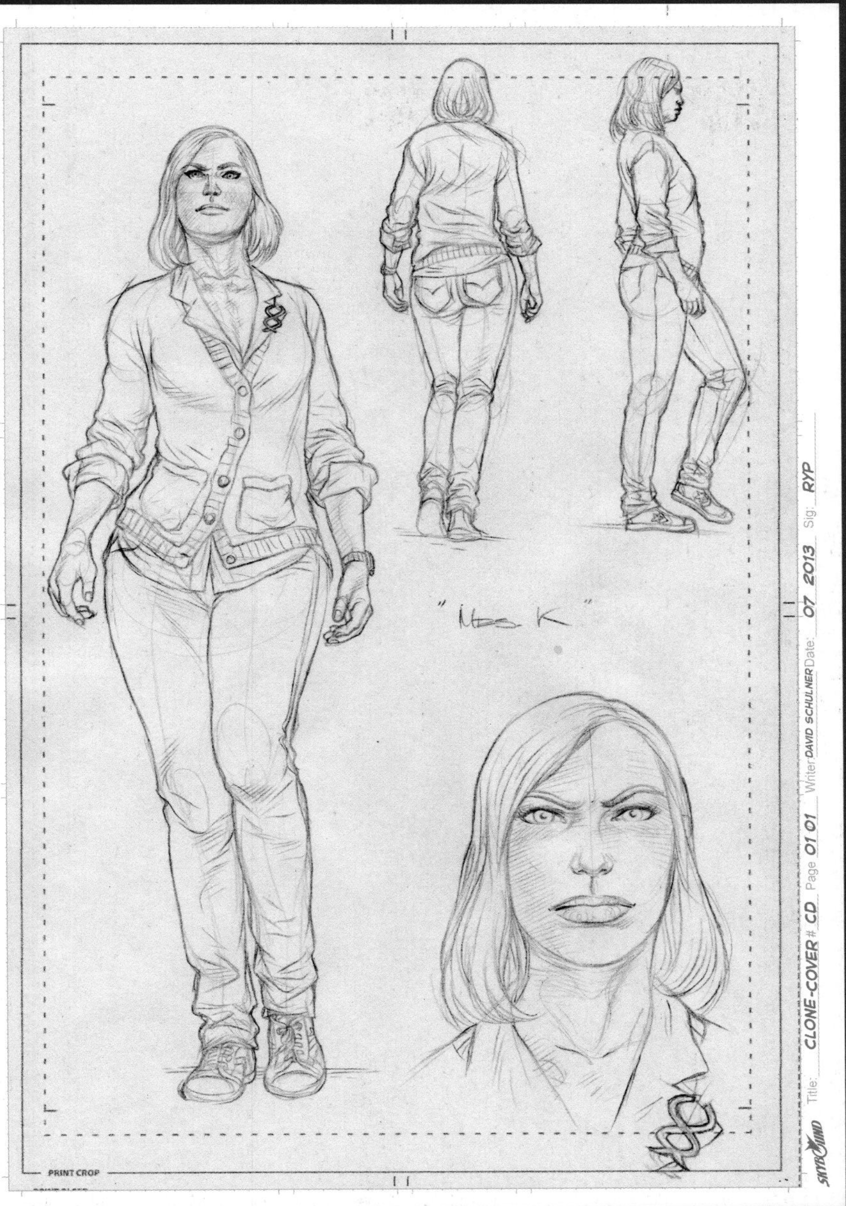
"Mrs. K"
Title: CLONE-COVER # CD Page 01 01 Writer DAVID SCHULNER Date: 07 2013 Sig: RYP
PRINT CROP
SKYBOUND

AARON: Looking back at Juan's character designs for Mrs. K, I was reminded of the day we created her. I remember there was some debate about how attractive she should be, how young, how old. At that point in the writing process, we didn't know her full backstory yet–that would come later. We just knew there was a story to tell. And we knew that Mrs. K would be the woman to help us tell it.

I dug back through our old CLONE scripts to find our initial description of her. I thought you guys might enjoy it:

Panel 5:
Looking up from the ground at A WOMAN.

She's in her 30s, blonde, stocky. If not for the SHOTGUN,
she'd look like a soccer mom in her jeans and a frumpy cardigan. But she's mean as hell. She is wearing a distinctive BLUE LAPEL PIN in the shape of a DOUBLE HELIX.

When Juan started sketching out his character design, he told us he used the movie SERIAL MOM by John Waters for reference, the 1994 comedy about a mom who happens to secretly be a serial killer. He explained that he pictured Mrs. K as a younger Kathleen Turner from this film, and we just laughed. Little did know Juan know how right he was... Oh, she's a killer, alright, and there's no end in sight.

MORE BOOKS FROM
ROBERT KIRKMAN
AND
SKYBOUND™

CLONE
VOLUME 2
SECOND GENERATION

VOL. 1: FIRST GENERATION TP
ISBN: 978-1-60706-683-5
$14.99
VOL. 2: SECOND GENERATION TP
ISBN: 978-1-60706-830-3
$14.99
VOL. 3: THIRD GENERATION TP
ISBN: 978-1-60706-939-3
$14.99

JOSHUA WILLIAMSON · GORAN SUDZUKA · MIROSLAV MRVA
GHOSTED
VOLUME ONE · HAUNTED HEIST

VOL. 1: HAUNTED HEIST TP
ISBN: 978-1-60706-836-5
$9.99

KIRKMAN · CERENO · GETTY · ANKA
GUARDING THE GLOBE
VOLUME ONE
UNDER SIEGE

VOL. 1: UNDER SIEGE TP
ISBN: 978-1-60706-356-8
$16.99
VOL. 2: HARD TO KILL TP
ISBN: 978-1-60706-673-6
$16.99

for more, visit
SKYBOUND.COM

SUPER DINOSAUR 3

VOL. 1
ISBN: 978-1-60706-420-6
$9.99
VOL. 2
ISBN: 978-1-60706-568-5
$12.99
VOL. 3
ISBN: 978-1-60706-667-5
$12.99
DELUXE COLORING BOOK
ISBN: 978-1-60706-481-7
$4.99

HESTER · NAUCK · ELTAEB
INVINCIBLE
UNIVERSE
VOLUME ONE
ON DEADLY GROUND

VOL. 1: ON DEADLY GROUND TP
ISBN: 978-1-60706-820-4
$16.99

THIEF OF THIEVES
VOLUME 3
"VENICE."

VOL. 1: "I QUIT."
ISBN: 978-1-60706-592-0
$14.99
VOL. 2: "HELP ME."
ISBN: 978-1-60706-676-7
$14.99
VOL. 3: "VENICE."
ISBN: 978-1-60706-844-0
$14.99

BRANDON SEIFERT
LUKAS KETNER
ANDY TROY
WITCH DOCTOR
VOLUME 2
MAL PRACTICE

VOL. 1: UNDER THE KNIFE TP
ISBN: 978-1-60706-441-1
$12.99
VOL. 2: MAL PRACTICE TP
ISBN: 978-1-60706-693-4
$14.99

THE ASTOUNDING WOLF-MAN
VOL. 1 TP
ISBN: 978-1-58240-862-0
$14.99
VOL. 2 TP
ISBN: 978-1-60706-007-9
$14.99
VOL. 3 TP
ISBN: 978-1-60706-111-3
$16.99
VOL. 4 TP
ISBN: 978-1-60706-249-3
$16.99

BATTLE POPE
VOL. 1: GENESIS TP
ISBN: 978-1-58240-572-8
$14.99
VOL. 2: MAYHEM TP
ISBN: 978-1-58240-529-2
$12.99
PILLOW TALK TP
677-0
751-7

EC 12 2014
#12.99

BRIT
VOL. 1: OLD SOLDIER TP
ISBN: 978-1-58240-678-7
$14.99
VOL. 2: AWOL
ISBN: 978-1-58240-864-4
$14.99
VOL. 3: FUBAR
ISBN: 978-1-60706-061-1
$16.99

CAPES
VOL. 1: PUNCHING THE CLOCK TP
ISBN: 978-1-58240-756-2
$17.99

HAUNT
VOL. 1 TP
ISBN: 978-1-60706-154-0
$9.99
VOL. 2 TP
ISBN: 978-1-60706-229-5
$16.99
VOL. 3 TP
ISBN: 978-1-60706-552-4
$14.99
THE IMMORTAL EDITION, VOL. 1 HC
ISBN: 978-1-60706-241-7
$34.99

THE INFINITE
VOL. 1 TP
ISBN: 978-1-60706-475-6
$9.99

SCIENCE DOG
OVERSIZED HC
ISBN: 978-1-60706-423-7
$19.99

SUPERPATRIOT
AMERICA'S FIGHTING FORCE
ISBN: 978-1-58240-355-1
$14.99

TALES OF THE REALM
HARDCOVER
ISBN: 978-1-58240-426-0
$34.95
TRADE PAPERBACK
ISBN: 978-1-58240-394-6
$14.95

TECH JACKET
VOL. 1: THE BOY FROM EARTH TP
ISBN: 978-1-58240-771-5
$14.99

TO FIND YOUR NEAREST COMIC BOOK STORE, CALL:
1-888-COMIC-BOOK

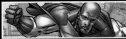

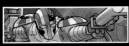

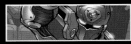